Beyond the Gap

SUSTAINABLE INFRASTRUCTURE SERIES

Beyond the Gap

How Countries Can Afford the Infrastructure They Need while Protecting the Planet

Julie Rozenberg and Marianne Fay, Editors

WORLD BANK GROUP

Contents

Acknowledgments xi
Key Messages xiii
About the Contributors xv
Abbreviations xix

Overview 1
Marianne Fay and Julie Rozenberg

Key Messages 1
Introduction 2
How Much New Infrastructure Is Needed? 3
Scenario Approaches Allow for Informed Policy Making 5
Operations and Maintenance Play a Major Role in Costs 21
In Sum 26
Notes 27
References 27

1   Making Infrastructure Needs Assessments Useful and Relevant 29
Marianne Fay and Julie Rozenberg

Key Messages 29
Introduction 29
Why Is Estimating Infrastructure Needs So Difficult? 31
A Framework to Make Infrastructure Investment Needs
Assessments Useful 37

In Sum 42
Notes 43
References 43

2   Water, Sanitation, and Irrigation..47
Charles J. E. Fox, Blanca Lopez-Alascio, Marianne Fay, Claire Nicolas,
and Julie Rozenberg

Key Messages 47
Introduction 48
Water and Sanitation: MDG or SDG Makes All the Difference 51
Irrigation: A Question of How Much to Expand...60
In Sum 68
Notes 68
References 69

3   Power 71
Claire Nicolas, Julie Rozenberg, and Marianne Fay

Key Messages 71
Introduction 71
Universal Access Costs Are Driven by Policy Choices regarding
the Strategy to Increase Access 74
Factoring Climate Change into Investment Needs Estimates.................84
South America: Bringing Climate and Demand Constraints Together....92
In Sum 94
Notes 95
References 95

4   Transport 99
Julie Rozenberg and Marianne Fay

Key Messages 99
Introduction 99
Rural Accessibility...103
Urban Transport 110
Global Transport Needs... 119
In Sum 125
Annex 4A: Transport Investment Can Have Positive Impacts on
Welfare but Hide Negative Impacts for Some Actors and for
the Environment... 126
Notes 128
References... 129

5   Flood Protection 133
Julie Rozenberg and Marianne Fay

Key Messages 133
Introduction 133
Costing Coastal and River Flood Protection Strategies 135
Future Investment Costs Depend on Construction Costs
and Risk Aversion 139
How Different Regions Fare Depends on the Protection Strategy 143

Protection Strategies Should Budget for Long-Term
Maintenance Expenses 146
In Sum 147
Notes 149
References 149

6   **Infrastructure and Disruptive Technologies 153**
Michael M. Leifman, Marianne Fay, Claire Nicolas, and Julie Rozenberg

Key Messages 153
Introduction 153
New Technologies Are Enabling Disruptions and Transformations 155
New Technologies Could Give Rise to Very Different Futures 159
What Governments Can Do (and Avoid Doing) 161
In Sum 167
Annex 6A: Methodology to Derive the Three Scenarios 168
Note 169
References 169

Technical Appendix...171

Boxes

2.1   International goals on water, sanitation, hygiene, and irrigation.......49
3.1   The multitier framework...75
3.2   Putting a price tag on transitioning to a carbon-free world..............85
3.3   By 2030, a 1.5C scenario is similar to a 2C scenario for
       electricity generation investments 91
5.1   Protecting New Orleans from flooding..148
6.1   How our experts see a likely technology future (by 2040-ish)......156
6.2   Our three technology-deployment scenarios.................................160

Figures

O.1   The cost for infrastructure investments ranges from 2 percent to
       8 percent of GDP per year in low- and middle-income countries........... 6
O.2   The goal and the choice of technology are the main drivers of
       investment costs... 8
O.3   Public support policies drive investment costs in irrigation 10
O.4   Within Sub-Saharan Africa, the financial burden of reaching
       universal electricity access varies significantly.......................12
O.5   A 2C world may cost less than the business-as-usual one—or
       a lot more 13
O.6   Models vary as to the extent to which decarbonization relies
       on stranded assets and reduced consumption.........................13
O.7   The choice of terrestrial mode and rail occupancy drive
       transport investment costs 14
O.8   The biggest burden in urban transport investment is on
       upper-middle-income countries 15
O.9   Upgrading rural roads in Sierra Leone becomes costly—fast............16
O.10   The cost of greater accessibility is much lower using gravel
       rather than paved roads in dry climates.......................................17

O.11 The choice of protection level, combined with construction costs, shapes river flood protection capital costs 18

O.12 Construction costs, combined with risk aversion, shape coastal protection capital costs...19

O.13 Operations and maintenance spending matters as much as capital spending for water and sanitation 22

O.14 The technology mix for electricity determines the variable cost burden..24

O.15 Maintenance may cost as much as or more than new investments in transport...25

2.1 In South Asia and Sub-Saharan Africa, new capital spending needs exceed replacement costs for existing assets............................55

2.2 The goal and the choice of technology are the main drivers of investment costs..56

2.3 Sub-Saharan Africa faces the highest capital cost of achieving universal access to water and sanitation.....................................57

2.4 Operations and maintenance spending matters as much as capital spending for water and sanitation 58

2.5 The affordability of expanding water and sanitation services could be an issue for Sub-Saharan Africa, unlike other regions.......59

2.6 Public support policies drive investment costs in irrigation.............63

2.7 South Asia and Sub-Saharan Africa bear the highest investment costs in irrigation...64

2.8 Public support for irrigation increases food security in low- and middle-income countries.. 64

B3.1.1 Improving attributes of energy supply leads to higher tiers of access 75

3.1 The cost of achieving universal access to electricity in Sub-Saharan Africa depends on the service tier targeted.................78

3.2 Within Sub-Saharan Africa, the financial burden of reaching universal electricity access varies significantly.......................................78

3.3 An increasing share of persons gaining access to electricity uses low-carbon options 79

3.4 The optimal mix of technology varies with the level of electricity service... 80

3.5 High variable power sector costs are a major challenge, especially in Sub-Saharan Africa...81

3.6 Electrification costs are much higher if the total cost of service is included..82

3.7 Sub-Saharan Africa faces high annual fixed operations and maintenance costs for electricity 83

3.8 High nominal access can mask low reliable access to electricity in major Sub-Saharan African cities 83

3.9 A 2C world may cost less than the business-as-usual one— or a lot more 86

3.10 Models disagree more in some regions than in others......................87

3.11 The low-carbon share of investment rises progressively...................88

3.12 Many models find many ways to meet the climate change constraint on the supply side 89

3.13 Electricity consumption falls as the climate constraint tightens.......90

3.14 Much of the coal-fired power infrastructure in the low- and middle-income world could become stranded assets by 2030......90

B3.3.1 Between 2015 and 2030, the 1.5C and the 2C investment paths for the power sector are very similar 91

3.15   Variable costs are lower than capital costs for power
       infrastructure in South America...93
3.16   Total costs of electricity in South America are driven by cost
       of capital, demand, and CO_2 constraint 93
4.1   Upgrading rural roads in Sierra Leone becomes costly—fast..........105
4.2   The cost of greater accessibility depends on many
       country-related factors...106
4.3   Road paving can have a major impact on forest cover 108
4.4   The cost of greater accessibility is much lower using gravel
       rather than paved roads in dry climates...109
4.5   A growing role exists for public transport 113
4.6   Better planning lowers urban transport needs by 20 percent......... 113
4.7   The biggest burden in urban transport investment is on
       upper-middle-income countries 114
4.8   Large differences in urban density around the world are
       maintained in the planning scenarios 115
4.9   Urban planning and climate change mitigation must be
       coordinated..116
4.10   Operating costs for urban transport are high 117
4.11   Global transport infrastructure investment needs are highest
       for road and rail...122
4.12   The choice of terrestrial mode and rail occupancy drive
       transport investment costs.. 123
4.13   Maintenance may cost as much as or more than new
       investments in transport..124
4A.1   Investments in transport corridors can create both winners
       and losers 127
5.1   Construction costs, combined with risk aversion, shape
       coastal protection capital costs..140
5.2   The optimal coastal protection strategy based on CBA
       reduces long-term costs.. 141
5.3   The choice of protection level, combined with construction
       costs, shapes river flood protection capital costs 142
5.4   For river floods, maintaining 2015 risk levels might be
       unaffordable in Sub-Saharan Africa 143
5.5   For coastal floods, the optimal protection strategy based on
       CBA invests more than the low-risk-tolerance strategy only in
       South Asia and Sub-Saharan Africa 144
A.1   Overview of the SSP space...174
A.2   Quantitative projections for demography, urbanization, and
       GDP in low- and middle-income countries, 2015–30...........................175

Maps

4.1   Sub-Saharan Africa stands out for rural accessibility issues 104
5.1   Using open or closed riverine coastal protection in
       the Netherlands..137

Tables

O.1   In the preferred scenario, investment costs are the highest for
       Sub-Saharan Africa and South Asia.. 7
O.2   Policy choices on tiers of service drive costs of electrification.............11

O.3   The preferred scenario uses low-carbon modes and accompanying policies for rail and public transport 15

O.4   Universal access to paved roads is not within countries' reach by 2030..17

1.1   The range of estimated annual infrastructure investment needs in the recent literature is quite large...36

1.2   Possible indicators for measuring infrastructure services, by sector......39

2.1   Overview of the assumptions and models used in this chapter 50

2.2   A long way to go to reach universal coverage on water and sanitation 51

2.3   Possible strategies for providing water and sanitation vary with the level and rollout of service...52

2.4   Various options are available for delivering water and sanitation services..54

2.5   Supporting irrigation helps to address hunger but is no panacea for climate change and biodiversity 66

2.6   Public support for irrigation induces shifts toward more water-intensive crops..67

3.1   Overview of the assumptions and models used in this chapter 73

3.2   What should the new level of customer consumption of electricity be?..76

3.3   Policy choices on tiers of service drive costs of electrification...........77

4.1   Overview of the assumptions and models used in this chapter 101

4.2   High road maintenance costs pose a hurdle in Sub-Saharan Africa 107

4.3   Universal access to paved roads is not within countries' reach by 2030 107

4.4   Drone delivery helps to increase social integration in rural areas.....110

4.5   Major gaps remain in the availability of mass transit infrastructure.......111

4.6   The preferred scenario uses low-carbon modes and accompanying policies for rail and public transport..............................125

5.1   Overview of the assumptions and models used in this chapter 134

5.2   Protection standards vary with wealth and location............................136

5.3   A wide range of sea-level rise scenarios 138

5.4   East and South Asia and Sub-Saharan Africa have the highest adaptation deficits in coastal protection 145

6.1   General levels of technology deployment, by scenario and sector......161

Acknowledgments

This report was written by a team composed of Julie Rozenberg (task team leader), Claire Nicolas, Charles J. E. Fox, Michael M. Leifman, and Blanca Lopez-Alascio, working under the supervision of Marianne Fay and with valuable contributions from Elco Koks and Mehdi Mikou.

Guidance was provided by the report's peer reviewers: Richard Damania, Vivien Foster, Stéphane Hallegatte, Javier Morales Sarriera, and Fernanda Ruiz Nunez (World Bank); Tomas Sebastian Serebrisky (Inter-American Development Bank); and Stephane Straub (Toulouse School of Economics).

The report benefited from comments and helpful suggestions from World Bank colleagues Moussa Blimpo, Matias Herrera Dappe, Soames Job, Brenden Jongman, Holly Krambeck, Ashok Kumar, Darwin Marcelo, Tatiana Peralta, Diego Rodriguez, Gustavo Saltiel, Benjamin Stewart, and Aiga Stokenberga.

The report draws from seven commissioned background papers:

- Fisch-Romito, V., and C. Guivarch. 2019. "Investment Needs for Transport Infrastructures along Low Carbon Pathways." Background paper prepared for this report, World Bank, Washington, DC.

- ITF (International Transport Forum). 2018. "The Billion Dollar Question: How Much Will It Cost to Decarbonise Cities' Transport Systems?" Background paper prepared for this report, World Bank, Washington, DC.

- Leifman, M. 2019. "Scenarios: Leapfrog, Lock-in, and Lopsided." Background paper prepared for this report, World Bank, Washington, DC.

- McCollum, D. L., W. Zhou, C. Bertram, H.-S. de Boer, V. Bosetti, S. Busch, J. Després, and others. 2018. "Energy Investment Needs for Fulfilling the Paris Agreement and Achieving the Sustainable Development Goals." *Nature Energy* 3 (7): 589–99.

- Moksnes, N., J. Rozenberg, O. Broad, C. Taliotis, and M. Howells. 2019. "Determinants of Energy Futures—A Scenario Discovery Method Applied to Cost and Carbon Emissions Futures for South American Electricity Infrastructure." Background paper prepared for this report, World Bank, Washington, DC.

- Nicholls, R. J., J. Hinkel, D. Lincke, and T. van der Pol. 2019. "Global Investment Costs for Coastal Defence through the 21st Century." Background paper prepared for this report, World Bank, Washington, DC.

- Palazzo, A., H. Valin, M. Batka, and P. Havlík. 2019. "Investment Needs for Irrigation Infrastructure along Different Socio-Economic Pathways." Background paper prepared for this report, World Bank, Washington, DC.

In addition, we made extensive use of two models developed by World Bank colleagues:

- Hutton, G., and M. C. Varughese. 2016. "The Costs of Meeting the 2030 Sustainable Development Goal Targets on Drinking Water, Sanitation, and Hygiene." Technical paper, Water and Sanitation Program. World Bank, Washington, DC.

- Jordan-Antoine, R., S. Banerjee, W. Blyth, and M. Bazilian. Forthcoming. "Estimates of the Cost of Reaching Universal Access to Electricity." Working paper, World Bank, Washington, DC.

The report was edited by Laura Wallace and copyedited by Elizabeth Forsyth.

Key Messages

This report aims to shift the debate regarding investment needs away from a simple focus on spending more and toward a focus on spending better on the right objectives using relevant metrics. It does so by offering a careful and systematic approach to estimating the funding needs (capital and operations and maintenance) to close the service gaps in water and sanitation, transportation, electricity, irrigation, and flood protection.

The main innovations of our work relative to other investment needs estimates are the following: (a) we developed all of the results presented here specifically for this report, following a consistent approach and timeline and based on clearly specified goals; (b) we used numerous scenarios to explore both uncertainty and the consequences of policy choices; (c) we estimated not only new investments, but also replacement capital costs, as well as maintenance for new and existing infrastructure; and (d) we provided estimates for both access and climate goals.

Key conclusions include the following:

- *How much countries need to spend on infrastructure depends on their goals, but also on the efficiency with which they pursue these goals.* By exploring thousands of scenarios, this report finds that new infrastructure could cost low- and middle-income countries (LMICs) anywhere between 2 percent and 8 percent of gross domestic product (GDP) per year to 2030, depending on the quality and quantity of service targeted and the spending efficiency achieved in reaching this goal.

- *With the right policies, investments of 4.5 percent of GDP will enable LMICs to achieve the infrastructure-related Sustainable Development Goals and stay on track to limit climate change to 2°C.* This report identifies policy mixes that could enable LMICs to achieve universal access to water, sanitation, and electricity; greater mobility; improved food security; better flood protection; and eventual full decarbonization—while limiting spending to 4.5 percent of GDP per year on new infrastructure.

- *Infrastructure investment paths compatible with full decarbonization by the end of the century need not cost more than more-polluting alternatives.* Investment needs remain between 2 percent and 8 percent of GDP even when looking only at the scenarios that achieve climate change stabilization at 2°C. Instead, spending efficiency is key and depends on the quality of the policies accompanying the investment.

- *Investing in infrastructure is not enough; maintaining it matters.* Improving services requires much than capital expenditure. Ensuring a steady flow of resources for operations and maintenance is a necessary condition for success. Good maintenance also generates substantial savings, reducing the total life-cycle cost of transport and water and sanitation infrastructure more than 50 percent.

About the Contributors

EDITORS

Julie Rozenberg is a Senior Economist in the Office of Chief Economist of the Sustainable Development Vice Presidency at the World Bank. Her work includes green growth and climate change mitigation strategies and climate change adaptation and disaster risk management. She is the author of many research articles and participated in the writing of several World Bank flagship reports, including *Decarbonizing Development: Three Steps to a Zero-Carbon Future* and *Shock Waves: Managing the Impacts of Climate Change on Poverty*. She also develops innovative methodologies to take long-term uncertainties into account in the economic analyses of projects in sectors like transport, water, or urbanization, helping World Bank clients to deal with climate change constraints and other long-term uncertainties in the preparation of projects and strategies. She holds an engineering degree from École Nationale Supérieure de Techniques Avancées and a PhD in economics from École des Hautes Études en Sciences Sociales in Paris.

Marianne Fay is the Chief Economist of the Sustainable Development Vice Presidency at the World Bank. She previously served as the Chief Economist for Climate Change. She has contributed to several *World Development Reports*, notably *World Development Report 2010: Development and Climate Change*, which she codirected, and has led various recent World Bank reports, such as *Inclusive Green Growth: The Pathway to Sustainable Development* and *Decarbonizing Development: Three Steps to a Zero-Carbon Future*. She has held positions in different Regions of the World Bank (Africa, Europe and Central Asia, and Latin America and the Caribbean), working on infrastructure, urbanization, and climate change. She is the author of articles and books on these topics. She is a founding member of the Green Growth Knowledge Platform, and she holds a PhD in economics from Columbia University.

AUTHORS

Charles J. E. Fox is an Analyst in the Office of Chief Economist of the Sustainable Development Vice Presidency at the World Bank. He has been heavily involved with the World Bank's Geospatial Operations Support Team (GOST) since its inception. He focuses on applying geospatial analytics and big data techniques to operational problems. Prior to joining the World Bank in 2016, he was an analyst with Lazard & Co. Services Ltd., specializing in transactions in the natural resources sector, and then leveraged transactions with a financial sponsor component. Before Lazard, he worked for Triple Point Investment Management. He holds a BA in economics and management from Oxford University.

Michael M. Leifman is the founder of Tenley Consulting, a firm offering advisory and strategic planning services to corporations, start-ups, multilateral banks, foundations, and nongovernmental organizations on a wide landscape of issues, including energy and environmental policy and economics, forecasting, and business and technology innovation. Before founding Tenley, he was Senior Strategist for the Business Innovations Group at General Electric (GE), where he focused on the power business, artificial intelligence, and the future of work and start-up businesses. He joined GE in 2008 and for many years was the Director of Forecasting and Analytics for GE Power and Water, as well as the Director of the Modeling Center of Excellence. Prior to working at GE, he worked for the U.S. Department of Energy's Office of Energy Efficiency and Renewable Energy, for the U.S. Environmental Protection Agency's Climate Change Division, and for an environmental policy consulting firm.

Blanca Lopez-Alascio is a Water and Sanitation Consultant at the Water Global Practice of the World Bank. She has seven years of experience in the design, preparation, and implementation of World Bank water supply and sanitation projects across the Latin America and Caribbean Region, mainly in Brazil, Honduras, Mexico, and Panama. She has collaborated on several analytical works on integrated urban water management, disaster risk management, and public expenditure review in the water sector. She holds a master's degree in international business administration from the Spanish

Foreign Trade Institute (ICEX/Spain) and is studying for a master's degree in water and environmental management from the Water, Engineering and Development Centre (WEDC) in the United Kingdom.

Claire Nicolas is an Energy Specialist in the Energy Global Practice at the World Bank. She previously held an Economist position in the Office of the Chief Economist of the Sustainable Development Vice Presidency. Her work focuses on power sector development, climate change mitigation, and decision making under uncertainty. She develops innovative tools and methodologies to help World Bank clients to take uncertainty into account in their power system and electrification strategies, whether it is long-term uncertainty like climate change or short-term uncertainty like renewable resource availability. Prior to joining the World Bank, she worked for four years as a Strategic Marketing Engineer in the oil refining industry. She holds an engineering degree from ENSTA ParisTech and a PhD in economics from Nanterre University in France.

Abbreviations

AFOLU	agriculture, forestry, and other land use
BAU	business as usual
CBA	cost-benefit analysis
CO_2	carbon dioxide
GDP	gross domestic product
GHG	greenhouse gas
IIoT	Industrial Internet of Things
IoT	Internet of Things
IPCC	Intergovernmental Panel on Climate Change
ITF	International Transport Forum
LMIC	low- and middle-income country
LUT	integrated land-use and transport planning
MDGs	Millennium Development Goals
MTF	multitier framework
NDC	nationally determined contribution to the Paris Agreement on Climate Change
NOx	nitrogen oxides
O&M	operations and maintenance
OECD	Organisation for Economic Co-operation and Development
RAI	rural access index

RCP   representative concentration pathway
ROG   robust governance
SDGs   Sustainable Development Goals
SSP   shared socioeconomic pathway
WASH water, sanitation, and hygiene

Overview

MARIANNE FAY AND JULIE ROZENBERG

KEY MESSAGES

- *How much countries need to spend on infrastructure depends on their goals, but also on the efficiency with which they pursue these goals.* By exploring thousands of scenarios, this report identifies the most important drivers of cost for future infrastructure investments and exposes the implications of different policy choices. It finds that new infrastructure could cost low- and middle-income countries (LMICs) anywhere between 2 percent and 8 percent of gross domestic product (GDP) per year to 2030 depending on the quality and quantity of service aimed for and the spending efficiency achieved to reach this goal.

- *With the right policies, investments of 4.5 percent of GDP will enable LMICs to achieve the infrastructure-related Sustainable Development Goals (SDGs) and stay on track to limit climate change to 2°C.* This report identifies policy mixes that could enable LMICs to achieve universal access to water, sanitation, and electricity; greater mobility; improved food security; better protection from floods; and eventual full decarbonization—while limiting spending to 4.5 percent of GDP per year on new infrastructure.

- *Infrastructure investment paths compatible with full decarbonization by the end of the century need not cost more than more-polluting alternatives.* Investment needs remain between 2 percent and 8 percent of GDP even when looking only at the scenarios that achieve climate change stabilization at 2°C. Instead, spending efficiency is key and depends on the quality of the policies accompanying the investment.

- *Investing in infrastructure is not enough; maintaining it also matters.* Improving services requires much more than capital expenditure. Ensuring a steady flow of resources for operations and maintenance (O&M) is a necessary condition for success. Good mainte-nance also generates substantial savings, reducing the total life-cycle cost of transport and water and sanitation infrastructure more than 50 percent.

INTRODUCTION

The infrastructure gap is large: 940 million individuals are without electricity, 663 million lack improved sources of drinking water, 2.4 billion lack improved sanitation facilities, 1 billion live more than 2 kilometers from an all-season road, and uncounted numbers are unable to access work and educational opportunities due to the absence or high cost of transport services. In LMICs, infrastructure—defined here as water and sanitation, electricity, transport, irrigation, and flood protection—falls short of what is needed to address public health and individual welfare, environmental considerations, and climate change risks, let alone achieve economic prosperity or middle-class aspirations.

The solution, many argue, is to spend more. Thus, the question of how to attract more resources to infrastructure (in particular, from the private sector) has dominated much of the conversation in international forums such as the Group of Twenty. The international community's SDGs and rising concerns about the urgency of action on climate change goals have added further impetus to the debate about how to entice the private sector to invest more in infrastructure.

But the story is not so simple. How much is needed depends on the objective pursued, and the objective pursued lies with the contexts, economic growth aspirations, and social and environmental objectives of individual countries. Further, the focus should be on the service gap, not the investment gap, and improving services typically requires much more than just capital expenditure. For example, ensuring that resources are reliably available to maintain existing and future infrastructure is a perennial challenge. And paying too much attention to the need to spend more risks diverting attention away from the need to spend better—an imperative for fiscally constrained LMIC economies—and the critical importance of establishing the needed institutions to pursue infrastructure goals sustainably.

This report aims to shift the debate regarding investment needs away from a simple focus on spending more and toward a focus on spending better on the right objectives with the use of relevant metrics. It contributes to that ambitious agenda by offering a careful and systematic approach to estimating the spending (capital as well as O&M) needed to close the service gap, moving away from single estimates of new capital investment needs. The objective is to highlight the sensitivity of the results to the ambition of the goals and the assumptions made—about pricing, technology, demand, climate change and climate policy, and other key factors—in ways that can help to inform policy choices.

In so doing, the report offers a framework for turning estimates of investment needs into useful tools for policy making. Estimates are structured in an "if-then" framework (*if* this is what is wanted and these are the assumptions made, *then* this is how much it would cost). To identify the most relevant objectives and assumptions in each sector, dozens and sometimes hundreds of scenarios are explored and the "cost drivers"—that is, the decisions and assumptions that best explain the spread in infrastructure costs—identified.

The report begins with a look at the complex relationship between infrastructure and growth and welfare, before presenting its methodological framework (chapter 1). It then presents detailed results for water and irrigation (chapter 2), electricity (chapter 3), transport (chapter 4), and flood protection (chapter 5). A final chapter examines what disruptive technologies could mean for the future of infrastructure services in LMICs.

The rest of this overview develops these messages and presents some sectoral results.

HOW MUCH NEW INFRASTRUCTURE IS NEEDED?

Infrastructure services depend on much more than just a stock of capital. Therefore, although a large literature on the impacts of infrastructure on growth, employment, and welfare has developed in the last decades, it is hardly conclusive. Possible explanations include the following:

- Most infrastructure is in the form of networks, which creates threshold effects and returns that vary with the stage of completion of the network and the number of users. Thus, the U.S. interstate highway system is believed to have had extremely large impacts on the U.S. economy up to its completion, after which additions to the network had limited effects.

- Transport and electricity services depend not only on roads and power plants but also on consumer durables (like cars, buses, trucks, and refrigerators) and machinery. The economic returns to these services are likely to be greater when the household or firm is located close to markets. In part because of this dependence on complementary inputs, impacts can be slow in coming. But because infrastructure is typically long-lived, the impacts may last a long time.

- Infrastructure may be built in pursuit of goals other than growth. Investments may be aimed at promoting social equity, environmental preservation, public health, political goals, or even personal enrichment. And in the absence of market signals, notably about future demand, it can be difficult to know where to build what and at what scale.

This complex relationship implies that it is not possible to determine an optimal level of infrastructure—and the existence of trade-offs between competing goals means that infrastructure planning and investment are inherently a political choice. Nevertheless, estimates of investment needs can help to inform that choice.

The most common methodology used to estimate infrastructure investment needs is, unfortunately, not the most useful. It relies on cross-country benchmarking that consists of looking at the average stock of infrastructure that countries typically have had at different levels of income, urbanization, and economic structure. Projections of future growth and socioeconomic change are then used to estimate the cost of maintaining the historical relationship derived from global estimates. This approach has several limitations: (a) there is no assumption of optimality—if infrastructure was under- or oversupplied in the past, the gap will remain, and (b) the estimates are highly sensitive to the projected values for growth and socioeconomic changes, with the sensitivity seldom explored.

A better approach, but one that applies only to cases where specific goals have been identified, is to price them using costing models. We use this approach for the access targets defined by the SDGs: universal access to safe water and sanitation, universal electrification, and improved accessibility to rural transport. For these targets, we rely on existing costing models, expanded and adapted to serve our needs.

Where objectives are more complex—such as a reliable electricity sector or a transport system adapted to a country's geography and trade patterns and compatible with low-carbon pathways—we use economic-engineering models. These are partial or general equilibrium models that, unfortunately, sometimes treat demand as exogenous. They do, however, offer a good representation of power systems and, more rarely, transport. Since no single model can do a good job of capturing the sectors in which we are interested, we rely on 14 different models that have been developed by various institutions for the different sectors and subsectors we study.

The main innovation of our approach, however, is in how we use these models. We draw from best-practice, long-term decision-making approaches to generate scenarios or "if-then" approaches. These approaches expose cost drivers and clarify the implications of assumptions, often implicitly made, about uncertain parameters (such as climate change policies or impacts, the evolution of technology, population growth, and urbanization). Our framework starts by identifying objectives and the metrics used to measure success; it then examines a variety of technical and policy options available to reach the objectives, along with exogenous factors that influence the cost and success of the investments in delivering the services.

As such, our approach has many advantages relative to previous estimates. First, we rely on numerous scenarios to explore uncertainty and the consequences of policy choices. Second, we use only models that have been published and peer reviewed and avoid proprietary, black-box models. Third, unlike many recent reports on investment needs that collate results from varying studies, we develop our results specifically for this report, following a consistent approach and timeline. Fourth, we systematically estimate not just capital expenditure for new investments, but also replacement capital costs as well as maintenance for new and existing infrastructure. Fifth, we provide estimates for both access and climate goals.

In the process, we make clear how misleading single-number estimates can be. Capital investments needed for electricity, transport, water and sanitation, irrigation, and coastal protection vary by a factor of 1 to 4 (or from 2 percent to 8 percent of GDP), depending on the ambition of the goal, the technologies adopted, how they are rolled out, their costs, and assumptions regarding socioeconomic pathways, notably population growth and urbanization (figure O.1). Even if we focus on investment plans that are compatible with a 2°C path, the range does not get narrower, as the goal of climate change mitigation is not the main driver of cost. We thus identify policy mixes that could enable countries to achieve the infrastructure-related SDGs: universal access to water, sanitation, and electricity; greater mobility; improved food security; better protection from floods; and eventual full decarbonization, while limiting spending on new infrastructure to 4.5 percent of GDP per year (table O.1).

We also offer an in-depth look at what disruptive technologies could mean for infrastructure. These technologies can come from enabling (and cross-cutting) innovations (such as the Internet of Things [IoT], artificial intelligence, machine learning, 3-D printing, and batteries) or from sector-specific ones (such as autonomous or electric vehicles and new biological water filtration techniques). But the disruption lies in how they are adopted, not simply in their availability.

SCENARIO APPROACHES ALLOW FOR INFORMED POLICY MAKING

Turning to sector-by-sector results, a clear finding is that, for every single sector, the two most important determinants of cost are the ambition of the goal in terms of access and quality—underscoring the need for policy debates on infrastructure to focus on this issue—and spending efficiency to reach the goal. Spending efficiency depends on the quality of complementary policies and on measures to reduce unit costs (like better procurement, planning, or execution). But the technologies used are also important given that they often involve trade-offs regarding the quality of service or other objectives (such as equity or environmental sustainability). The time horizon also matters: the solution that is least expensive over the next 15 years may result in higher costs later on.

Water: Lower-Cost Technologies Can Help to Achieve the SDGs

SDG targets 6.1 and 6.2 set out the goal of universal access to *safely managed* water, sanitation, and hygiene services and an end to open defecation by 2030. This goal can be achieved using more or less expensive technologies (for example, relying on septic tanks rather than on sewerage systems with treatment) and following different pathways. One option is to roll out universal access to *basic* water and sanitation services (an "indirect" pathway) before upgrading to safely managed

FIGURE O.1 The cost for infrastructure investments ranges from 2 percent to 8 percent of GDP per year in low- and middle-income countries

Average annual cost to develop infrastructure for the preferred scenario and full range of results, by sector, 2015–30

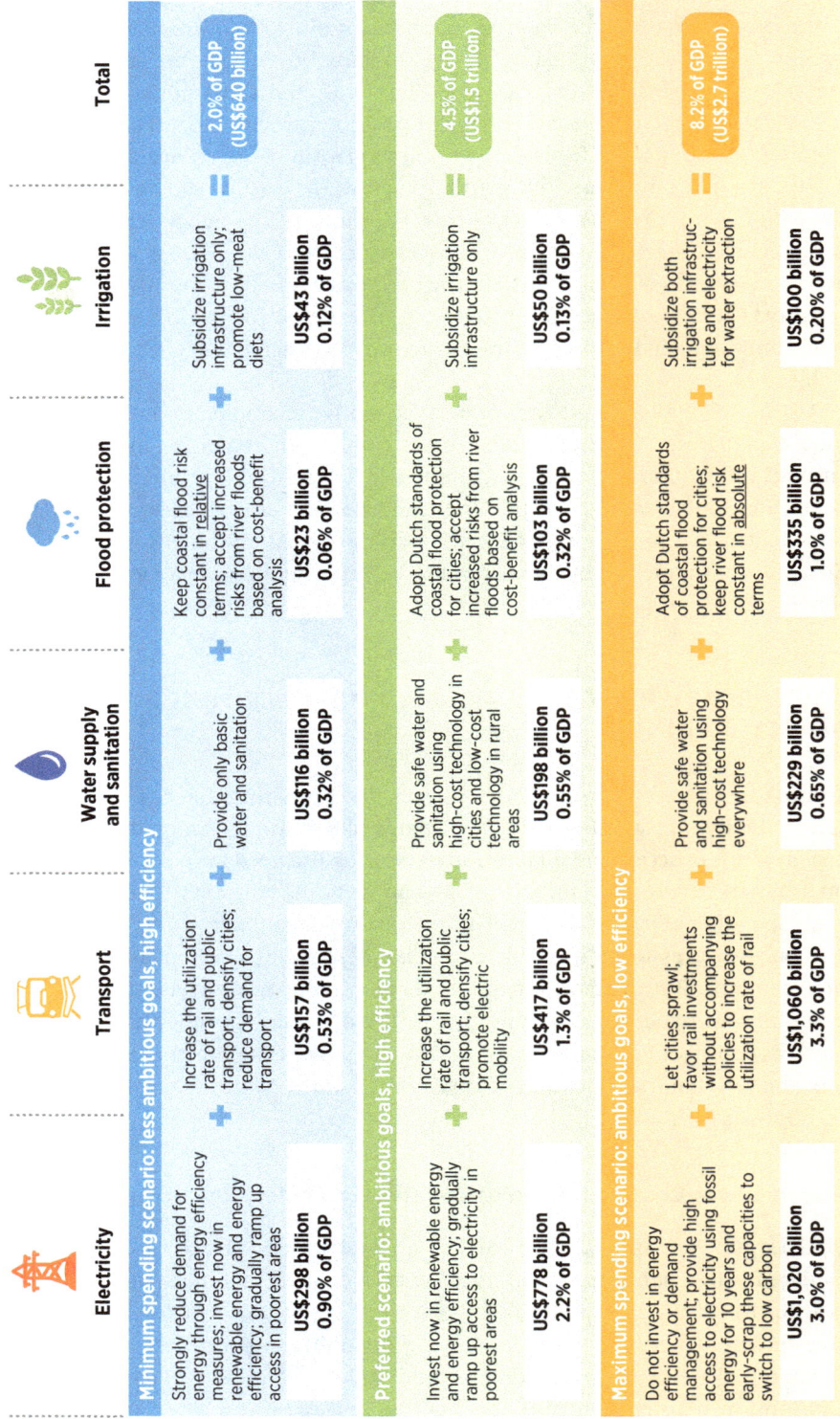

	Electricity	Transport	Water supply and sanitation	Flood protection	Irrigation	Total
Minimum spending scenario: less ambitious goals, high efficiency	Strongly reduce demand for energy through energy efficiency measures; invest now in renewable energy and energy efficiency; gradually ramp up access in poorest areas	Increase the utilization rate of rail and public transport; densify cities; reduce demand for transport	Provide only basic water and sanitation	Keep coastal flood risk constant in relative terms; accept increased risks from river floods based on cost-benefit analysis	Subsidize irrigation infrastructure only; promote low-meat diets	2.0% of GDP (US$640 billion)
	US$298 billion 0.90% of GDP	**US$157 billion** 0.53% of GDP	**US$116 billion** 0.32% of GDP	**US$23 billion** 0.06% of GDP	**US$43 billion** 0.12% of GDP	
Preferred scenario: ambitious goals, high efficiency	Invest now in renewable energy and energy efficiency; gradually ramp up access to electricity in poorest areas	Increase the utilization rate of rail and public transport; densify cities; promote electric mobility	Provide safe water and sanitation using high-cost technology in cities and low-cost technology in rural areas	Adopt Dutch standards of coastal flood protection for cities; accept increased risks from river floods based on cost-benefit analysis	Subsidize irrigation infrastructure only	4.5% of GDP (US$1.5 trillion)
	US$778 billion 2.2% of GDP	**US$417 billion** 1.3% of GDP	**US$198 billion** 0.55% of GDP	**US$103 billion** 0.32% of GDP	**US$50 billion** 0.13% of GDP	
Maximum spending scenario: ambitious goals, low efficiency	Do not invest in energy efficiency or demand management; provide high access to electricity using fossil energy for 10 years and early-scrap these capacities to switch to low carbon	Let cities sprawl; favor rail investments without accompanying policies to increase the utilization rate of rail	Provide safe water and sanitation using high-cost technology everywhere	Adopt Dutch standards of coastal flood protection for cities; keep river flood risk constant in absolute terms	Subsidize both irrigation infrastructure and electricity for water extraction	8.2% of GDP (US$2.7 trillion)
	US$1,020 billion 3.0% of GDP	**US$1,060 billion** 3.3% of GDP	**US$229 billion** 0.65% of GDP	**US$335 billion** 1.0% of GDP	**US$100 billion** 0.20% of GDP	

TABLE O.1 In the preferred scenario, investment costs are the highest for Sub-Saharan Africa and South Asia

Average annual cost of investment in the preferred scenario, by sector and region, 2015–30

% of regional GDP

Sector	Type of investment	Africa and Middle East		Asia			Latin America and Caribbean	Latin America and Caribbean[a]	Former Soviet Union[b]	Eastern Europe and Central Asia[b]
		Middle East and North Africa	Sub-Saharan Africa	South Asia	Asia	East Asia and Pacific	Latin America and Caribbean			
Electricity	Capital	1.3			2.4			1.2	5.3	
	Maintenance	0.3			0.7			0.2	1.1	
Transport	Capital	3.2			0.8			1.4	0.0	
	Maintenance	1.0			1.6			0.6	1.8	
Water supply and sanitation	Capital	0.9	1.6	0.8		0.3	0.5			0.4
	Maintenance	0.3	0.6	0.3		0.1	0.2			0.1
Irrigation	Capital[c]	0.1	0.4	0.3		0.1	0.1			0.0
Flood protection	Capital	0.2	0.8	0.5		0.3	0.2			0.06
	Maintenance	0.04	0.11	0.07		0.08	0.08			0.01
Total[d]	Capital	5.6	7.2	4.8		4.0	3.4			
	Maintenance	1.6	2.0	2.7		2.5	1.1			

Note: Columns are grouped by SSP region and World Bank region.

Note: Country groups differ between sectors due to the different regional aggregation of models used. SSP = shared socioeconomic pathway, as used by the Intergovernmental Panel on Climate Change.

a. The following countries and territories are included in the SSP country group, but not in the World Bank country group: Aruba, The Bahamas, Barbados, Chile, French Guiana, Guadeloupe, Martinique, and Uruguay.

b. The Russian Federation is included in the SSP Former Soviet Union group, but not in the World Bank Eastern Europe and Central Asia group because it is classified as a high-income country.

c. Includes maintenance.

d. Based on countries that are included in all studies.

FIGURE O.2 **The goal and the choice of technology are the main drivers of investment costs**

Average annual cost of capital investment in water and sanitation, by access goal, strategy, and choice of technology, 2015–30

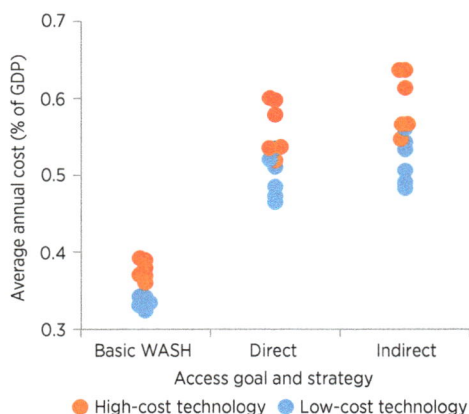

Source: Based on Hutton and Varughese 2016.
Note: Each dot corresponds to 1 of 36 scenarios based on variations across three goals (basic WASH, direct, indirect), two technologies (high cost, low cost), three possible rates of population growth and associated urbanization, and a high and a low estimate of capital cost. The graph (like others in this overview) is a "beeswarm" plot, which plots data points relative to a fixed reference axis (the x-axis) in a way that no two data points overlap, showing not only the range of values but also their distribution. The "direct" pathway is one in which every new household served is provided with safely managed water and sanitation; the "indirect" pathway first rolls out universal access to basic services before upgrading to safely managed services. Estimates include capital costs both to expand access and to preserve it for those currently served. WASH = water, sanitation, and hygiene.

services, as opposed to providing all newly served households directly with *safely managed* services (the "direct" pathway). We therefore examine the cost of achieving access to both basic and safely managed water and sanitation (two different levels of ambition) by varying technologies, pathways, and assumptions regarding population growth and urbanization as well as capital costs.

Our results show that while the total capital cost to achieve universal access to basic water and sanitation ranges from US$116 billion to US$142 billion, the cost to achieve the SDG targets ranges from US$171 billion to US$229 billion (0.5 percent to 0.6 percent of GDP). This cost includes the capital costs of extending coverage to persons who are currently unserved—which ranges from US$67 billion to US$129 billion (0.2 percent to 0.4 percent of GDP) for achieving SDG targets 6.1 and 6.2—as well as the cost of replacing *existing* assets that have reached the end of their useful life (US$100 billion).[1]

The principal driver of capital cost beyond the ambition of the goal is the choice of technology (figure O.2). The high-cost-technology option divides the results into two distinct groups, meaning that, regardless of capital cost overruns and population and urbanization rates, the low-cost technology remains less expensive. The pathway chosen (direct or indirect) makes little difference overall, although the indirect one is slightly more expensive.

The low-cost-technology option thus appears to be the most cost-effective means of achieving SDG targets 6.1 and 6.2. For most countries, it could make sense to start with low-cost technologies where the conditions (population density, urbanization) allow, notably for wastewater and sanitation, and then phase in the implementation of conventional sewerage and wastewater treatment—at least in the less densely populated areas. Such an approach facilitates building up the economic and financial sustainability of both the service and the utilities tasked with providing it.

There are several caveats to this point. First, in many countries, unfortunately, water quality norms and laws force cities to comply with very strict standards without allowing for gradualism. Second, non-network solutions (our low-cost option) are cost-effective in periurban areas, but not necessarily in dense urban areas. Non-network solutions may simply be impractical in very large, dense cities, while networked solutions create economies of scale in large cities. Finally, the low-cost option does not allow countries to achieve SDG target 6.3 ("By 2030, improve water quality by reducing pollution, … halving the proportion of untreated wastewater") and target 6.6 ("By 2020, protect and restore water-related ecosystems")—both of which require wastewater treatment facilities. As such, the choice is not so simple. Besides, new technologies described in chapter 6 of this report, like ultraviolet rays and photocatalysts powered by solar panels and new trencher systems to make pipe laying much quicker and less costly, have the potential to accelerate progress toward targets 6.1 and 6.2 at a relatively lower cost.

Irrigation: Public Support Boosts Food Security but Can Pose Issues for Other SDGs

Where irrigation investments are justified, public support for irrigation is necessary because transforming traditional rainfed systems or upgrading water-inefficient irrigation systems to become productive irrigation systems typically requires investments that go well beyond the economic means of farmers. We thus model two strategies for public support for irrigation, which differ in the degree to which they subsidize irrigation capital and water use. We assess the cost of these two strategies across multiple scenarios, varying trade openness for food markets, climate change, and changes in diets.

The primary driver of future investment costs for irrigation is the extent of public support. Under the high public support policies—which fully subsidize water for farmers, resulting in irrigated land extending to its full potential—irrigation investments reach 0.15 percent to 0.25 percent of GDP per year, on average, between 2015 and 2030 in LMICs. This cost is substantially higher than under moderate public support policies that cover only capital expenditure (figure O.3). As with water and sanitation infrastructure, a large share of total spending is to replace existing capital (0.05 percent of GDP per year between 2015 and 2030).

At the regional level, the relative importance of new investment versus replacement of existing capital varies greatly, given that 33 percent of the world's total irrigated area in 2010 was in South Asia and 32 percent was in East Asia and Pacific, but only 6 percent was in Latin America, and only a few percent was in the other low- and middle-income regions. Total costs range between 0.08 percent to 0.16 percent of GDP annually for the

FIGURE O.3 Public support policies drive investment costs in irrigation

Average annual cost of investment in irrigation, by investment type and level of public support, 2015–30

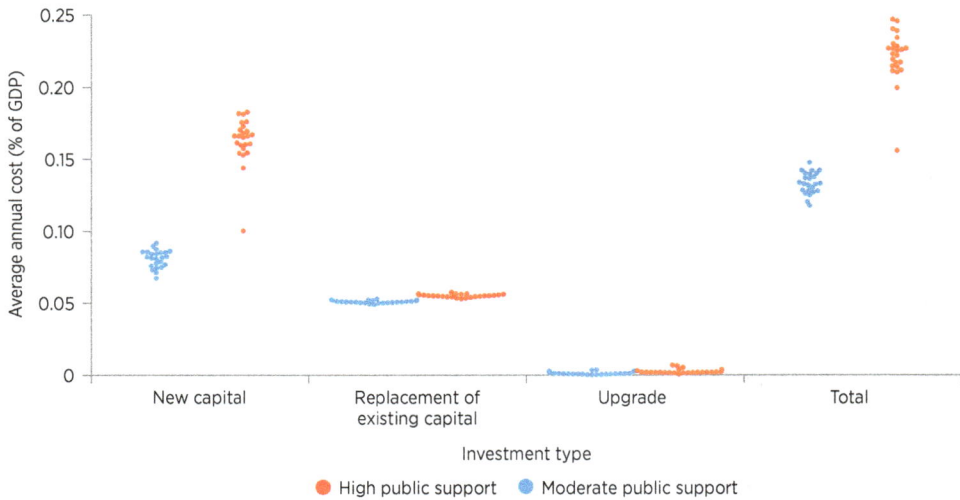

● High public support   ● Moderate public support

Source: Based on Palazzo and others 2019.
Note: High public support policies fully subsidize irrigation capital expenditures and water for farmers. Moderate public support policies cover only capital expenditures.

Middle East and North Africa and 0.32 percent to 0.72 percent of GDP annually for Sub-Saharan Africa.

Moreover, while investments in irrigation would lead to improved food security overall under both high and moderate public support strategies—and in all scenarios—regional outcomes vary. In fact, similar public support policies to increase irrigation to its full potential would lead to unequal outcomes across regions with regard to an increase in food availability—from 10 kilocalories per capita per day in Europe and Central Asia to 51 kilocalories per capita per day in South Asia.

In addition, investments in irrigation can have negative impacts on environmental flows and on forests (because of the rebound effect created by higher yields, which increase the expansion of cultivated land) and thus on greenhouse gas emissions and biodiversity. Further, in dry areas, irrigation can lead to maladaptation, whereby farmers drain finite underground water resources or specialize in "thirsty" crops ill-suited for the local climate. Thus, complementary policies are needed to limit the negative impacts on ecosystems and provide farmers with climate-smart practices and technologies.

The most desirable strategy in our analysis is perhaps to provide moderate public support for irrigation, which subsidizes irrigation equipment but not water, so that farmers gain a sense of increased water scarcity when too much water is extracted. This strategy would cost LMICs around 0.13 percent of GDP per year.

Power: A Choice of "Basic" Electrification or Much More?

As with water, the SDGs set a goal for electricity, namely, universal access by 2030. To understand the cost drivers for universal electrification, we rely on a costing tool created to estimate country-level funding requirements for Sub-Saharan Africa and extend it to another six countries (Afghanistan, Bangladesh, India, Myanmar, the Philippines, and the Republic of Yemen) that, together with Africa, account for around 95 percent of the population without access to electricity.

The analysis explores several strategies pertaining to the tier of service (or consumption level it allows—from enough power to charge a phone and power a few light bulbs for a few hours per day to enough power to run high-consumption appliances reliably). Each tier is assessed across multiple scenarios built with uncertain parameters (like rate of population growth and urbanization, growth of industrial demand, evolution of technology cost, and fuel price).

The analysis shows that what drives the investment cost for universal electrification is the tier of service offered to newly connected households (table O.2). Governments may choose first to offer basic service to newly connected households or instead to offer high-quality service immediately. The annual investment required to reach universal access by 2030 varies between US$45 billion and US$49 billion (0.9 percent of countries' GDP) for the basic-service strategy to between US$53 billion and US$58 billion (1.1 percent of GDP) for the high-service strategy.

Providing access via lower tiers of service may also help to tackle demand-side constraints such as consumers' low willingness or ability to pay. A recent World Bank study estimates that, in Africa, demand-side constraints account for some 40 percent of the access deficit (Blimpo and Cosgrove-Davies 2018). Adapting the tier of electrification offered to the socioeconomic situation of the households or regions targeted could help to reduce these demand-side constraints. Newly connected households need not stay in low tiers of service in the long run.

TABLE O.2 Policy choices on tiers of service drive costs of electrification

Average annual cost of investment in electrification, by tier of service provided, 2015–30

Indicator	Basic	Middle range	High quality
Amount (US$, billions)	45–49	47–52	53–58
% of GDP	0.92–0.94	0.95–0.98	1.1–1.2

Note: Costs are for Sub-Saharan Africa, Afghanistan, Bangladesh, India, Myanmar, the Philippines, and the Republic of Yemen. "Basic" corresponds to tiers 1 and 2 of the multitier framework of the Sustainable Energy for All global tracking framework; "middle range" refers to tier 3; and "high quality" refers to tiers 4 and 5. Variations within tiers of service are driven by assumptions regarding population growth, urbanization rate, industrial demand growth, technology cost evolution, and fuel price.

FIGURE O.4 Within Sub-Saharan Africa, the financial burden of reaching universal electricity access varies significantly

Average annual cost of investment in electrification in Sub-Saharan Africa, by targeted tier of service provision, 2015–30

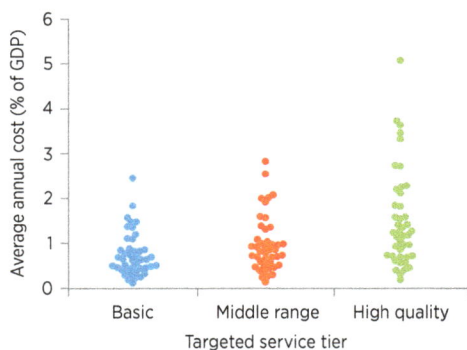

Note: Each dot represents one Sub-Saharan African country. All uncertain parameters are set to "reference scenario" values. See Nicolas and others (2019) for a presentation of the reference scenario (demography parameters: SSP 2; fossil fuel prices: medium; technology cost evolution: medium; industrial demand growth rate: growing with SSP 2 GDP). SSP = shared socioeconomic pathway.

However, the electrification pathway could begin with tailored technological solutions instead of directly aiming to connect the whole population to the grid. This pathway may also be the only affordable way forward for many countries (figure O.4). The emergence of new technologies and business models for mini-grid and off-grid electrification should help to reduce costs and facilitate the journey toward universal access.

In addition to providing access to the millions without it, the goal is to continue to provide reliable and affordable electricity while moving toward a decarbonized power system that is consistent with the 2°C target or the 1.5°C target of the Paris Agreement. Many economic engineering models have examined this challenge by relying on different assumptions and strategies. We examine six of them to compare the costs of a business-as-usual strategy with those of a 2°C strategy (the costs associated with a 1.5°C target are discussed in box 3.3 in chapter 3).

The conclusion that emerges from this multimodel analysis is that, depending on the assumptions made regarding socioeconomic pathways, technological change, and policy choices, a 2°C pathway could be either more or less expensive than a business-as-usual one for the power sector. Two models anticipate higher investment costs (up to 3 percent of GDP), while the more optimistic one anticipates lower costs regardless of the pathway chosen (0.96 percent of GDP) (figure O.5).

The variables (or cost drivers) that explain this divergence of estimates across models include (a) the capital cost of low-carbon technologies (renewable and carbon capture and storage), (b) energy efficiency improvements and demand management (as captured by the elasticity of demand parameters in the models), and (c) the extent to which the transition results in stranded assets (for example, thermal power plants that need to be retired early). Each model has a different way of employing these levers, which results in very different possible costs and futures. The only consistent finding across models is that costs increase with stranded assets and consumption per capita, but models vary significantly regarding the extent to which they rely on stranded assets and lower per capita consumption as levers in achieving a low-carbon pathway (figure O.6).

FIGURE O.5 **A 2C world may cost less than the business-as-usual one—or a lot more**

Average annual cost of investment in the power sector, by policy scenario and integrated assessment model used, 2015–30

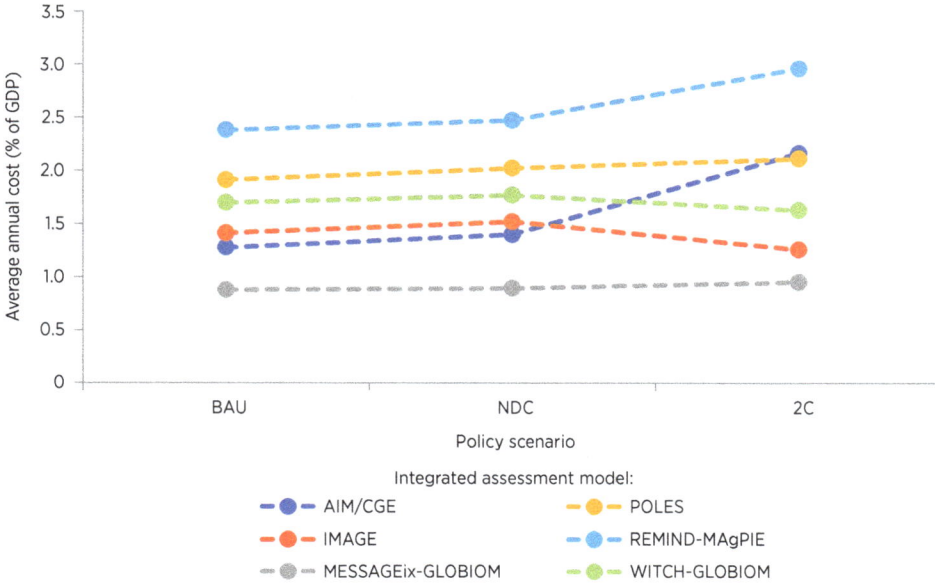

Source: Based on McCollum and others 2018.
Note: Results exclude high-income countries. BAU = investment needed if countries follow a business-as-usual trajectory; NDC = cost of implementing measures announced by countries in their nationally determined contribution to the Paris Agreement on Climate Change; 2C = measures needed for an emissions trajectory consistent with keeping climate warming below 2°C.

FIGURE O.6 **Models vary as to the extent to which decarbonization relies on stranded assets and reduced consumption**

Extent to which decarbonization relies on stranded assets and reduced consumption, by integrated assessment model used

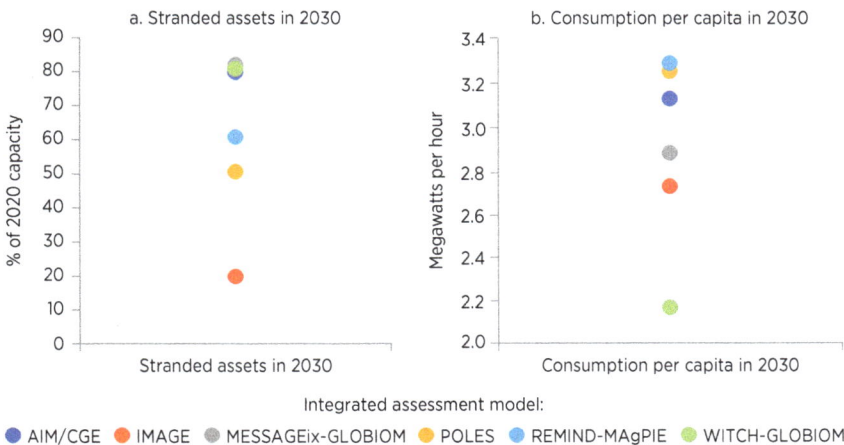

Source: Based on McCollum and others 2018.
Note: Stranded assets are calculated as total early retired and idle coal power plants in 2030 as a percentage of 2020 capacity. The assumptions are shown for a pathway consistent with a 2°C goal.

Our "preferred" pathway limits stranded assets, has a relatively high per capita consumption due to electric mobility, and invests mostly in renewable energy and storage. It results in capital costs of 2.2 percent of GDP per year, on average, for LMICs to increase electricity supply while decarbonizing their power systems.

Transport: Costs Are Shaped by Choice of Mode and Complementary Policies

Transport investments need to respond to demand for mobility and to manage pollution, including emissions of greenhouse gases. But demand for mobility is endogenous and varies with socioeconomic changes. As such, we use one of the rare models that not only simulates decarbonization pathways but also captures a detailed evolution of the transport sector within the global economy. This model allows us to simulate future mobility scenarios for both freight and passenger transport across hundreds of scenarios that combine varying socioeconomic pathways, consumer preferences, spatial organization, climate policies and ambitions, and technical challenges to mitigation policies (such as availability and cost of low-carbon technologies).

The range of estimates across these many scenarios is extremely large. Transport investment pathways could cost anywhere from 0.9 percent to 3.3 percent of LMICs' GDP per year, depending on the assumptions made and the policy instruments rolled out. Among the dozens of parameters explored, the two main cost drivers are the choice of mode shift for terrestrial transport—constant shares or shift to more rail and bus rapid transit—combined with policies to increase rail transport occupancy (figure O.7).

The message is similar if we focus on urban transport—which we do using a separate model that allows for a much more detailed analysis of urban transport. We compare three strategies: (a) "business as usual," (b) "robust governance," which relies on classic instruments to promote low carbon use (such as pricing and regulatory policies, including stringent fuel and vehicle efficiency standards, and investments in public transport), and (c) "integrated land-use and transport planning," which adds land-use policies to the previous toolbox. The third strategy is

FIGURE O.7 **The choice of terrestrial mode and rail occupancy drive transport investment costs**

Average annual cost of capital investment in transport, by choice of terrestrial mode and rail occupancy, 2015–30

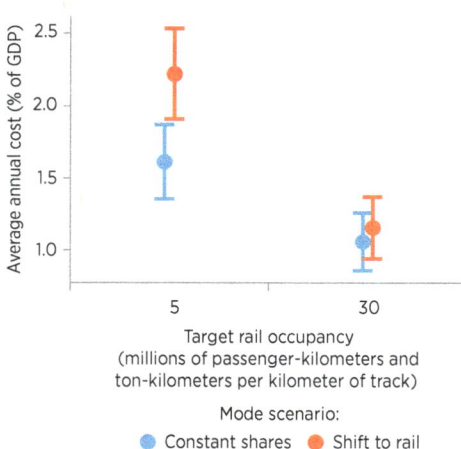

Mode scenario:
● Constant shares ● Shift to rail

Source: Based on Fisch-Romito and Guivarch 2019.
Note: Numbers exclude Organisation for Economic Co-operation and Development countries. The bars represent the range of estimates, generated by hundreds of scenarios, while the central dots represent the median value across estimates.

systematically less costly than any of the others, a finding that holds across regions (figure O.8).

A clear result of these two studies is that future demand for mobility can be supplied at relatively low infrastructure investment costs and low carbon dioxide (CO_2) emissions with a shift toward more rail and urban public transport—if it is accompanied by policies that ensure high rail occupancy and land-use policies to densify cities (table O.3).

FIGURE O.8 The biggest burden in urban transport investment is on upper-middle-income countries

Average annual cost of investment in urban transport, by region and planning scenario, 2015–30

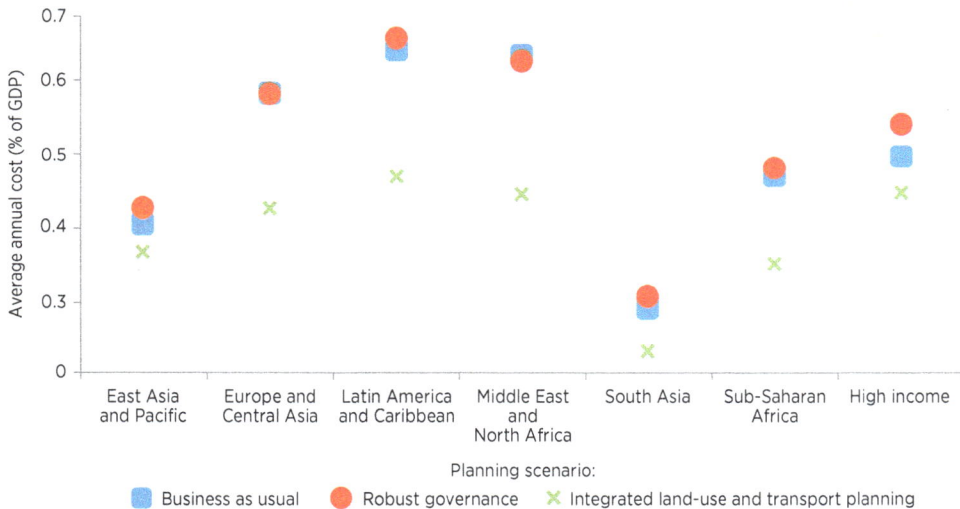

Source: Based on ITF 2018.

TABLE O.3 The preferred scenario uses low-carbon modes and accompanying policies for rail and public transport

Average annual cost of investment in transport infrastructure, by scenario, 2015–30

% of GDP

Mode	Entire transport sector		Urban transport sector only	
	Accompanying policy for high rail occupancy	No accompanying policy	Land-use planning	No land-use planning
Low carbon (rail, bus rapid transit)	**1.3**	2.3	**0.37**	0.47
Business as usual (roads)	n.a.	1.7	n.a.	0.45

Note: The preferred scenario is in bold. n.a. = not applicable.

Our "preferred scenario" for the entire transport sector would cost 1.3 percent of LMICs' GDP per year and would be consistent with full decarbonization after 2050. For urban areas, our preferred scenario is the integrated land-use and transport planning strategy, which would cost 0.37 percent of GDP per year.

We also look at the rural transport subsector, for which an indicator is mentioned in SDG 9 ("Proportion of the rural population who live within 2 kilometers of an all-season road"). However, no target is specified for this indicator—likely because it is unclear how a global target regarding rural accessibility could be set. To explore the challenge, we build a model to prioritize rural road investments based on two simple criteria: (a) maximizing the rural access index (RAI), which is defined as "the number of rural people who live within 2 kilometers of an all-season road as a proportion of the total rural population," and (b) providing connectivity with the primary and secondary network.[2] We price the investment option of upgrading existing tertiary roads or track to an all-season (paved) road.

Results show that setting a simple universal goal—for example, 80 percent accessibility—is neither realistic nor appropriate. The incremental cost of increasing rural accessibility increases rapidly with the ambition of the goal and, for many countries, rapidly becomes prohibitive. To illustrate: paving Sierra Leone's tertiary roads would increase its RAI from 28 percent to 70 percent but cost more than the country's GDP in 2017 (figure O.9). Increasing the country's RAI by 1 percentage point would cost US$30 million when the RAI is 30 percent (about 1 percent of GDP), but US$200 million when it is 70 percent.

Given that it is impossible to cost rural access overall, because goals and costs are too country-dependent, we reverse the question and examine how much access countries could gain by 2030 by spending 1 percent of their GDP on new rural roads every year. Our results show that with optimistic assumptions regarding GDP growth, the increase in access could range from 9 percentage points, on average, in East Asia to 17 percentage points, on average, in Sub-Saharan Africa (table O.4). But across all LMICs, rural accessibility would increase only from 39 percent to 52 percent.

The implication, then, is that achieving universal access to paved roads may not be a realistic goal for many countries. Instead, rural roads should be prioritized carefully and other solutions sought for increasing social integration in

FIGURE O.9 Upgrading rural roads in Sierra Leone becomes costly—fast

Cumulative cost of increasing access from 28% to 70%

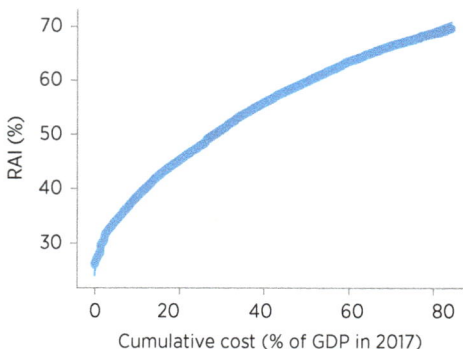

Note: RAI = rural access index.

TABLE O.4 Universal access to paved roads is not within countries' reach by 2030

Ability to achieve universal access to paved roads by 2030, by level of spending and region

% of rural population within 2 kilometers of a primary or secondary road

Region	2017	If all countries in the region spend 1% of their GDP per year by 2030
East Asia and Pacific	52	61
Europe and Central Asia	29	40
Latin America and Caribbean	34	45
Middle East and North Africa	39	51
South Asia	43	57
Sub-Saharan Africa	29	46

Note: GDP for each country grows following the shared socioeconomic pathway 5, which has the highest growth rate.

low-density areas. Options might include cabotage in coastal areas, smaller roads better suited for bicycle and motorcycle traffic, gravel roads (figure O.10), or even drones to deliver medical supplies and other essentials.

Floods: The Desired Levels of Protection Matter More Than Socioeconomics or Climate Change

Flood damages are expected to increase significantly over the 21st century as sea-level rise, more intense precipitation, extreme weather events, and socioeconomic developments combine to threaten an ever-increasing number of people and an ever-more expensive value of assets at risk in coastal and riverine floodplains (where cities and economic activities have often flourished). We therefore propose a comprehensive quantification of future investment needs in coastal protection infrastructure and complement it with an existing quantification of investment needs in riverine flood protection. These two studies rely on specialized models that consider (a) different *levels* of protection (reflecting different levels of risk aversion); (b) different *means* of providing that protection (through different protection technologies, like surge barriers or river dikes); and (c) uncertainties surrounding the cost of protection, future socioeconomic changes, and climate change (Nicholls and others 2019; Ward and others 2017).

FIGURE O.10 The cost of greater accessibility is much lower using gravel rather than paved roads in dry climates

Cumulative cost of increasing rural access with gravel and paved roads in Morocco

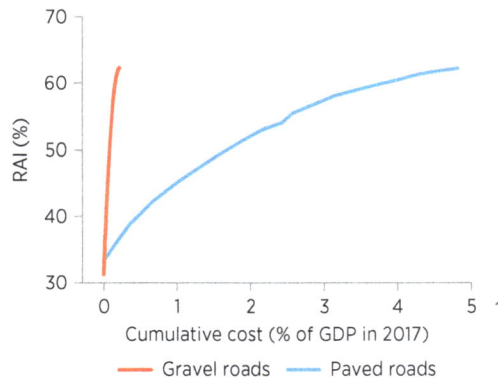

Note: RAI = rural access index.

Three strategies are studied for river floods: (a) achieving an optimal level of protection based on a simple cost-benefit analysis (CBA) that minimizes the sum of protection cost (capital and maintenance) and residual flood damage (to assets) to 2100; (b) keeping the current *absolute* level of flood risk constant in each country, in U.S. dollars; and (c) keeping the current *relative* level of flood risk constant in each country, as a percent of GDP.

The same three strategies are explored for coastal protection, along with a fourth: (d) the "low-risk-tolerance" strategy, which entails keeping average annual losses below 0.01 percent of local GDP for protected areas (defined on the basis of density). This is the level of protection that Amsterdam and Rotterdam set for themselves in 2005. We take this (high) Dutch standard as the acceptable risk standard in a low-risk-tolerance world.

Capital costs for river flood protection are an annual average of 0.04 percent to 0.47 percent of LMICs' GDP for the least expensive strategy (optimal protection), but 0.15 percent to 2.4 percent of GDP for the most expensive strategy (constant absolute risk) (figure O.11).

For coastal protection, future investment needs in LMICs also span a wide range depending on construction costs and the protection strategy pursued. Costs are between 0.006 percent and 0.05 percent of LMICs' GDP, on average, every year for the least expensive strategy (constant relative risk) and between 0.04 percent and 0.19 percent of GDP, on average, every year for the

FIGURE O.11 **The choice of protection level, combined with construction costs, shapes river flood protection capital costs**

Average annual cost of investment in river flood protection, by construction costs and risk-taking strategy, 2015–30

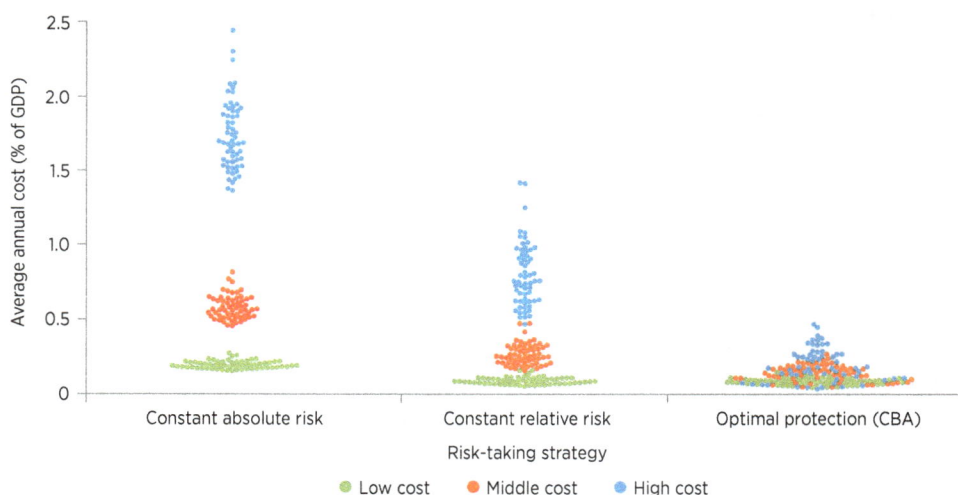

Source: Based on Ward and others 2017.
Note: Each dot represents one scenario, with the 60 scenarios in each subgroup derived by combining the three socioeconomic pathways, four radiative forcing scenarios (representative concentration pathways), and five global climate models. Numbers exclude high-income countries. CBA = cost-benefit analysis.

FIGURE O.12 **Construction costs, combined with risk aversion, shape coastal protection capital costs**

Average annual cost of investment in coastal protection, by construction costs and risk-taking strategy, 2015–30

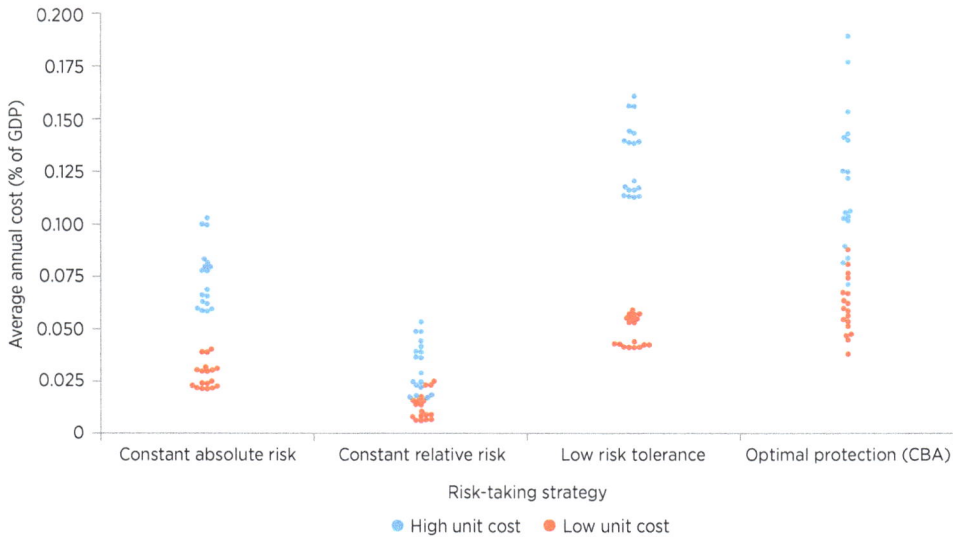

Source: Based on Nicholls and others 2019.
Note: Each dot represents one scenario, with the 18 scenarios in each subgroup derived by combining the three socioeconomic pathways, three representative concentration pathways, and two choices of technology (river dike or storm surge barrier). Numbers exclude high-income countries. If low- and middle-income countries with no coast were excluded, the points would be between 0.05 percent and 0.20 percent. CBA = cost-benefit analysis.

most expensive strategy (optimal protection based on CBA) (figure O.12). Uncertainty surrounding sea-level rise or socioeconomic change plays a secondary role, while the choice of technology for hard protection has only a minor impact on overall costs. Although these costs appear low, this is partly because the cost of what is a very localized and partial protection is being spread over national GDPs.

Construction costs for dikes are difficult to assess, because they are highly heterogeneous (they depend on soil characteristics and availability of nature-based solutions) and vary with the selected technology and with material costs that are challenging to predict (like availability and cost of sand and cement). Although Nicholls and others (2019) found in their detailed analysis of unit costs that costs can vary up to threefold within one country, Ward and others (2017) explored unit costs that vary from one to nine between the "low" and "high" scenarios.

If we use the middle-cost estimate from Ward and others (2017), which falls within the range defined by Nicholls and others (2019), investment costs in river flood protection range between 0.05 percent and 0.26 percent of LMICs' GDP for the optimal protection strategy based on CBA and between 0.45 percent and 0.81 percent of GDP for the constant absolute risk strategy.

Overall, in our "preferred" strategy (which minimizes overall costs and relies on what we consider "reasonable" assumptions), LMICs would have to spend 0.33 percent of their GDP annually on capital investments for both coastal and river flood protection by 2030. (This is an average over all climate change scenarios.) Although these estimates appear relatively modest, investment costs might be higher in practice if protection strategies have to be made robust to the many different futures that could arise as a result of unpredictable patterns of future climate change and urbanization. In addition, flood protection investments will need to be accompanied by complementary policies such as land-use planning to prevent people from settling in flood-prone areas or nature-based solutions to increase water storage and decrease runoff (and decrease investment costs in hard infrastructure). These investments will also have to be complemented by early-warning systems and communication about residual risk.

Disruptive Technologies: Governance Trumps Innovation

How might new technologies shape the future of infrastructure in LMICs? We explore scenarios depicting the ways in which infrastructure sectors can evolve as a result of cross-cutting innovations (such as IoT, artificial intelligence, machine learning, 3-D printing, and batteries) or sector-specific ones (such as autonomous vehicles, electric vehicles, and new biological water filtration techniques). But here, instead of using models, we used expert elicitation in structured interviews and workshops. The resulting three scenarios—"leapfrog," "lopsided," and "lock-in"—describe how various policy choices and external forces can lead to contrasting futures for infrastructure.

One aspect of the disruption is that these new technologies allow for more decentralization of infrastructure services, thus making it possible for people who can afford it to buy the service directly from the private sector and thereby get around large-scale infrastructure networks and the cross-subsidies that historically have funded service for poorer individuals. For example, in cities the availability of ride sharing and autonomous vehicles can encourage the better-off to shift from mass transit to private rides, thus threatening to bankrupt mass transit agencies.

Another aspect is the fact that technology disruptions create losers and winners. A failure to smooth the transition sufficiently for incumbents or, alternatively, excessive protection for incumbents are twin risks that need to be navigated carefully.

The key message that emerges from this expert elicitation is that the main forces that shape the way technology will affect infrastructure and the services it provides are the ability and success of governments, planning authorities, and regulatory authorities to fulfill their enabling and distributive functions. By enabling function, we mean their ability to put in place backbone infrastructure, financial incentives, and regulatory frameworks.

By distributive function, we mean their role in enacting measures to ensure that the spread of new technologies is not limited to the wealthy and does not decrease opportunities and access for the rest of the population.

Thus, the uncertainty regarding technology relevant to infrastructure over the next 15 or 20 years is not about the success of technology research and development, but rather its deployment in LMICs. That deployment, in turn, depends on how effective governments are in their enabling and distributive function.

OPERATIONS AND MAINTENANCE PLAY A MAJOR ROLE IN COSTS

O&M is a perennial challenge in infrastructure. All countries—rich and poor—struggle to assess properly the O&M resources needed to turn infrastructure stocks into reliable flows of services. While not unique to LMICs, this struggle is particularly central to the development agenda, given the general preference of donors to "cut ribbons" on new infrastructure rather than to finance what they consider to be the country's or the users' responsibility. Efforts have been made to resolve the issue by strengthening institutions (such as utilities or budgetary rules), creating a reliable source of funds (such as the Road Funds common in Africa), and increasing cost recovery at least to cover recurrent costs.

Yet this challenge is not systematically incorporated as an element to consider while deciding on an investment strategy. This is a serious problem, given that different types of infrastructure have very different implications for recurrent costs. Think about electricity: renewables have high capital (up-front) costs but negligible O&M costs; in contrast, thermal plants are typically much less expensive to build, but have high O&M costs, with volatile fossil fuel prices introducing great uncertainty as to future O&M costs.

The argument, therefore, is that "investment needs"—or rather the strategic decisions made about what technology to use to increase infrastructure stock—should be based on an analysis of *total* costs, with careful consideration of the choices or assumptions made about the cost of capital, discount rate, and future ability to cover O&M costs. CBAs and associated expected rates of return on infrastructure investments typically assume that the power plant, road, or water treatment plant will be functional during its expected lifetime. If that does not occur—due to the absence of fuel, chemicals, or maintenance—the economic calculus and associated ranking of options change dramatically.

This said, options with lower O&M costs will not always be the best ones, as they may reduce the flexibility of the investment. For example, in urban transport, a choice may be made to favor more flexible solutions (like buses rather than light rail) even if they exhibit higher operating costs. One reason to favor more flexible solutions, even if more expensive, could be the uncertainty surrounding new technologies that can disrupt the sector (see chapter 6 for a discussion).

Water and Sanitation: O&M Costs Account for More Than Half of Financing Needs

For water and sanitation, average annual O&M costs exceed capital costs in all of the scenarios considered, accounting for 54 percent to 58 percent of the total annual expenditure needed to deliver the service. When operations and maintenance are included, meeting SDG targets 6.1 and 6.2 costs between 1.1 percent and 1.4 percent of LMICs' GDP (figure O.13). Failure to perform routine maintenance would reduce the useful life of installed capital and increase overall capital replacement costs by at least 60 percent.

The fact that O&M constitutes the bulk of overall costs means that countries need to think about the affordability of expansion plans. It is not enough for donors to raise funds and for governments to make room for capital investments. Allowance for an equivalent amount, or more, must be made for O&M in order to ensure service sustainability. Whether this is

FIGURE O.13 Operations and maintenance spending matters as much as capital spending for water and sanitation

Average annual cost of capital and operations and maintenance in water and sanitation, by access goal and strategy, 2015–30

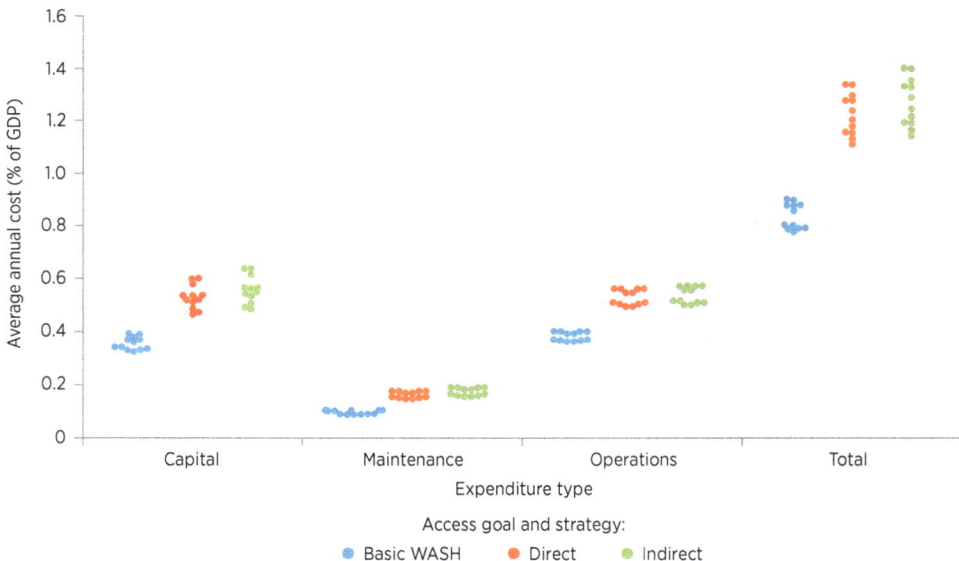

Source: Based on Hutton and Varughese 2016.
Note: Capital, operations, and maintenance costs are for both new and existing users. They represent the amount needed both to expand service and to continue serving existing users. The "direct" pathway is one in which every new household served is provided with safely managed water and sanitation; the "indirect" pathway first rolls out universal access to basic services before upgrading to safely managed services. WASH = water, sanitation, and hygiene.

covered through tariffs or paid for by taxpayers is a choice that each country or municipality will need to make, based on the population's ability to pay. (Currently, only 60 percent of utilities in LMICs fully cover O&M through user fees.) But a failure to raise the resources needed for operations and timely maintenance will result in the waste of scarce capital resources.

Beyond investing in infrastructure, additional resources will be required to strengthen water and sanitation institutions and regulations, given that infrastructure alone has never been enough to achieve sustainable provision of water, sanitation, and hygiene services. Policy, institutions, and appropriate regulations are needed if financial flows are to deliver the infrastructure needed and if this infrastructure, in turn, is to deliver the service desired.

Power Sector: O&M Costs, Especially Fuel Costs, Are Critical

The low uptake and willingness to pay that prevail across Africa can be explained (at least partially) by the poor reliability of power supply. In most African countries (79 percent), less than a third of firms report reliable access to electricity. In 2014, more than 50 percent of connected households in Liberia reported that they never have power; this share was around 30 percent in Sierra Leone and Uganda. In Madagascar, only about 300 megawatts of the 500 megawatts of installed capacity was operating in 2017, while in the Democratic Republic of Congo, 29 percent of hydropower plants and 57 percent of thermal plants are currently unable to operate. In Benin, the Comoros, Guinea-Bissau, and Sierra Leone, less than 20 percent of installed generation capacity is functioning and available.

Thus, the question of universal access cannot be restricted to capital investment needs. It has to include improving existing service, maintaining future infrastructure, and weighing the financial implications of today's investment choices on tomorrow's variable costs.

In the power sector, annual maintenance costs are generally estimated at around 3 percent of the cost of investment, on average, across all installed capacity (costs vary between 1 percent and 6 percent, depending on the plant technology). Given our estimates of the total installed capacity in LMICs, we estimate that maintenance costs add up to around US$136 billion. For Sub-Saharan Africa alone, maintenance costs could represent between US$2.5 billion and US$3.6 billion, on average, per year over the 2015–30 period, on top of the US$14.5 billion to US$22.6 billion needed for capital costs.

Making matters worse, maintenance costs pale in comparison with fuel costs, at least for countries heavily dependent on thermal plants. In Africa, variable costs, such as fuel costs, add up to US$24 billion to US$35 billion, which is significantly more than what will be needed in new investments. The exact amount depends on the extent to which access is expanded on- or off-grid (and new investments favor renewables), but it remains extremely high across all scenarios. This is because the current energy

FIGURE O.14 **The technology mix for electricity determines the variable cost burden**

Ratio of variable to total investment costs in South America and Sub-Saharan Africa

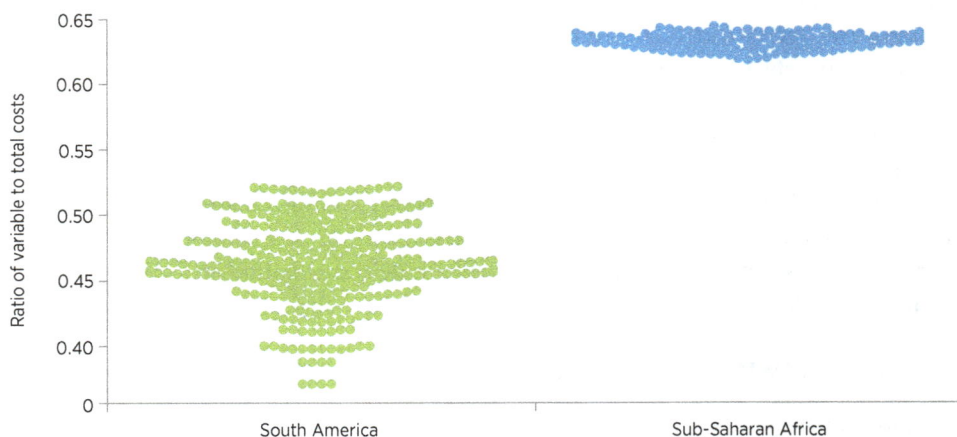

Note: Each dot represents a scenario. There are many more scenarios for South America than for Sub-Saharan Africa, as more sources of uncertainty are explored. The large difference in the ratio of variable to total costs between them can be explained by the fact that Africa relies largely on thermal plants, while South America gets the bulk of its electricity from hydropower.

mix is dominated by thermal plants—in contrast with a region such as Latin America, whose electricity is derived primarily from low-variable-cost hydroelectricity and whose O&M (including fuel) costs are substantially lower as a result (figure O.14).

Transport: Overall Maintenance Costs as Much as New Investment

Maintenance costs for all existing and future transport infrastructure in LMICs could amount to 1.1 percent to 2.1 percent of GDP per year, on average, between 2015 and 2030—which is almost as high as what is needed for new capital investment. The costs of maintenance are even higher than the costs of new investment in countries that already have large transport networks, such as those in Asia and the former Soviet Union (figure O.15). Failure to perform routine maintenance would increase overall capital and rehabilitation costs by 50 percent.

For urban areas, operating costs for public transport dwarf the costs of both maintenance and new investment. While total maintenance costs amount to 0.19 percent to 0.21 percent of GDP per year, on average, over 2015–30, depending on the strategy, the operation of public transport infrastructure could represent 1 percent to 1.3 percent of GDP per year, on average, in LMICs—or twice as much as new investment costs. This represents between 1 percent of countries' GDP in South Asia and 2.3 percent in Sub-Saharan Africa annually. While some of these operating costs should be recouped through passenger fares, cost recovery is typically low. In European countries, subsidies for public transport represent up to 60 percent of the total

FIGURE O.15 **Maintenance may cost as much as or more than new investments in transport**

Average annual cost of investment in maintenance and new transport infrastructure, by region, 2015–30

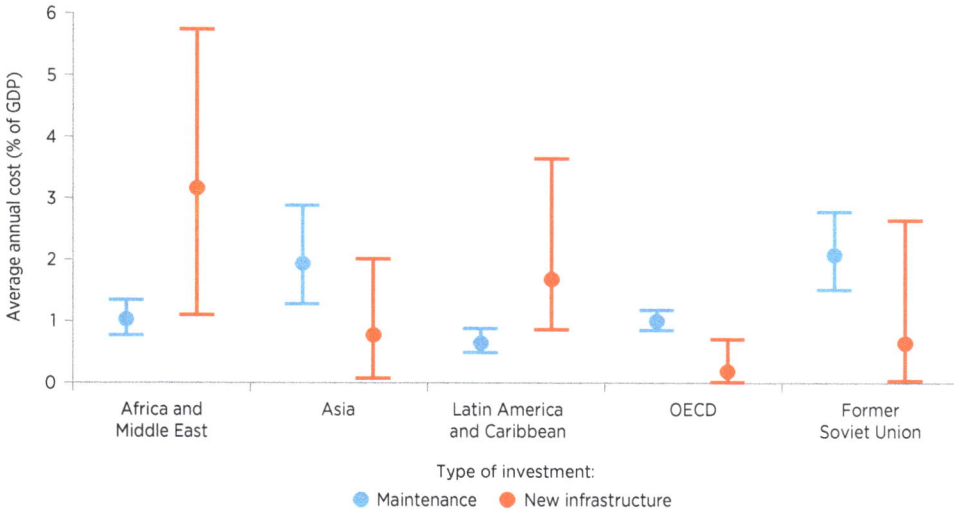

Type of investment:
● Maintenance   ● New infrastructure

Source: Based on Fisch-Romito and Guivarch 2019.
Note: The bars represent the range of estimates, generated by hundreds of scenarios, while the central dots represent the median value across estimates. The regional breakdown is that of the IMACLIM-R model and is *more* aggregated than the usual World Bank regional breakdown. OECD = Organisation for Economic Co-operation and Development.

operation costs. Cities should be prepared to spend on the operation of their public transport system at least as much as they spend on new infrastructure, on average, every year.

Flood Protection: Lives Depend on Good Maintenance

Flood protection infrastructure creates countervailing risks—that is, risks that arise as a result of an action taken to reduce a target risk—because it creates an incentive for people to settle in at-risk locations that now appear safer. These countervailing risks reinforce the importance of the commitment made by the initial capital investment. Failure to maintain the protective infrastructure can create the risk of catastrophic failures and put lives, not just assets, at risk.

By 2030, the cost of maintaining existing and future coastal protection infrastructure is between 0.02 percent and 0.07 percent of LMICs' GDP, on average, every year—depending on the protection strategy and construction costs (maintenance costs are estimated as a fixed fraction of construction costs). For river flood protection, the cost of maintaining new infrastructure is between 0.002 percent and 0.04 percent of LMICs' GDP annually by 2030.

While these costs appear affordable, the development of appropriate institutions and governance mechanisms to deliver maintenance, as well as the necessary funding streams, is essential for an infrastructure-based protection strategy to be effective. The Netherlands and the Thames Estuary (London) offer good examples of major flood defense systems that have been actively maintained over decades and upgraded as needed. These systems are linked to strong flood management institutions and long-term planning looking many decades into the future. For protection to be successful elsewhere, similar arrangements would be required, including guaranteed funding streams for maintenance.

If this commitment cannot be delivered, alternative coastal adaptation approaches are recommended—such as accommodation, nature-based solutions, or retreat. Further, even if well-maintained, defenses are always associated with residual risk, and appropriate measures need to be put in place for their management, especially in coastal cities. Appropriate flood warnings and disaster preparedness mechanisms remain essential, even if a good protection and maintenance regime is in place.

IN SUM

We have demonstrated that exercises to estimate infrastructure investment needs could generate helpful policy insights if carried out within a scenario framework and designed to identify cost-effective ways of achieving a given goal. This report attempts to shift the debate on infrastructure needs and should be seen as a starting point for further analysis. In particular, the approach explored here can be used at a more local level to help decision makers to build long-term infrastructure plans.

The choices and uncertainties driving future infrastructure needs at the local level might differ from the ones assessed in this report, but the method that decision makers can use to identify them would be the same. The key message is that it is both possible, and important, to explore how multiple investment and policy choices would play out in multiple futures, according to multiple objectives and metrics for success. This approach allows identifying the factors that matter, the trade-offs between objectives, and the most robust policy choices.

Looking ahead, a few questions stand out that we could not do full justice to in the context of the present work. First is the issue of nature-based infrastructure and how it may be a critical complement to hard infrastructure, reducing costs and increasing resilience. We touch on the subject in chapter 5 on flood protection, but wetlands, floodplains, forests, and mangroves are critical for water services (including hydroelectricity) and resilience of infrastructure more generally. This subject is now the focus of a separate World Bank report (Browder and others, forthcoming).

Another issue is that of spending efficiency. Unit costs vary greatly across countries in a way that defies easy explanations. Reporting this variation—and exploring its sources and potential ways of reducing costs—is a much-needed undertaking. For example, the U.K. government reports having reduced construction costs in public sector projects by 20 percent, thanks to the adoption of digital construction modeling. A 20 percent reduction in construction costs would be equivalent to tripling or quadrupling private investments in infrastructure from their current level.

Spending better, rather than just spending more, is at the center of the infrastructure challenge. Thus, for an investment needs assessment to be useful, it must be designed to shed light on how to do so.

NOTES

1. All existing assets—be they for basic or for safely managed service provision—are assumed to be replaced at the end of their useful life, creating new investment needs, irrespective of the choice of policy strategy.
2. An "all-season road" refers to "a road that is motorable all year round by the prevailing means of rural transport." The RAI is below 60 percent in most LMICs—meaning that less than 60 percent of the rural population live more than 2 kilometers from an all-season road—and is below 20 percent in 24 countries (Mikou and others 2019).

REFERENCES

Blimpo, M., and M. Cosgrove-Davies. 2018. *Electricity Uptake for Economic Transformation in Sub-Saharan Africa.* Washington, DC: World Bank.

Browder, G., S. Ozment, I. Rehberger Bescos, T. Gartner, and G. M. Lange. Forthcoming. *Integrating Green and Grey: Creating Next Generation Infrastructure.* Washington, DC: World Bank and World Resources Institute.

Fisch-Romito, V., and C. Guivarch. 2019. "Investment Needs for Transport Infrastructures along Low Carbon Pathways." Background paper prepared for this report, World Bank, Washington, DC.

Hutton, G., and M. C. Varughese. 2016. "The Costs of Meeting the 2030 Sustainable Development Goal Targets on Drinking Water, Sanitation, and Hygiene." Technical paper, Water and Sanitation Program. World Bank, Washington, DC.

ITF (International Transport Forum). 2018. "The Billion Dollar Question: How Much Will It Cost to Decarbonise Cities' Transport Systems?" Background paper prepared for this report, World Bank, Washington, DC.

McCollum, D. L., W. Zhou, C. Bertram, H.-S. de Boer, V. Bosetti, S. Busch, J. Després, and others. 2018. "Energy Investment Needs for Fulfilling the Paris Agreement and Achieving the Sustainable Development Goals." *Nature Energy* 1 (June). doi: 10.1038/s41560-018-0179-z.

Mikou, M., J. Rozenberg, E. Koks, C. Fox, and T. Peralta-Quiros. 2019. "Assessing Rural Accessibility and Rural Roads Investment Needs Using Open Source Data." Background paper prepared for this report, World Bank, Washington, DC.

Nicholls, R. J., J. Hinkel, D. Lincke, and T. van der Pol. 2019. "Global Investment Costs for Coastal Defence through the 21st Century." Background paper prepared for this report, World Bank, Washington, DC.

Nicolas, C., J. Rozenberg, and B. Samson. 2019. "Meeting the SDGs for Electricity Access—Using a Multi Scenario Approach to Understand the Cost Drivers of Power Infrastructure in Sub-Saharan Africa." Background paper prepared for this report, World Bank, Washington, DC.

Palazzo, A., H. Valin, M. Batka, and P. Havlík. 2019. "Investment Needs for Irrigation Infrastructure along Different Socio-Economic Pathways." Background paper prepared for this report, World Bank, Washington, DC.

Ward, P. J., B. Jongman, J. C. Aerts, P. D. Bates, W. J. Botzen, A. D. Loaiza, S. Hallegatte, J. M. Kind, J. Kwadijk, and P. Scussolini. 2017. "A Global Framework for Future Costs and Benefits of River-Flood Protection in Urban Areas." *Nature Climate Change* 7 (9): 642–46.

1

Making Infrastructure Needs Assessments Useful and Relevant

MARIANNE FAY AND JULIE ROZENBERG

KEY MESSAGES

- Estimating how much infrastructure is needed is a complex undertaking due to multiple and sometimes competing goals (economic, social, environmental, political) and the indirect link between physical infrastructure and the services to be delivered.

- Most assessments of infrastructure investment needs produce a single number that cannot inform the debate about the ambitions and goals of infrastructure investments or about cost drivers and critical assumptions.

- Scenarios, or "if-then" approaches, allow for informed policy making by exposing cost drivers and shedding light on the implications of assumptions, often implicitly made, about uncertain parameters. Such scenarios can be built on the basis of debates about goals and metrics to measure success, the technical and policy options available to reach the objectives, and the exogenous factors that influence the cost and success of the investments.

INTRODUCTION

The infrastructure gap is large: 940 million individuals are without electricity, 663 million lack improved drinking water sources, 2.4 billion lack improved sanitation facilities, 1 billion live more than 2 kilometers from an all-weather road, and uncounted numbers are unable to access work and educational opportunities due to the absence or high cost of transport services. Infrastructure in low- and middle-income countries (LMICs) falls short of what is needed for public health and individual welfare, environmental considerations, and climate change risks—let alone economic prosperity or middle-class aspirations.

The solution, many argue, is to spend more. Thus, the question of how to attract more resources to infrastructure (in particular, from the private sector) has dominated much of the conversation in international forums such as the Group of Twenty. The international community's Sustainable Development Goals (SDGs) and rising concerns about the urgency of action on climate change have added further impetus to the push to spend more on infrastructure.

But the story is not so simple. The question of "how much is needed?" should always be accompanied by a clarification as to "for what?" And the answer to "for what?" lies with the contexts, economic growth aspirations, and social and environmental objectives of individual countries. For example, geography matters: households in Malawi will never need as much heating as those in Sweden. And the answer to "for what?" should be about services—not infrastructure per se. Improved mobility can be generated from better land-use planning and denser housing, not just transport investments; flood protection can rely on dikes or well-preserved ecosystems (or both).

Further, an emphasis on spending more focuses attention on the need to raise funds rather than on the need to spend better. Efficiency and demand management policies can significantly reduce investment needs and help to close service gaps much more cost-effectively than new infrastructure investments alone. For instance, "shaving" peak electricity demand with smart meters can reduce the need for new power plants. Similarly, achieving a better balance between capital and operations and maintenance (O&M) spending can reduce overall spending needs while improving service.

As such, the commonly used approaches to investment needs—which typically produce a single quantified estimate of capital expenditure—are neither helpful nor accurate. They are commonly used because single numbers are attractive in their simplicity, and they avoid potentially difficult debates about the appropriate goals and trade-offs. But single estimates of capital investments cannot inform questions around what are the appropriate goals, the best way to pursue them, and the means available to improve public spending efficiency. And how much is needed depends on many factors, including the country's goals and its efficiency in pursuing those goals.

This report aims to shift the debate regarding investment needs away from a simple focus on spending more and toward a focus on spending better on the right objectives, using relevant metrics. Spending more may still be needed, but that decision should be based on a careful and systematic approach to investment needs estimates, one that emphasizes the importance of clearly defining the vision and accounting for the sensitivity of the results to assumptions.

This chapter proposes a framework to help decision makers to identify the objectives they want to achieve with infrastructure investments and to make infrastructure needs assessments relevant for policies. It draws from best-practice, long-term decision making, which involves debating three key areas: (a) the multiple objectives that the decision is trying to achieve and the metrics used to measure success, (b) the technical and policy options available to reach the objectives, and (c) the exogenous factors that influence the cost and success of the investments in delivering the services for which they are built. This approach generates scenarios, or "if-then" approaches, that expose cost drivers and the implications of assumptions, often implicitly made, about uncertain parameters, such as climate change, evolution of technology, population growth, and urbanization.

The discussion that follows is organized around the two key messages of this report: first, it is difficult to estimate how much infrastructure is needed, and single-number estimates of investment needs are neither accurate nor helpful; second, it is possible to make investment estimation exercises useful for decision making by using the kind of scenarios, or "if-then" approaches, that have been developed for long-term decision making.

WHY IS ESTIMATING INFRASTRUCTURE NEEDS SO DIFFICULT?

Infrastructure is only as useful as the services it provides—and these services depend on many factors other than infrastructure, making it complex to model the relationship between infrastructure and growth or welfare. This complexity has spawned a large literature on the topic as well as some rather heroic attempts at estimating "the" global infrastructure investment need.

The Relationship between Infrastructure and Growth Is Complex

Economic infrastructure—such as water and sanitation, electricity, transport, and protective infrastructure such as dikes and levees—is clearly necessary for the functioning of modern economies and the well-being of populations.[1] However, it does not necessarily follow that more infrastructure will bring more growth or greater prosperity. The constraints may lie elsewhere—with human or private capital or with weak institutions and the rule of law. And, of course, infrastructure is expensive to build and maintain, much of it financed through costly and often distortive taxation, implying heavy trade-offs.

As such, a large literature has developed over the last 25 years to assess whether countries are investing "enough" or "too much" in infrastructure and to identify the optimal amount of infrastructure investment. Unfortunately, this literature is hardly conclusive (Bom and Ligthart 2014; Estache and Fay 2010; Holmgren and Merkel 2017; Straub 2008, 2011). While the majority (though not all) of the studies tend to find a positive causal relationship between infrastructure and growth, the magnitude of the relationship varies widely. A meta-analysis of 78 studies (covering mostly high-income countries) found that elasticities of output with respect to infrastructure range from −0.06 to 0.52 (Holmgren and Merkel 2017), meaning that infrastructure investments sometimes have a slightly negative impact on growth and sometimes have a significantly positive impact.

Why is it so difficult to establish precisely what appears to most observers in most countries to be an obvious need for more and better infrastructure? The reasons are several.

To begin with, most infrastructure is in the form of networks, which creates threshold effects, with returns that vary with the stage of completion and the number of users. For example, construction of the U.S. interstate highway system is believed to have had extremely large impacts on U.S. total factor productivity up to the point of its completion, after which returns to additional domestic road building declined steeply (Fernald 1999). Similarly, in Indian villages, significantly reducing diarrhea and improving health seem to require interventions that provide the *entire* village with access to both safe water and sanitation, making it difficult to measure the return on marginal investments (Duflo and others 2015).

Also, unlike private capital, infrastructure is unlikely to be a simple argument in a country's production function:

- Better infrastructure may lead to a reorganization of economic activities with increased trade and deeper labor markets, thereby creating agglomeration economies. Indian colonial districts saw a 16 percent increase in income following the building of the country's railroad network, as railways massively improved transport and enabled trade (Donaldson 2018).

- Impacts vary depending on the availability of complementary inputs and the local context. Peripheral counties in China appear to have been hurt by the construction of the highway system that benefited the nodal counties (Storeygard 2016). Rural electrification substantially increased female employment and enabled microenterprises in South Africa (Dinkelman 2011), but had no measurable impact on employment or welfare in Kenya (Lee and others 2016). The explanation could be that Kenya's villages were too poor or credit-constrained or the electricity service was too unreliable for the newly connected households to make much use of this electrification.

- Impacts may also take time in coming, because of this interaction with complementary inputs. But given that infrastructure typically has a lifetime of several decades to centuries, and given the effects already mentioned, impacts are possibly very long-lasting. In Ghana, the impact of colonial railroads on the distribution of economic activity across the country persists today, long after these railroads have collapsed (Jedwab and Moradi 2015). In the United States, many former portage sites (sites that required overland hauling due to obstacles to water navigation) are still important nodes for the transport network, long after their historical advantage has become obsolete (Bleakley and Lin 2012). And a large amount of future greenhouse gas emissions is already committed by existing energy and transport infrastructure (Davis and others 2010; Guivarch and Hallegatte 2011).

Then, too, not all infrastructure is created equal. The civil servants and politicians who decide on the type and placement of infrastructure do not always do so with the objective of maximizing growth. They may be pursuing goals of social equity (such as integration of remote areas), public health (such as rural water and sanitation programs), electoral ambitions, or even personal gain. Or, in the absence of a market signal to equate demand and supply, they may simply find it difficult to determine the optimal type and placement of infrastructure. Besides, infrastructure is "lumpy," so that most LMICs still in the process of developing their transport networks and electricity systems are likely to have too much or too little infrastructure at any point in time.

Finally, infrastructure is hard to measure. Much of the early infrastructure research used total public investment flows to construct a measure of the stock of infrastructure capital.[2] This is problematic, as the share of public investment that is allocated to economic infrastructure varies across countries and across time, as does the importance of private investment in infrastructure. As such, total public investment will overestimate or underestimate infrastructure investment. In addition, since the effectiveness of public spending varies across and within countries, infrastructure investments may not even be a good proxy for the stock of capital, prompting many researchers to rely directly on measures of stocks of infrastructure. Unfortunately, even those measures are problematic, as they seldom capture differences in service quality and reliability—having a piped water connection in a house does not guarantee that the water flows or that it is safe.

Approaches to Estimating Investment Needs Typically Aim to Derive a Single Number Rather Than to Inform about Cost Drivers and Critical Assumptions

Various methodologies have been used to estimate investment needs. They include (a) "top-down" growth-maximizing macro-level estimates, (b) "top-down" benchmarking using a variety of benchmarks (such as historical evolution or high-income countries) and differing levels of sophistication, (c) "bottom-up" approaches based on the costing of specific goals, (d) general or partial equilibrium models, and (e) "mix and match" approaches.

Growth-Maximizing Macro-Level Estimates

It should be clear by now that any attempt to use the macro literature to establish a growth-maximizing level of investment is risky at best. A few studies have attempted to do it using a production function approach in an endogenous growth model (Crafts 2009; Kamps 2006), relying on heroic assumptions in the process. For example, Crafts (2009) assumes that the elasticity of output with respect to infrastructure is 0.2 among his European country sample, which, for a given depreciation rate, translates into a growth-maximizing ratio of public to private capital of 31 percent and associated public investment of 2.5 percent to 4 percent per year, depending on the country. Crafts does warn, however, that his approach ignores the indirect and nonlinear effects of infrastructure discussed earlier and thus is more applicable to countries with mature infrastructure systems (like high-income countries) than to LMICs. But even for high-income countries, it is anyone's guess whether 0.2 is the right elasticity.

Benchmarking and Top-Down Approaches

The most commonly used approach to estimating investment needs—at least in the context of LMICs—has been the benchmarking developed in Fay (2001) and popularized in Fay and Yepes (2003). It looks at how infrastructure and income (gross domestic product [GDP]) evolved together in the past (correcting for factors such as urbanization and industrialization) and assumes that this relationship will remain stable in the future. The investment needed to keep this relationship constant is then derived based on projected GDP growth, urbanization, and industrialization. This approach assumes no optimality, which means that if past demand is rationed, if the structure of the economy changes, or if the relationship between infrastructure and growth changes, projected investment needs will bear little relation to demand-satisfying investments, let alone growth-maximizing ones.

One redeeming trait of the Fay and Yepes approach, however, is that it captures and highlights maintenance needs, which are generally fairly simple to establish at the aggregate level, at least for a network in decent condition (this report relies on similar techniques for estimates of maintenance needs per sector). Such standardized ratios can be used to determine the resources needed to ensure that a given investment achieves its expected useful life and impact, but their use would not be appropriate for a country or sector with a large backlog of maintenance.

Closely related "top-down" efforts use various econometric techniques directly to estimate global, regional, national, and sectoral investment needs in infrastructure (Ruiz Nunez and Wei 2015; Serebrisky and others 2015). Improvements on the standard Fay and Yepes model came from Perrotti and Sánchez (2011) and Kohli and Basil (2011). In particular, Perrotti and Sánchez (2011) updated the estimates from the original Fay and Yepes model by adjusting for recent investment behaviors—instead of relying exclusively on historical trends.

An alternative benchmarking approach that has been proposed is to measure the infrastructure gap by the distance to the advanced-economy frontier (a proxy for optimal infrastructure endowment). This approach poses several problems:

- For transport, optimality will depend more on geography (density) and trade patterns than on income levels.

- Affordability matters: there is no point in building a network that a country cannot afford to maintain. In Romania, the European Union–subsidized upgrade of the water and sanitation systems to the required European Union standards cost the equivalent of 16 percent of GDP, raising the question of both opportunity cost and the country's ability to afford the O&M of such a complex, expensive system.

- Complementary investments also matter, given that poorer countries may not have the consumer durables that turn infrastructure into services.

"Bottom-Up" Approaches: Pricing Set Goals

The superiority of bottom-up approaches over others is that they require the explicit identification of a goal. They then estimate the costs of achieving specific goals before aggregating them at the desired regional or sectoral level (Bhattacharyay 2010; Briceño-Garmendia and Foster 2009; Hutton and Varughese 2016; Schmidt-Traub 2015). Some studies rely on existing goals, like the SDGs, while others derive their own. For example, Briceño-Garmendia and Foster (2009) developed a set of infrastructure service goals for Africa through a consultative process and priced them using micro-level data that they had collected.

Alternatively, it is possible to use economic-engineering models, such as those that exist for the power and water sectors (on which national utilities usually rely) and those that exist at the regional or even global level. Such models are designed to estimate the investment needed to maintain the integrity of the network and satisfy predicted expansion in demand. And they usually optimize investments to meet demand given cost constraints or to maximize the sum of users' and producers' surplus. One weakness is that, since they are partial equilibrium models, demand is exogenous, and the demand response to price is limited (at best, it is modeled through an elasticity).

General Equilibrium Models or Energy-Economy-Environment Models

Macroeconomic estimates based on general equilibrium models (rather than benchmarking) assess implicit infrastructure needs in scenarios guided by demographic trends and technical change, in which households maximize their consumption, firms maximize their profits, and government maximizes welfare through redistribution. Infrastructure is often derived from households' consumption and firms' production. Some macroeconomic models explicitly represent energy infrastructure—such as those of research institutes and agencies such as the Centre International de Recherche sur l'Environnement et le Développement (CIRED), the International Energy Agency (IEA), the International Institute for Applied Systems Analysis (IIASA), or the Potsdam Institute for Climate Impact Research (PIK)—and have been used to price the cost of alternative energy emissions scenarios and climate mitigation policies. They typically cover the electricity system, sometimes transport, and occasionally other sectors. In the transport sector, spatially explicit general equilibrium models have been used recently at the city level to assess the impacts of various infrastructure investment strategies.

"Mix and Match" Approaches

Some recent reports have produced estimates of infrastructure investment needs by compiling sectoral estimates from various sources. The most recent (Mirabile and others 2017) used IEA models for electricity and transport and an average of estimates from various other sources for water and sanitation (Booz Allen Hamilton 2007; OECD 2006, 2012; Global Water Intelligence database). McKinsey & Company (Woetzel and others 2016) and the New Climate Economy (NCE 2014) use a mix of older IEA and Organisation for Economic Co-operation and Development (OECD) estimates and Global Water Intelligence data for water.

As table 1.1 shows, estimates cover a wide range—from 2.5 percent to 8 percent of GDP. However, these estimates seldom discuss cost drivers and are used to identify financial need rather than investment strategies. The exceptions are the general equilibrium models used to estimate the cost of climate policy goals, which typically present both a base case and a climate mitigation scenario.

TABLE 1.1 The range of estimated annual infrastructure investment needs in the recent literature is quite large

Estimated cost of infrastructure investment needed, by coverage and period

Source	Coverage	Period	% of GDP	Cumulative amount (US$, trillions)
OECD 2006	Global	2010–30	3.5	64
Bhattacharyay 2010	Asia and the Pacific	2012–20	6.5	—
Fay and others 2011	Low- and middle-income	2008–15	6.6	—
Kohli and Basil 2011	Latin America and Caribbean	2011–40	3.8–4.0	—
Perrotti and Sánchez 2011	Latin America and Caribbean	2006–20	2.5	—
NCE 2014	Global	2015–30	—	89
Ruiz Nunez and Wei 2015	Low- and middle-income	2014–20	6.1	—
Woetzel and others 2016	Global	2016–30	3.8	57
OECD 2017	Global	2016–30	5.3	80.6

Note: All reports include transport, electricity, water and sanitation, and telecommunication infrastructure. The OECD (Organisation for Economic Co-operation and Development) and NCE (New Climate Economy) present results for both baseline scenarios (shown here) and pathways consistent with 2°C warming. — = not available.

A FRAMEWORK TO MAKE INFRASTRUCTURE INVESTMENT NEEDS ASSESSMENTS USEFUL

This report proposes a framework to help decision makers build a vision of what they want to achieve with infrastructure investments and understand how they can reach this vision. The approach used can be described as an "agree on decisions" approach (Kalra and others 2014), as opposed to an "agree on assumptions" approach. It builds on a growing body of literature that argues that long-term decisions should be based not on an agreement regarding what the future will bring, but rather on (a) an agreement regarding the multiple objectives that the decision is trying to reach and the metrics used to measure success and (b) an understanding of the vulnerabilities of the system, under current and multiple future conditions (Brown and others 2012; Haasnoot and others 2013; Hallegatte 2009; Kwakkel and van der Pas 2011; Kwakkel and Walker 2010; Lempert and others 2006; Walker and others 2013).

Many tools and processes have been developed to apply these principles. They all start by building an understanding of the system for which decisions have to be made. This exercise should be done by a broad team, which includes stakeholders with opposite views or objectives. It also involves identifying (a) the multiple objectives motivating infrastructure investments, (b) the multiple metrics required to assess success, (c) the technical and policy options available to reach the objectives, and (d) the exogenous factors that influence the cost and success of the investments. We address these in turn below.

Identifying the Objectives of Infrastructure Investment

Public infrastructure investments have multiple objectives, including non-economic ones like physical and social integration of a country, pollution management, or public health and safety. Further, infrastructure services are both final consumption goods for households and intermediate inputs for firms' production functions (Straub 2011). Although the boundaries are sometimes unclear (for example, is transportation to school a consumption good?), estimates suggest that about one-third to half of infrastructure services go to households, and the rest go to firms (Straub 2011).

Assessing infrastructure investment needs begins with building a vision of what the investments are meant to achieve along several dimensions, using multiple metrics. The following are examples of objectives that decision makers can aim for while making infrastructure investment decisions for the sectors included in our study (transport, water and sanitation, electricity services, and flood protection):

- *Economic growth: infrastructure services for firms.* Firms in all sectors need energy and water for their production processes; they need access to transport infrastructure for their workers and for the goods coming from their suppliers and going to their clients; and they need protective infrastructure against natural disasters to ensure the robustness and resilience of their economic activities.

- *Welfare: infrastructure services for households (improved human capital and consumption).* People's well-being is dependent on having access to electricity, domestic water and sanitation, and transport services—all of which bring health and education benefits as well as access to jobs.

- *Environmental sustainability: infrastructure services that limit climate change.* Environmental protection has been an objective of the international community since the United Nations Conference on the Human Environment, which was held in Sweden in 1972. With the Paris Agreement (United Nations 2015), countries have committed to limit global temperature increase to "well below 2°C." The Paris Agreement has major implications for future infrastructure, especially transport and energy, because it requires reaching zero global net emissions before the end of the century (Fay and others 2015; Steffen and others 2015).

- *Societal goals: infrastructure services for integration and peace.* Access to infrastructure services in rural areas can sometimes be motivated by objectives related to social inclusion rather than economic welfare (Narayan 2002; Shucksmith 2010). In fragile states, inequity in infrastructure provision is a major source of conflict.

- *Political goals: infrastructure services for social efficiency (or political expediency).* Pork barrel politics play an important role in infrastructure spending. For example, a study that modeled how investment decisions were made in France concluded, "Roads and railways are not built to reduce traffic jams; they are built essentially to get politicians elected" (Cadot and others 2006, 28). Some "white elephant" projects might indeed be preferred over socially efficient ones because of their political outcomes (Alesina and others 1999; Rauch 1994; Robinson and Torvik 2005). A study found that, in the postindependence period in Kenya, districts that shared the ethnicity of the president received twice as much expenditure on roads and had five times the length of paved roads built as other districts (Burgess and others 2015).

Although decision makers can aim for socially efficient outcomes, infrastructure spending alone clearly does not guarantee that these outcomes will be reached. Besides, these objectives can have trade-offs, and policy packages and compensations are often required to ensure that everybody wins from the investment (Roberts and others 2018).

Identifying the Metrics to Monitor Infrastructure Services

Infrastructure's ability to deliver on these economic and social objectives requires that the services provided be effectively available to individuals and firms. This connection implies that the service needs to be of reasonable quality and reliability, be affordable, and be provided in a financially

TABLE 1.2 Possible indicators for measuring infrastructure services, by sector

Sector	Access	Quality and reliability	Affordability	Financial sustainability	Environmental sustainability
Energy	Number of people connected to the grid; amount of kilowatt-hours per capita consumed	Frequency of brownouts and blackouts	Electricity tariff; connection cost	Share of operating costs and capital costs covered by tariffs	Air quality; water quality; CO_2 emissions
Transport	Number of people living within 2 kilometers of an all-weather road; number of people served by public transportation	Road roughness index	Road user cost; user fees	Adequate and regular maintenance budget	Air quality; CO_2 emissions
Water	Number of people with access to basic sanitation; number of people with access to safe water	Water quality; number of hours of continuous service	Tariff; connection cost	Share of operating costs and capital costs covered by tariffs	Sustainability of groundwater extraction
Flood protection	Number of people protected by the infrastructure	Absence of infrastructure failure in case of extreme event	Local taxes; land prices	Adequate and regular maintenance budget	Ecosystems destruction

sustainable manner. As such, each sector (transport, energy, water, and flood protection) should be monitored along five dimensions: (a) access, (b) quality and reliability, (c) affordability, (d) financial sustainability, and (e) environmental sustainability. Table 1.2 gives examples of metrics that can be used to monitor these dimensions.

Identifying the Types of Options Available to Reach the Objectives

Multiple options are available to help decision makers to reach the objectives described above. In each sector, options include both technology and policy instruments that can influence demand and choices.

"Hard" or Nature-Based Infrastructure

While infrastructure services have traditionally relied on concrete and metal, new solutions are emerging in some sectors to use nature more efficiently (Browder and others, forthcoming). Along the Gulf coast of the United States, nature-based solutions for flood protection (conservation and expansion) can be more cost-effective for the same level of protection (Reguero and others 2018). New York City filters only 10 percent of its water, relying instead on policies that protect its upstate watershed, saving billions of dollars in capital investments (Hu 2018).

Optimization, Safety Margins, or Flexible Designs

Most infrastructure investments are immobile capital with a long lifetime. While many designs are tentatively "optimized" for the future, in some cases it can make sense to build in safety margins to avoid future surprises. Alternatively, similar services can sometimes be provided with more flexible policies. For example, flood protection can be provided by wetlands and mangroves instead of dikes. Although it is impossible to reverse the decision to build a dike, it is possible to reverse the decision to protect a wetland.

Increased Provision of Services or Demand Management

Since infrastructure systems are often designed for peak demand for transport and energy—or for the worst-case scenario for water and flood protection—using demand management to smooth the peaks can yield large cost reductions. The most obvious example is the use of smart meters to reduce peak demand for electricity, but demand management also includes land-use planning to increase density—and thus reduce mobility needs—or the avoidance of new construction in flood-prone areas.

Centralized or Decentralized Systems

While power systems were traditionally centralized—power services are delivered through one interconnected network that allows for economy of scale on the supply side—over the past 10 years, technological progress has made decentralized systems more affordable. Mini-grids and off-grid power supply are introducing a paradigm change in the power sector, because these technologies are often powered by renewable energy sources, are faster to install than traditional technologies, and can be financed by private actors more easily.

Complementary Policies

Infrastructure pricing policies are key to managing demand, and hence environmental impact, but they also have equity implications. For instance, road pricing in cities helps to reduce congestion, and higher water and electricity tariffs are key to ensuring efficient use—although the efficiency gains can be at the expense of excluding the poor. Thus, complementary social protection policies are needed to protect the needs of poorer individuals. Social tariffs are typically poorly targeted, which means that, where they exist, social safety nets and cash transfer schemes would work better (Komives and others 2005).

Identifying the Uncertainties

External factors, many out of the control of decision makers, can challenge decision making because they influence the success and cost of the various options.

Technological Disruptions and Future Costs of Different Technologies

The future costs of electricity storage technologies (for example, the lithium-ion battery) will have major impacts on the costs of renewable energy and electricity transport (see chapter 4). Similarly, vehicle automation and ride-sharing platforms will also strongly influence urban mobility.

Future Demand

Demography and urbanization, as well as future consumption per capita, will affect infrastructure needs (the quantity of investments and technologies). In the absence of demand management, future (peak) electricity demand can be the main driver of investment needs (see chapter 3). Rapid penetration of electric cars can also change the demand for electricity, especially the structure of this demand, as vehicle charging will likely occur at quite different times than traditional demand for electricity.

Future Environmental Stresses

Climate change impacts on temperature, rainfall, and sea-level rise can have a significant impact on the cost of infrastructure systems (see chapters 2 and 5). Declining water resources—whether due to climate change or overuse—constrain the choice not only of water and sanitation infrastructure but also of electricity infrastructure.

Financial Resources (So-Called "Fiscal Space")

Perhaps the most critical determinant of the rate of return on an infrastructure investment is the availability of resources for O&M. Most investments are made assuming that resources will be available, yet they often are not—at least not in the expected amount. Similarly, the cost of capital is an important uncertainty when making technological choices for long-lived investments. This is particularly relevant for renewable energy, which has much higher up-front capital costs and lower recurrent costs than thermal power plants (see chapter 3).

Political Environment and Institutions

The long-term sustainability of some infrastructure investments depends on future public institutions, especially their ability to manage the infrastructure over time and adapt it to changing conditions. For example, some investments in coastal protection might be too risky if the institutions to maintain them in the future are not in place.

Final Phase: Stress Tests

Once there is agreement on the objectives, the metrics, and the options available, the next phase is to stress test various policy or investment options over a wide range of futures, using computer models or qualitative methods like expert elicitation. The stress test results in a concise description of the conditions under which the infrastructure system is likely to fail to meet one or more objectives. Often these conditions are summarized as scenarios that capture the mix of factors that, when combined, yield successes or failures. For infrastructure investment costs, this exercise would entail identifying the conditions under which infrastructure services could not be delivered or could be delivered only at very high financial, social, or environmental costs.

The options that emerge from the stress test are then organized into potential robust and flexible strategies, and the trade-offs among these strategies are examined—for example, between growth and environmental sustainability and between growth and equality (Roberts and others 2018).

This process promotes consensus around decisions and can help to manage deep uncertainty regarding future changes like climate change. It also encourages decision makers to debate important questions openly:

- Are the conditions under which our option performs poorly sufficiently likely that we should choose a different option?

- What level of risk are we comfortable with?

- What trade-offs do we wish to make between robustness and cost?

- Which options leave us with the most flexibility to respond to future changes?

This process can help policy makers to make informed decisions regarding infrastructure investment needs, despite the many complex relationships and uncertainties. Different levels of complexity can be used, depending on the size of the system studied and the scope of the exercise (high-level strategic planning versus selection of specific investment options). But no single quantitative model can represent all of the factors described in this section for all infrastructure sectors and thus determine, at a global level, the infrastructure in which the world should invest. Besides, most of the factors in these four categories are context-specific. Moreover, the objectives and pathways to achieve them are policy choices that each country or community needs to determine for itself, giving due consideration to external impacts.

IN SUM

In the following chapters, the primary focus is on generating global (rather than country-specific) numbers and on achieving the SDGs, with a special focus on access and climate change mitigation goals. Our proposed framework is used to identify the main choices and uncertainties driving the future infrastructure needs across LMICs. That said, although the choices and uncertainties driving future infrastructure needs at the local level might be different, the method that decision makers can use to identify them would be the same.

The key message of this report is that it is both possible and important to explore how multiple investment and policy choices would play out in multiple futures, according to multiple objectives and metrics for success. Doing so will enable decision makers to identify the factors that matter, the trade-offs among objectives, and the most robust policy choices.

Chapter 2 now turns to our first sector, water and sanitation, which benefits from a clear goal set by the international community through the SDGs, making it a good case with which to begin to apply our framework.

NOTES

1. Economic infrastructure is defined by a unique set of characteristics, including networked delivery systems, sunk investments, and economies of scale, that lead to natural monopolies; it typically includes water and sanitation, electricity, transport (air, rail, road, and ports), and the backbone of information and communication technologies. Some analysts include irrigation infrastructure as well and, more rarely, protective infrastructure (such as dikes and levees), as we do in this report.
2. This approach, which has been largely discredited (Pritchett 1996; Straub 2011), appears to be making a comeback, at least in the gray literature (IMF 2014).

REFERENCES

Alesina, A., R. Baqir, and W. Easterly. 1999. "Public Goods and Ethnic Divisions." *Quarterly Journal of Economics* 114 (4): 1243–84.

Bhattacharyay, B. 2010. "Estimating Demand for Infrastructure in Energy, Transport, Telecommunications, Water, and Sanitation in Asia and the Pacific: 2010–2020." ADBI Working Paper 248, Asian Development Bank Institute, Tokyo.

Bleakley, H., and J. Lin. 2012. "Portage and Path Dependence." *Quarterly Journal of Economics* 127 (2): 587–644.

Bom, P. R. D., and J. E. Ligthart. 2014. "What Have We Learned from Three Decades of Research on the Productivity of Public Capital?" *Journal of Economic Surveys* 28 (5): 889–916.

Booz Allen Hamilton. 2007. "The Global Infrastructure Investment Deficit." Booz Allen Hamilton, McLean, VA.

Briceño-Garmendia, C. M., and V. Foster. 2009. *Africa's Infrastructure: A Time for Transformation.* Africa Development Forum. Washington, DC: World Bank.

Browder, G., S. Ozment, I. Rehberger Bescos, T. Gartner, and G. M. Lange. Forthcoming. *Integrating Green and Grey: Creating Next Generation Infrastructure.* Washington, DC: World Bank and World Resources Institute.

Brown, C., Y. Ghile, M. Laverty, and K. Li. 2012. "Decision Scaling: Linking Bottom-Up Vulnerability Analysis with Climate Projections in the Water Sector." *Water Resources Research* 48 (9): 9537.

Burgess, R., R. Jedwab, E. Miguel, A. Morjaria, and G. Padró i Miquel. 2015. "The Value of Democracy: Evidence from Road Building in Kenya." *American Economic Review* 105 (6): 1817–51.

Cadot, O., L.-H. Röller, and A. Stephan. 2006. "Contribution to Productivity or Pork Barrel? The Two Faces of Infrastructure Investment." *Journal of Public Economics* 90 (6–7): 1133–53.

Crafts, N. 2009. "Transport Infrastructure Investment: Implications for Growth and Productivity." *Oxford Review of Economic Policy* 25 (3): 327–43.

Davis, S. J., K. Caldeira, and H. D. Matthews. 2010. "Future CO_2 Emissions and Climate Change from Existing Energy Infrastructure." *Science* 329 (5997): 1330–33.

Dinkelman, T. 2011. "The Effects of Rural Electrification on Employment: New Evidence from South Africa." *American Economic Review* 101 (7): 3078–108.

Donaldson, D. 2018. "Railroads of the Raj: Estimating the Impact of Transportation Infrastructure." *American Economic Review* 108 (4–5): 899–934.

Duflo, E., M. Greenstone, R. Guiteras, and T. Clasen. 2015. "Toilets Can Work: Short- and Medium-Run Health Impacts of Addressing Complementarities and Externalities in Water and Sanitation." NBER Working Paper 21521, National Bureau of Economic Research, Cambridge, MA.

Estache, A., and M. Fay. 2010. "Current Debates on Infrastructure Policy." World Bank, Washington, DC.

Fay, M. 2001. *Financing the Future: Infrastructure Needs in Latin America, 2000–05.* Washington, DC: World Bank.

Fay, M., S. Hallegatte, A. Vogt-Schilb, J. Rozenberg, U. Narloch, and T. Kerr. 2015. *Decarbonizing Development: Three Steps to a Zero-Carbon Future.* Washington, DC: World Bank.

Fay, M., M. Toman, D. Benitez, and S. Csordas. 2011. "Infrastructure and Sustainable Development." In *Postcrisis Growth and Development: A Development Agenda for the G-20*, edited by S. Fardoust and Y. Kim. Washington, DC: World Bank.

Fay, M., and T. Yepes. 2003. "Investing in Infrastructure: What Is Needed from 2000 to 2010?" Policy Research Working Paper 3102, World Bank, Washington, DC.

Fernald, J. G. 1999. "Roads to Prosperity? Assessing the Link between Public Capital and Productivity." *American Economic Review* 89 (3): 619–38.

Guivarch, C., and S. Hallegatte. 2011. "Existing Infrastructure and the 2°C Target." *Climatic Change* 109 (3–4): 801–05.

Haasnoot, M., J. H. Kwakkel, W. E. Walker, and J. ter Maat. 2013. "Dynamic Adaptive Policy Pathways: A Method for Crafting Robust Decisions for a Deeply Uncertain World." *Global Environmental Change* 23 (2): 485–98.

Hallegatte, S. 2009. "Strategies to Adapt to an Uncertain Climate Change." *Global Environmental Change* 19 (2): 240–47.

Holmgren, J., and A. Merkel. 2017. "Much Ado about Nothing? A Meta-Analysis of the Relationship between Infrastructure and Economic Growth." *Research in Transportation Economics* 63 (August): 13–26.

Hu, W. 2018. "A Billion Dollar Investment in New York's Water." *New York Times*, January 18. https://www.nytimes.com/2018/01/18/nyregion/new-york-city-water-filtration.html.

Hutton, G., and M. C. Varughese. 2016. "The Costs of Meeting the 2030 Sustainable Development Goal Targets on Drinking Water, Sanitation, and Hygiene." Technical Paper, Water and Sanitation Program. World Bank, Washington, DC.

IMF (International Monetary Fund). 2014. *World Economic Outlook: Legacies, Clouds, Uncertainties.* Washington, DC: IMF.

Jedwab, R., and A. Moradi. 2015. "The Permanent Effects of Transportation Revolutions in Poor Countries: Evidence from Africa." *Review of Economics and Statistics* 98 (2): 268–84.

Kalra, N., S. Hallegatte, R. Lempert, C. Brown, A. Fozzard, S. Gill, and A. Shah. 2014. "Agreeing on Robust Decisions: New Processes for Decision Making under Deep Uncertainty." Policy Research Working Paper 6906, World Bank, Washington, DC.

Kamps, C. 2006. "New Estimates of Government Net Capital Stocks for 22 OECD Countries, 1960–2001." *IMF Economic Review* 53 (1): 120–50.

Kohli, H. A., and P. Basil. 2011. "Requirements for Infrastructure Investment in Latin America under Alternate Growth Scenarios: 2011–2040." *Global Journal of Emerging Market Economies* 3 (1): 59–110.

Komives, K., V. Foster, J. Halpern, Q. Wodon, and R. Abdullah. 2005. "Water, Electricity, and the Poor: Who Benefits from Utility Subsidies?" Water P-Notes 20, World Bank, Washington, DC.

Kwakkel, J. H., and J. W. G. van der Pas. 2011. "Evaluation of Infrastructure Planning Approaches: An Analogy with Medicine." *Futures* 43 (November): 934–46.

Kwakkel, J. H., and W. E. Walker. 2010. "Grappling with Uncertainty in the Long-Term Development of Infrastructure Systems." In *Next Generation Infrastructure Systems for Eco-Cities: 11–13 November 2010, Shenzhen, China: Conference Proceedings*, 1–6. Piscataway, NJ: Institute of Electrical and Electronics Engineers.

Lee, K., E. Miguel, and C. Wolfram. 2016. "Experimental Evidence on the Demand for and Costs of Rural Electrification." National Bureau of Economic Research, Cambridge, MA.

Lempert, R. J., D. G. Groves, S. W. Popper, and S. C. Bankes. 2006. "A General, Analytic Method for Generating Robust Strategies and Narrative Scenarios." *Management Science* 52 (4): 514–28.

Mirabile, M., V. Marchal, and R. Baron. 2017. "Technical Note on Estimates of Infrastructure Investment Needs." Background note to the report, *Investing in Climate, Investing in Growth*, Organisation for Economic Co-operation and Development, Paris.

Narayan, D. 2002. "Bonds and Bridges: Social Capital and Poverty." In *Social Capital and Economic Development: Well-Being in Developing Countries*, 58–81. Northampton, MA: Edward Elgar.

NCE (New Climate Economy). 2014. *Better Growth, Better Climate: The New Climate Economy Report*. Washington, DC: Global Commission on the Economy and Climate.

OECD (Organisation for Economic Co-operation and Development). 2006. *Infrastructure to 2030: Telecom, Land Transport, Water, and Electricity*. Paris: OECD Publishing.

———. 2012. *Strategic Transport Infrastructure Needs to 2030*. Paris: OECD Publishing.

———. 2017. *Investing in Climate, Investing in Growth*. Paris: OECD Publishing.

Perrotti, D. E., and R. Sánchez. 2011. *La brecha de infraestructura en América Latina y el Caribe*. Santiago: Comisión Económica para América Latina y el Caribe.

Pritchett, L. 1996. "Mind Your P's and Q's: The Cost of Public Investment Is Not the Value of Public Capital." Policy Research Working Paper 1660, World Bank, Washington, DC.

Rauch, J. E. 1994. "Bureaucracy, Infrastructure, and Economic Growth: Evidence from U.S. Cities during the Progressive Era." NBER Working Paper 4973, National Bureau of Economic Research, Cambridge, MA.

Reguero, B. G., M. W. Beck, D. N. Bresch, J. Calil, and I. Meliane. 2018. "Comparing the Cost-Effectiveness of Nature-Based and Coastal Adaptation: A Case Study from the Gulf Coast of the United States." *PLOS ONE* 13 (4): e0192132.

Roberts, M., M. Melecky, T. Bougna, and Y. Xu. 2018. "Transport Corridors and Their Wider Economic Benefits: A Critical Review of the Literature." World Bank, Washington, DC.

Robinson, J. A., and R. Torvik. 2005. "White Elephants." *Journal of Public Economics* 89 (2–3): 197–210.

Ruiz Nunez, F., and Z. Wei. 2015. "Infrastructure Investment Demands in Emerging Markets and Developing Economies." Policy Research Working Paper 7414, World Bank, Washington, DC.

Schmidt-Traub, G. 2015. *Investment Needs to Achieve the Sustainable Development Goals: Understanding the Billions and Trillions*. New York: Sustainable Development Solutions Network.

Serebrisky, T., A. Suárez-Alemán, D. Margot, and M. C. Ramirez. 2015. "Financing Infrastructure in Latin America and the Caribbean: How, How Much, and by Whom?" Inter-American Development Bank, Washington, DC.

Shucksmith, M. 2010. "Disintegrated Rural Development? Neo-Endogenous Rural Development, Planning, and Place-Shaping in Diffused Power Contexts." *Sociologia Ruralis* 50 (1): 1–14.

Steffen, W., K. Richardson, J. Rockström, S. E. Cornell, I. Fetzer, E. M. Bennett, R. Biggs, and others. 2015. "Planetary Boundaries: Guiding Human Development on a Changing Planet." *Science* 347 (6223): 1259855.

Storeygard, A. 2016. "Farther on Down the Road: Transport Costs, Trade, and Urban Growth in Sub-Saharan Africa." *Review of Economic Studies* 83 (3): 1263–95.

Straub, S. 2008. *Infrastructure and Growth in Developing Countries*. Washington, DC: World Bank.

———. 2011. "Infrastructure and Development: A Critical Appraisal of the Macro-Level Literature." *Journal of Development Studies* 47 (5): 683–708.

United Nations. 2015. Paris Agreement. New York: United Nations.

Walker, W. E., M. Haasnoot, and J. H. Kwakkel. 2013. "Adapt or Perish: A Review of Planning Approaches for Adaptation under Deep Uncertainty." *Sustainability* 5 (3): 955–79.

Woetzel, J., N. Garemo, J. Mischke, M. Hjerpe, and R. Palter. 2016. "Bridging Global Infrastructure Gaps." McKinsey & Company, New York.

2

Water, Sanitation, and Irrigation

CHARLES J. E. FOX, BLANCA LOPEZ-ALASCIO, MARIANNE FAY, CLAIRE NICOLAS, AND JULIE ROZENBERG

KEY MESSAGES

- Universal coverage of safe water, sanitation, and hygiene (WASH) could be achieved at the relatively modest cost of 0.32 percent to 0.65 percent of gross domestic product (GDP) per year. Perhaps the most realistic scenario would involve low- and middle-income countries (LMICs) gradually rolling out safely managed water and sanitation using high-cost technology where appropriate. This would cost 0.55 percent of GDP per year for new capital.

- Achieving universal coverage will require much more than a one-off injection of capital. Total cost amounts to 1.1 percent to 1.4 percent of GDP per year. Operations and maintenance (O&M) account for more than half of the spending needed under any scenario, with the other half split about equally between the capital cost of extending access to those unserved and the capital investments needed to preserve service for those currently served. Failure to perform routine maintenance could increase total capital costs by more than 60 percent. Institutions, policies, and appropriate regulations, rather than just capital investments, are needed.

- Extending irrigation to the full extent of available water (after satisfying human and industrial consumption) would cost 0.15 percent to 0.25 percent of GDP per year, depending on policy choices pertaining to subsidies. A reasonable scenario of moderate public support—that is, subsidies for irrigation equipment, but not for water consumption—would cost around 0.13 percent of GDP per year for capital and maintenance. In all scenarios, complementary policies are needed to limit the negative impacts on ecosystems and provide farmers with climate-smart practices and technologies.

INTRODUCTION

The international community has defined a series of goals regarding access to water and sanitation in recent decades, and it has committed substantial resources to achieving them—starting with Millennium Development Goal (MDG) 7 on ensuring environmental sustainability. This target calls for cutting by half, by 2015, the proportion of people lacking sustainable access to safe drinking water and basic sanitation from its 1990 level (box 2.1).

Considerable progress has been made on MDG 7: since 1990, 2.1 billion people have gained access to improved sanitation facilities, and 2.6 billion have gained access to improved drinking water. Nevertheless, as of 2015, 663 million lacked improved sources of drinking water, 2.4 billion lacked access to basic sanitation, and 892 million continued to practice open defecation (WHO and UNICEF 2017).

In 2015, the international community raised the bar with its 2030 Sustainable Development Goals (SDGs). Not only do these include a dedicated goal for water and sanitation (SDG 6), but the targets are more ambitious—regarding both the population to be served and the level of service to which countries should aspire (defined as "safely managed services").

Irrigation goals, however, are more complex to define. Intensification of agriculture through irrigation is seen as a way to make progress toward SDG 2 on "ending hunger, achieving food security, improving nutrition, and promoting sustainable agriculture" by increasing the productivity of land and reducing the sector's exposure to the impacts of climate change (Leclère and others 2014; Müller and others 2011; Roudier and others 2011). Yet economic and political justifications for future investments in irrigation depend on (a) the local availability of water, which is influenced by climate change and the growing competition for water from other sectors (households, energy, and industry), (b) global food markets (does it make sense to invest in irrigation in arid regions if they can reliably import food from other regions?), and (c) competition for land.

Against this backdrop, what are the drivers for water, sanitation, hygiene (WASH), and irrigation investment costs, and how will these costs vary with service targets and investment pathways? This chapter uses two methodologies to answer this question: (a) a model that estimates global costs for SDG targets 6.1 and 6.2 (henceforth referred to simply as targets 6.1 and 6.2) and (b) a global land-use and irrigation model (which touches on climate change). The chapter begins with the WASH question, before turning to irrigation. All the assumptions are described in table 2.1, following the framework developed in chapter 1.

The following are the key findings of these studies:

On the water and sanitation front,

- Reaching the goal of universal coverage of safe water and sanitation will require much more than a one-off injection of capital. The capital

BOX 2.1

INTERNATIONAL GOALS ON WATER, SANITATION, HYGIENE, AND IRRIGATION

The following is the relevant 2015 Millennium Development Goal (MDG):

MDG 7. Ensure environmental sustainability

- Target 7.C. Halve, by 2015, the proportion of the population without sustainable access to safe drinking water and basic sanitation.

The following are the relevant 2030 Sustainable Development Goals (SDGs):

SDG 2. End hunger, achieve food security and improved nutrition, and promote sustainable agriculture

SDG 6. Ensure availability and sustainable management of water and sanitation for all

- Target 6.1. By 2030, achieve universal and equitable access to safe and affordable drinking water for all.
- Target 6.2. By 2030, achieve access to adequate and equitable sanitation and hygiene for all and end open defecation, paying special attention to the needs of women and girls and those in vulnerable situations.
- Target 6.3. By 2030, improve water quality by reducing pollution, eliminating dumping, and minimizing release of hazardous chemicals and materials, halving the proportion of untreated wastewater and substantially increasing recycling and safe reuse globally.
- Target 6.6. By 2020, protect and restore water-related ecosystems, including mountains, forests, wetlands, rivers, aquifers, and lakes.

The following are the definitions of the World Health Organization and United Nations Children's Fund Joint Monitoring Programme for "basic" and "safely managed" services:

- *Basic water service.* Drinking water from an improved source within a 30-minute round trip
- *Basic sanitation service.* An improved facility that is not shared with other households
- *Safely managed water service.* Drinking water from an improved water source located on the premises, available when needed, and free of fecal and priority chemical contamination
- *Safely managed sanitation.* An improved facility that is not shared with other households and where excreta are safely disposed of in situ or off-site.

TABLE 2.1 Overview of the assumptions and models used in this chapter

Sector and objectives	Models	Source	Metrics	Policy scenarios	Uncertain parameters
Water supply and sanitation					
Provide universal access to safely managed water and sanitation services and hygiene services and bring an end to open defecation by 2030 (SDG targets 6.1 and 6.2)	World Bank costing model	Hutton and Varughese 2016	Capital costs; operations and maintenance costs	Basic water and sanitation; direct strategy to attain SDG targets 6.1 and 6.2; indirect strategy to attain SDG targets 6.1 and 6.2	Technology choice; population growth; capital costs
Irrigation					
End hunger (SDG 2); mitigate climate change (SDG 13); protect biodiversity (SDG 15)	GLOBIOM (land-use and agriculture partial equilibrium model), with irrigation module	Palazzo and others 2019	Capital costs; maintenance costs; average daily per capita calorie availability; sustainable water use; terrestrial biodiversity; greenhouse gas emissions from agriculture, forestry, and other land uses	Moderate public support for irrigation (subsidies for investments); high public support for irrigation (subsidies for investments and water)	Magnitude of climate change impact; change in dietary patterns; trade openness; water use efficiency; socioeconomic context from the shared socioeconomic pathways (population, GDP, yields, water demand from other users)

Note: The structure of the table follows the framework developed in chapter 1. SDG = Sustainable Development Goal.

cost of extending access represents only about a quarter of the financing needs of the sector. Preserving service for those currently served requires as much or more in capital costs, while O&M costs again double financing needs.

- For most regions, the overall cost (capital and O&M for existing and new service) remains relatively modest at 1.1 percent to 1.4 percent of GDP per year to achieve targets 6.1 and 6.2—with the exception of Sub-Saharan Africa, where it could reach 4 percent of GDP or more. Financing needs can be reduced somewhat by adopting lower-cost technologies and phasing in the implementation of sewerage—at least in the less densely populated areas.

On the irrigation front,

- While public support to irrigation improves food security globally, investment in irrigation is by no means a panacea across the SDGs and across low- and middle-income regions.

- In South Asia, an investment of 0.3 percent to 0.4 percent of GDP per year would improve food availability by 1.3 percent to 2.7 percent, depending on climate change and global markets, while in Sub-Saharan Africa, an investment of 0.6 percent to 0.7 percent of GDP per year would improve food availability by 0.3 percent to 0.9 percent.

- Complementary policies will be needed to limit the harm to ecosystems and provide farmers with climate-smart practices and technologies.

WATER AND SANITATION: MDG OR SDG MAKES ALL THE DIFFERENCE

Although access to water and sanitation services has increased greatly in recent decades, coverage rates in 2015 show that countries need to keep investing to close the gap for universal access even to "basic" services—with the 2015 coverage rate at 81 percent for basic water and at 61 percent for basic sanitation (table 2.2). Achieving universal access to "safely managed" water and sanitation services poses an even greater challenge, given the significantly lower coverage rates (43 percent for water and 30 percent for sanitation) and higher investment costs for "safe" water and sanitation.[1] Moreover, the population in LMICs will continue to grow rapidly in the coming decades, increasing the number of people who will need access.

Using Simple Tools to Model Investment Needs for WASH

What would it take to achieve the targets for WASH within the MDGs and SDGs by 2030, under different assumptions about demography, technology, capital expenditure, and service upgrade strategy? For this exercise,

TABLE 2.2 **A long way to go to reach universal coverage on water and sanitation**

WASH coverage rates in 2015 and population to be served by 2030 to achieve universal coverage

Goal	Coverage rate in 2015 (% of population)	Population to be served by 2030 in the SSP 2 scenario (millions)
Universal basic services: basic water	81	2,101
No open defecation: basic sanitation	61	3,328
Universal safely managed services: hygiene	66	3,228
Any type of sanitation[a]	72	1,014
Safely managed water	43	4,416
Safely managed sanitation	30	5,186

Source: Hutton and Varughese 2016 for 2015 coverage rates.
Note: Population to be served by 2030 is the number of people who will need access in 2030, including the current gap plus population growth between 2015 and 2030, based on the shared socioeconomic pathway (SSP) 2 (demography and urbanization projections). WASH = water, sanitation, and hygiene.
a. For example, simple pit latrine.

we iterate the approach and costing tool developed by Hutton and Varughese (2016), with two additions:[2]

- *We include the cost of preserving service for those currently served.* Besides estimating the cost of meeting the service needs of the currently unserved, we estimate the cost of preserving service for those currently served, including capital replacement and O&M.

- *We further explore uncertainty and cost drivers.* The assumptions made in Hutton and Varughese on demography and urbanization, capital spending, service upgrade pathway, and choice of technology are varied systematically and combined to explore a larger set of scenarios than in the initial study.

We costed two policy goals:

- An ambitious version of the WASH-related MDG target: universal access to basic water, sanitation, and hygiene services by 2030

- Achievement of SDG targets 6.1 and 6.2: universal access to safely managed water and sanitation services and hygiene services and an end to open defecation by 2030.

Given that achieving targets 6.1 and 6.2 is more ambitious, and therefore costlier, countries may need to work toward these more ambitious objectives in stages—providing more basic services first, before upgrading to safely managed ones. For that reason, we also examine two strategies for reaching targets 6.1 and 6.2, as summarized in table 2.3:

- *Direct strategy.* Assumes that countries go directly to providing safely managed services for all citizens

TABLE 2.3 Possible strategies for providing water and sanitation vary with the level and rollout of service

Possible strategies for providing universal access to water, sanitation, and hygiene services, by level of service and rollout

% of population covered

Service	Universal access to basic WASH	SDG targets 6.1 and 6.2	
	Strategy 1: Basic WASH	Strategy 2: Direct	Strategy 3: Indirect
Basic water	100	n.a.	100
Basic sanitation	100	100	100
Hygiene	100	100	100
Safely managed water	n.a.	100	100
Safely managed sanitation	n.a.	100	100
Simple pit latrine to end open defecation	n.a.	n.a.	100

Note: "Basic sanitation" covers only the cost of latrines. "Safely managed sanitation" is an incremental cost that covers the service chain from fecal sludge extraction through conveyance to treatment and disposal. By contrast, "safely managed water" and "basic water" services are direct substitutes. The "direct" pathway is one in which every new household served is provided with safely managed water and sanitation; the "indirect" pathway first rolls out universal access to basic services before upgrading to safely managed services. SDG = Sustainable Development Goal; WASH = water, sanitation, and hygiene; n.a. = not applicable.

- *Indirect strategy.* Assumes that countries first deliver universal access to basic water and sanitation services to all of their citizens, before working to upgrade everyone to safely managed services.

Each strategy has its pros and cons. The indirect one is likely to facilitate a quicker achievement of universal access (although only to basic services), but it is more expensive because it involves an initial investment followed by an upgrade. In addition, achieving universal access to basic services first and then upgrading to safely managed services before 2030 might not be realistic. Doing so may strain capacity and be costlier than in our assumptions if the availability of suppliers is limited. The direct strategy is less costly overall, but slower, because it requires more financial resources up-front. In practice, most countries will choose a pathway somewhere between these two strategies.

Further, we analyze the impact of three other variables on spending outcomes:

- *Population and urbanization.* The analysis considers shared socioeconomic pathways (SSPs) 2, 3, and 4, as used by the Intergovernmental Panel on Climate Change (Dellink and others 2017; Grubler and others 2007; KC and Lutz 2014; O'Neill and others 2017). These pathways include different estimates of future population and urbanization rates. The urban share of the population strongly influences cost estimates, as the technologies used for providing services vary between rural and urban settings.

- *Technology choice.* A given service can be delivered using different technologies. Sanitation, for example, can be provided in numerous ways, ranging from a simple pit latrine to a conventional sewerage system with full treatment of wastewater, with significant variations in the capital expenditure required for hardware construction as well as O&M. To assess the impact of choice of technology on investment costs, we allow for one "low-cost" and one "high-cost" technology solution for (a) basic water and (b) basic sanitation and (c) safely managed sanitation services. However, only one solution is considered for providing safe water and hygiene services (table 2.4). Of course, the type of technology chosen affects capital and O&M expenditures, and numerous technologies, especially recent ones, could be considered (see chapter 6). For example, recent innovations using ultraviolet rays and photocatalysts powered by solar panels can make desalination and water purification a viable option even in remote areas and on a small scale. New trencher systems are also replacing traditional excavators to make pipe laying much quicker and less costly. However, at this stage, too little data are available on the possible cost implications of these technologies in different countries.

- *Capital spending.* Capital spending on new infrastructure is notoriously uncertain; overspending is common, even though new technologies and energy sources can significantly lower costs. The analysis defines two cases

TABLE 2.4 Various options are available for delivering water and sanitation services

Choice of technology for delivering water and sanitation services to urban and rural areas, by cost

| | "Low-cost" technology choice | | "High-cost" technology choice | |
Service	Urban	Rural	Urban	Rural
Basic water	Dug well	Dug well	Tubewell or borehole	Tubewell or borehole
Basic sanitation	Any pit latrine	Dry pit latrine	Septic tank	Wet pit latrine
Safely managed sanitation	Septic tank with fecal sludge management	Dry pit latrine with fecal sludge management	Sewerage with treatment	Septic tank with fecal sludge management
Safely managed water	On-plot piped water supply	On-plot piped water supply	On-plot piped water supply	On-plot piped water supply
Hygiene	Station with access to soap and water	Station with access to soap and water	Station with access to soap and water	Station with access to soap and water

of capital spending—"low" and "high"—which correspond to 100 percent and 125 percent, respectively, of the baseline estimates from Hutton and Varughese's tool for capital expenditure.

Infrastructure unit costs vary widely across countries. For example, the unit cost of sewerage collection and treatment as collected by Hutton and Varughese is below US$100 in Guinea, Nepal, and Somalia, but is more than US$1,000 in Costa Rica, Papua New Guinea, and Sudan. Similar spreads exist for all of the technologies considered. Many factors can explain these spreads—from variations in the costs of local labor and materials to vast differences in public spending efficiency and the prevalence of corruption. However, understanding why building infrastructure is far more expensive in some countries than in others is beyond the scope of this report.

In our analysis of uncertainty, we do not apply the full cross-country range of costs to each country estimate, as the cost of building, say, sewerage will likely never be as low in Costa Rica as in Guinea, even with high spending efficiency. Instead, we use two options per country—either estimated unit costs for this country or a 25 percent higher one—to reflect overspending or possible changes in material costs or efficiency.

Combinations of these variables (population, technology choice, and capital cost) define 12 scenarios for each of our three service upgrade strategies, for a total of 36 future scenarios. Investment needs based on these scenarios are presented as a range. All scenarios assume that full service coverage is achieved by 2030.

Capital Costs Are Driven by the Ambition of the Target and the Technology Adopted

Achieving targets 6.1 and 6.2 is more expensive by about a third or more than the basic alternative. The capital costs of extending coverage to the currently unserved population could range from US$15 billion to US$40 billion (equivalent to 0.04 percent to 0.1 percent of LMICs' GDP) per year from 2015 to 2030 for basic WASH, and US$67 billion to US$129 billion (0.2 percent to 0.4 percent of GDP) for targets 6.1 and 6.2.

However, capital expenditures to replace existing assets turn out to be as significant as or more significant than those needed to expand coverage. These provisions add about US$100 billion under all policy strategies and in all scenarios (all existing assets, be they for basic or safely managed service provision, are assumed to be replaced at the end of their useful life, creating new investment needs, irrespective of the choice of policy strategy).[3]

Thus, total capital costs to achieve targets 6.1 and 6.2 could be between US$171 billion and US$229 billion (0.5 percent to 0.6 percent of GDP). Expanding services would account for about half (39 percent to 55 percent) of total capital investment needs, with the rest (45 percent to 62 percent) needed to continue serving the already served population.

At the regional level, the breakdown between replacement costs for existing and new capital investment varies greatly (figure 2.1). In regions with low access, such as South Asia and Sub-Saharan Africa, funding needed for new capital spending is higher than funding needed to replace

FIGURE 2.1 In South Asia and Sub-Saharan Africa, new capital spending needs exceed replacement costs for existing assets

Average annual cost of capital spending on new and existing assets in water and sanitation, by region, 2015–30

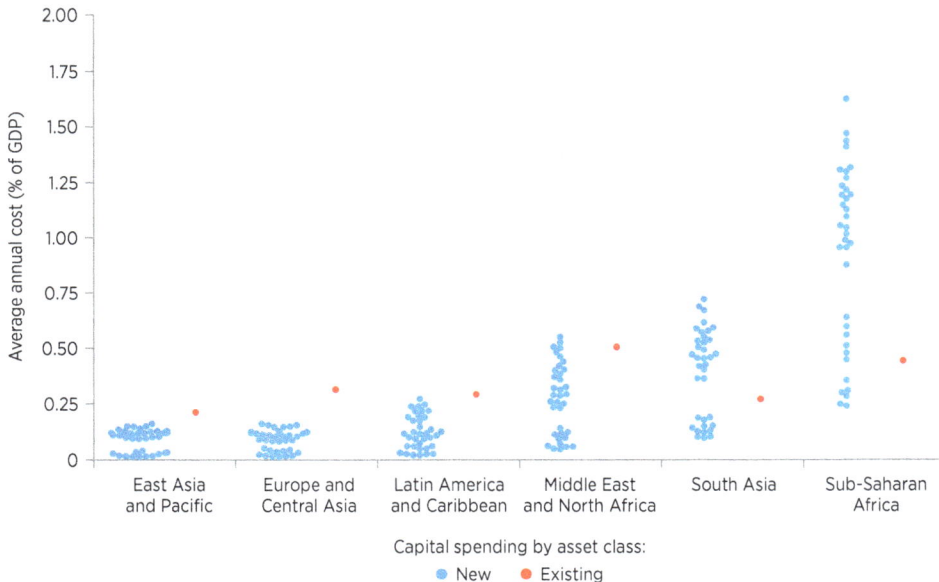

Source: Based on Hutton and Varughese 2016.
Note: The model does not explore the possible uncertainty regarding the cost of replacing existing capital. The cost is assumed to be the same in all scenarios. The graph (like others in this chapter) is a "beeswarm" plot, where data points are plotted relative to a fixed reference axis (the x-axis) in a way that no two data points overlap, showing not only the range of values but also their distribution.

existing capital spending in almost all of the scenarios; the opposite is true in other regions.

The key cost driver turns out to be the ambition of the goal (figure 2.2). Our analysis shows that the least-cost strategy would be to provide universal access just to basic WASH. Even in the most expensive case (a combination of choice of "high-cost" technologies, assumption of "high" capital spending, and the largest increase in population and urbanization), the costs of achieving universal basic WASH are lower than the costs of achieving targets 6.1 and 6.2, under any circumstances.

The next most important driver is the choice of technology. Here, we find that the results for high- and low-cost options fall into two distinct groups. This means that even if there are capital overruns and high population and urbanization rates, in most cases the low-cost technology remains less expensive than the high-cost technology, with no overrun and lower population growth (figure 2.2).

Thus, the low-cost technology option appears to be the most cost-effective means of achieving targets 6.1 and 6.2. For most countries, it would make sense to start with low-cost technologies when the conditions (population density, urbanization, topography, water consumption, and cultural beliefs) permit it and then to phase in conventional sewerage and wastewater treatment—at least in the less densely populated areas. Such an approach would allow time to build up the economic and financial sustainability of the utilities tasked with providing the service.

But there are several caveats. First, in many countries, water quality norms and laws force cities to comply with very strict standards, without allowing for gradualism. Second, non-network solutions (our low-cost option) are more likely to be cost-effective in periurban areas than in dense urban areas (Whittington and others 2009). Third, non-network solutions may simply be impractical in very large, very dense cities, while networked solutions create economies of scale. Fourth, the low-cost option would not allow countries to achieve SDG target 6.3 ("By 2030, improve water quality by reducing pollution, ... halving the proportion of

FIGURE 2.2 The goal and the choice of technology are the main drivers of investment costs

Average annual cost of capital investment in water and sanitation, by access goal, strategy, and choice of technology, 2015–30

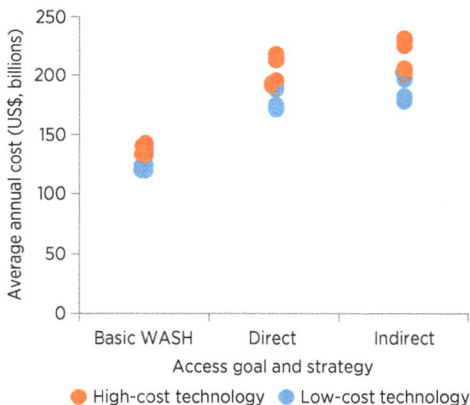

● High-cost technology ● Low-cost technology

Source: Based on Hutton and Varughese 2016.
Note: A 6 percent discount rate was used. Each dot corresponds to 1 of 36 scenarios based on variations across three goals (basic WASH, direct, indirect), two technologies (high cost, low cost), three possible rates of population growth and associated urbanization, and a high and a low estimate of capital cost. The "direct" pathway is one in which every new household served is provided with safely managed water and sanitation; the "indirect" pathway first rolls out universal access to basic services before upgrading to safely managed services. Estimates include capital costs both to expand access and to preserve it for those currently served. WASH = water, sanitation, and hygiene.

untreated wastewater") and SDG target 6.6 ("By 2020, protect and restore water-related ecosystems"), both of which require wastewater treatment facilities.

As to whether a direct or indirect strategy should be pursued, this decision matters much less than the choice of goal or technology (figure 2.2). Nevertheless, it is somewhat less costly to provide the population directly with safely managed water and sanitation services (as noted in Hutton and Varughese 2016). As such, countries may have to balance the need to make limited resources go a long way with the goal of quickly providing at least some type of service to as many households as possible. This finding is especially true in Sub-Saharan Africa—the region with both the largest number of unserved households and the largest need for capital investment in service expansion. Indeed, the cost per year for achieving universal access to basic WASH and meeting targets 6.1 and 6.2 could range between US$33 billion and US$51 billion (1.3 percent to 2.1 percent of GDP) (figure 2.3).

For LMICs as a whole, assumptions about population growth and urbanization—that is, the choice of SSP scenario—make very little difference.

FIGURE 2.3 **Sub-Saharan Africa faces the highest capital cost of achieving universal access to water and sanitation**

Average annual capital cost of achieving universal access to water and sanitation, by access goal, strategy, and region, 2015–30

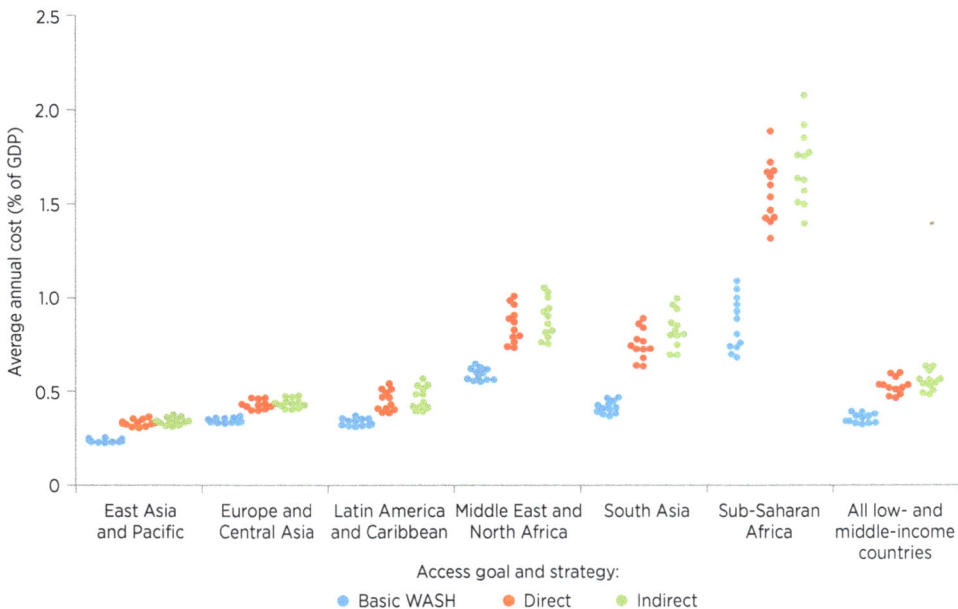

Source: Based on Hutton and Varughese 2016.
Note: Capital costs include both provision of new access and preservation of access for those currently served. The "direct" pathway is one in which every new household served is provided with safely managed water and sanitation; the "indirect" pathway first rolls out universal access to basic services before upgrading to safely managed services. WASH = water, sanitation, and hygiene.

But at the regional level, significant differences emerge. The SSP is a bigger driver of total spending for Sub-Saharan Africa than for any other region, given the stark population increase modeled for Africa under certain SSPs (figure 2.3). Indeed, the population scenario used can change the capital cost estimate by up to 10 percent, whereas for other regions, the impact of the choice of SSP is much smaller.

Beyond Capital Costs: Incorporating Operations and Maintenance

Capital costs are only part of the financing challenge of providing water and sanitation services—the bulk of costs under any scenario are related to O&M. Average annual O&M costs exceed capital costs in all of the scenarios considered, accounting for 54 percent to 58 percent of the total annual expenditure needed to deliver the service. When O&M spending is included, achieving universal basic WASH coverage costs between US$284 billion and US$327 billion (0.8 percent to 0.9 percent of LMICs' GDP) annually, while

FIGURE 2.4 Operations and maintenance spending matters as much as capital spending for water and sanitation

Average annual cost of capital and operations and maintenance in water and sanitation, by access goal and strategy, 2015–30

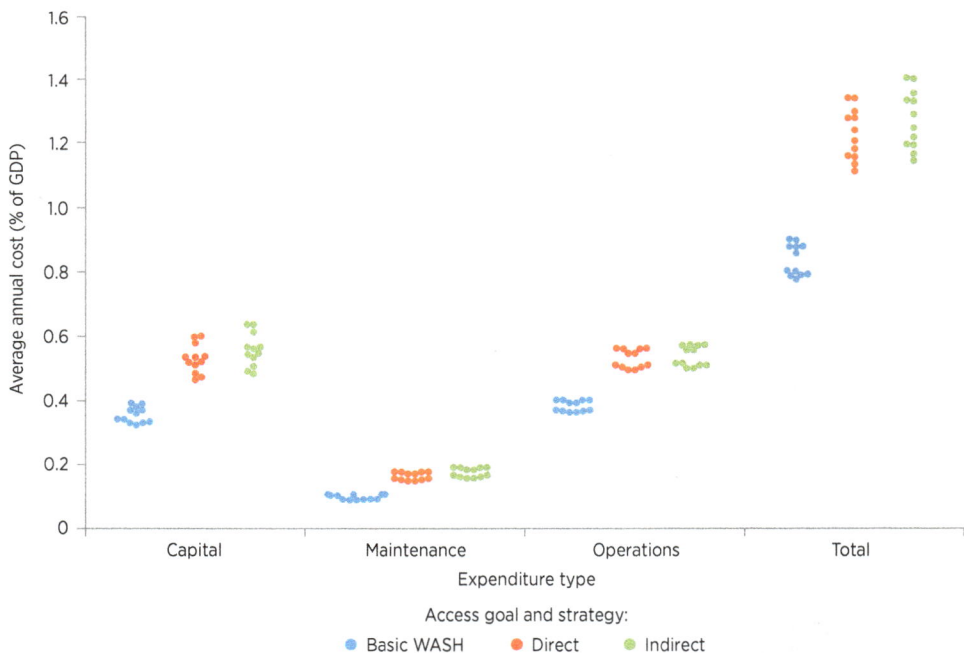

Source: Based on Hutton and Varughese 2016.
Note: Capital, operations, and maintenance costs are for new and existing users, representing the amount needed both to expand service and to continue serving existing users. The "direct" pathway is one in which every new household served is provided with safely managed water and sanitation; the "indirect" pathway first rolls out universal access to basic services before upgrading to safely managed services. WASH = water, sanitation, and hygiene.

meeting targets 6.1 and 6.2 costs between US$406 billion and US$509 billion (1.1 percent to 1.4 percent of LMICs' GDP) (figure 2.4).

Further, the choice of high- or low-cost technology continues to divide annual cost estimates into two distinct groups, once accounting for the policy strategy. This can be seen in the groups of "parallel points" for each policy strategy in figure 2.4, especially for O&M costs. Operations expenditure is considerably more sensitive than maintenance expenditure to the choice of technology.

At the regional level, affordability does not appear to be an issue for the relatively richer regions with already good coverage, such as East Asia and Pacific, Europe and Central Asia, and Latin America and the Caribbean. Even for the Middle East and North Africa and South Asia, total costs could rise at most to about 2 percent of GDP. However, for Sub-Saharan Africa, total costs could amount to close to 4 percent of GDP (figure 2.5). Further, even richer countries struggle with funding water and sanitation services given low willingness to pay, chronically low cost recovery, and the general unreliability of public transfers and subsidies.

The fact that O&M costs will constitute the bulk of total spending means that countries need to consider the affordability of expansion plans. It is not

FIGURE 2.5 **The affordability of expanding water and sanitation services could be an issue for Sub-Saharan Africa, unlike other regions**

Average annual cost of expanding water and sanitation services, by access goal, strategy, and region, 2015–30

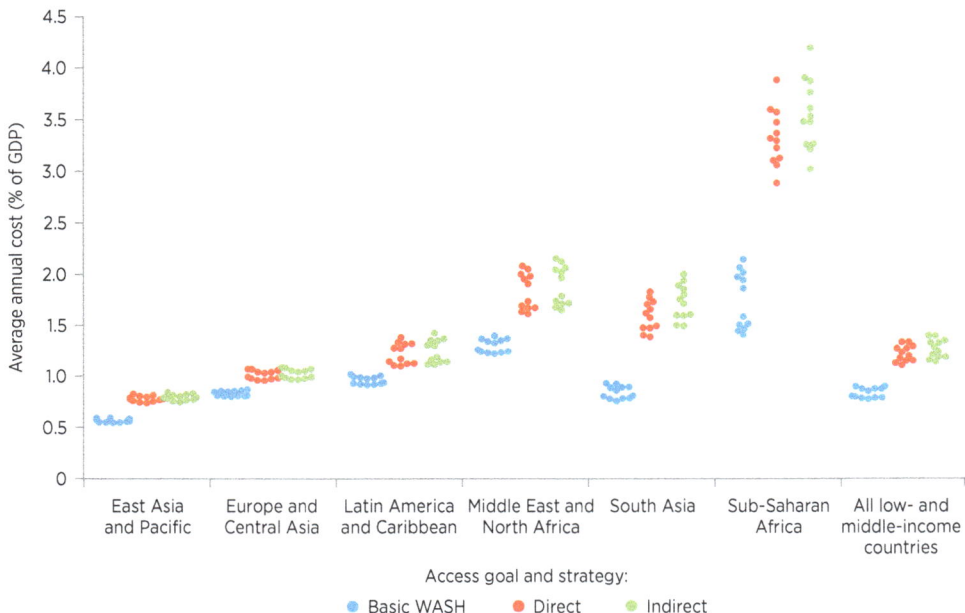

Source: Based on Hutton and Varughese 2016.
Note: The "direct" pathway is one in which every new household served is provided with safely managed water and sanitation; the "indirect" pathway first rolls out universal access to basic services before upgrading to safely managed services. WASH = water, sanitation, and hygiene.

enough for donors to raise funds and for governments to make room for capital investments. Allowance for an equivalent amount, or more, has to be made for O&M to ensure the sustainability of service provision. Whether this amount is covered through tariffs or paid for by taxpayers is a choice that each country or municipality will have to make based on the population's ability to pay. But a failure to raise the resources needed for operations and timely maintenance will result in the waste of scarce capital resources. We estimate that failure to perform routine maintenance would cost 60 percent more in capital costs due to more frequent rehabilitation.

Additional resources will be required to strengthen water and sanitation institutions and regulations, given that infrastructure alone has never been enough to achieve sustainable provision of WASH services. Policy, institutions, and appropriate regulations are needed if financial flows are to deliver the infrastructure needed and, in turn, if infrastructure is to deliver the desired service (Mumssen and others 2018).

IRRIGATION: A QUESTION OF HOW MUCH TO EXPAND

Irrigation investments increase the productivity of land and reduce the impacts of climate change, which are estimated to be significant for rainfed agriculture (Leclère and others 2014; Müller and others 2011; Roudier and others 2011). They can thus contribute to SDG 2 on ending hunger, achieving food security, improving nutrition, and promoting sustainable agriculture. The potential is significant, given that only about 43 percent of land with irrigation potential was irrigated in 2010, when irrigated cropland accounted for only 30 percent of total global cropland (FAO 2017; Frenken 2012).

However, the economic and political justifications for future irrigation investments depend on (a) local availability of water, which depends on local conditions, climate change, and growing competition for water from other sectors (households, energy, and industry); (b) global food markets (does investing in irrigation in arid regions make sense if they can reliably import food from other regions?); and (c) competition for land.

How to Model the Investment Needs for Irrigation

To investigate the impacts and costs of investment strategies for maintaining, upgrading, and expanding irrigated agriculture globally, we use a global land-use model, GLOBIOM (Havlík and others 2011; Havlík and others 2014; Palazzo and others 2019). The supply of and demand for agricultural products are modeled at a high spatial resolution in an integrated approach that considers the impacts of global change (socioeconomic and climatic) on both the demand for food and fiber as well as the availability of land to produce these products. The model assesses the conditions and investments required to transform rainfed cropland into productive and efficient irrigated cropland—considering the biophysical availability of water, the growing competition for water from other sectors (households, energy, and industry), and the impacts of upgraded and expanded irrigation systems on regional crop production, land-use change and emissions, food security, and demand for water.[4]

In many regions, transforming traditional rainfed systems or upgrading water-inefficient irrigation systems into productive irrigation systems will require investments that go well beyond the economic means of farmers. Partial subsidies for capital costs from government agencies or basin authorities are common even in high-income countries (like Australia, Canada, France, Greece, Italy, and Spain). In many LMICs, including China, India, and Pakistan, all capital costs and part of O&M costs are subsidized by state agencies and water user organizations (Toan 2016). Training, which is essential to use and maintain irrigation systems effectively, is often publicly funded, as in Sub-Saharan Africa (Van Koppen and others 2005). Therefore, two policy strategies are modeled: "moderate" public support and "high" public support for irrigation. Those two policies are compared with a benchmark of no expansion of irrigation systems after 2010.

Moderate Public Support Strategy

Public investment supports capital costs to build large-scale dams and water delivery systems and some of the costs to expand irrigated areas or upgrade existing areas to more efficient irrigation systems. However, farmers are responsible for the parts and materials for farm irrigation equipment, and they face a water price that reflects the relative scarcity of water due to increasing demand from other sectors. The irrigated area thus expands only if doing so is profitable for farmers, given increasing water prices.

High Public Support Strategy

Public investments support all capital costs (including replacement of existing capital), parts, and materials for farm irrigation equipment, along with training. In addition, water is subsidized for irrigation, so that the water price that farmers face is not subjected to the impacts of scarcity. Water used for irrigation is limited only by the quantity that is physically available after household and industrial demands have been satisfied. The irrigated area thus expands to the fullest extent of the physically available water.

Subsidizing the price of water for irrigation was common practice until recently in Europe and the United States to encourage agricultural development. However, many of these policies are being reformed due to their environmental impacts, including overextraction and water pollution (Wichelns 2010). In low- and middle-income regions, irrigation water is commonly available for free or at very low prices (Toan 2016).

These strategies are then implemented in a "business-as-usual" scenario based on SSP 2 "middle of the road" (O'Neill and others 2017) and under various scenarios reflecting the uncertainty around the following issues:

- *Future socioeconomic changes.* Future socioeconomic changes include population growth and economic development—factors that will affect future demand for food, regional investments, and advances in agricultural productivity. Two alternative pathways are used: SSPs 1 and 3.

- *Future climate change impacts.* Impacts of future climate change include the decline in productivity of crops under extreme heat and water stress. Representative concentration pathway (RCP) 8.5 simulations with six different global climate models are used.

- *Future dietary preferences.* The evolution of diets will have large impacts on future demand for cropland and pasture and, therefore, on irrigation needs. Three scenarios are considered: one business-as-usual scenario based on Food and Agriculture Organization projections, one with lower meat intake in high-income countries, and one with lower meat intake in all large meat-consuming regions.

- *Future trade agreements.* Shocks in the agricultural supply chain that stem from conflicts or climate change can have profound effects and limitations on trade that can affect food security (Baldos and Hertel 2015; Mosnier and others 2014; Simson and Tang 2013; van Dijk 2011). Two different assumptions based on those of the SSPs are considered. In the "open trade" scenario, trade elasticities rise 50 percent to represent lower international transaction costs. In the "restricted trade" scenario, elasticities fall 50 percent to reflect trade barriers.

- *Water use efficiency.* The water application efficiency of irrigation systems improves over time, but future improvement rates are uncertain. In the high-efficiency scenario, water application efficiency improves 5 percent per decade, while in the low-efficiency scenario, it does not improve.

The costs resulting from the model are the results of an optimization in each grid cell, so that the two strategies can result in very different cost outcomes, depending on the region.

New Capital Investment Costs Are Driven by the Public Support Strategy

The primary driver of future investment costs for irrigation is the extent of public support (figure 2.6). Under high public support policies—which fully subsidize water for farmers—irrigation investments in LMICs reach 0.15 percent to 0.25 percent of GDP per year, on average, between 2015 and 2030. This is

FIGURE 2.6 Public support policies drive investment costs in irrigation

Average annual cost of investment in irrigation, by investment type and level of public support, 2015–30

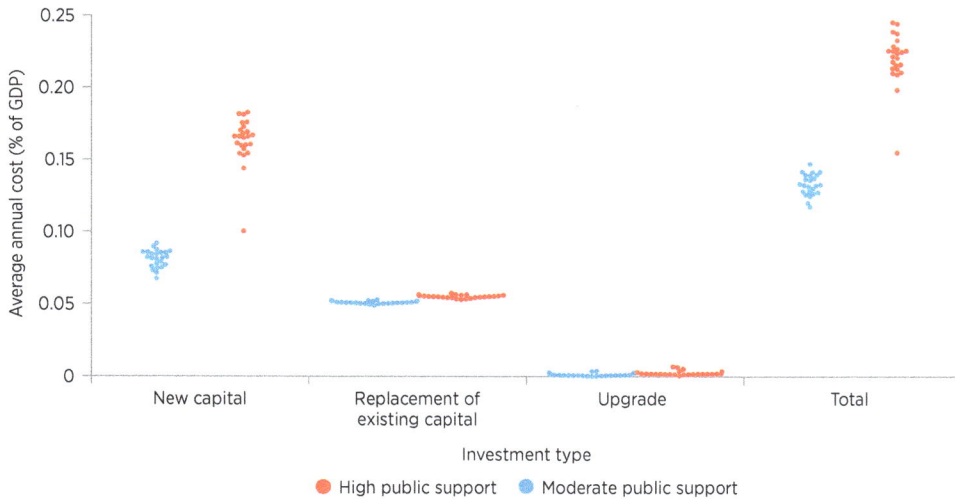

Source: Based on Palazzo and others 2019.
Note: High public support policies fully subsidize irrigation capital expenditures and water for farmers. Moderate public support policies cover only capital expenditures.

substantially more than under moderate public support policies that cover only capital expenditure. As with water and sanitation infrastructure, a large share of total spending comes from the need to replace existing capital (0.4 to 0.6 percent of LMICs' GDP per year between 2015 and 2030).

At the regional level, the share of new and replacement of existing capital varies greatly, given that 33 percent of the world's total irrigated area in 2010 was in South Asia and 32 percent was in East Asia and Pacific, but only 6 percent was in Latin America, and only a few percent was in the other low- and middle-income regions. Total costs range from a low of between 0.08 percent to 0.16 percent of GDP annually for the Middle East and North Africa and a high of 0.32 percent to 0.72 percent of GDP for Sub-Saharan Africa (figure 2.7).

Food security—measured by the per capita availability of kilocalories per day—increases under both high and moderate public support strategies and in all scenarios (climate change, trade openness, water efficiency, and diets) compared with the benchmark strategy of no expansion of irrigation (figure 2.8). The impact of public support increases with climate change, with some uncertainty depending on the global climate model used. Conversely, the two strategies have a smaller impact on food security under low-meat-diet scenarios, since demand for agricultural production is lower in these scenarios, due to a reduction of cropland required for feeding livestock.

The greatest impact of expanded irrigation on food security is in scenarios with restricted trade. Expanded irrigation has limited impact for scenarios with

FIGURE 2.7 **South Asia and Sub-Saharan Africa bear the highest investment costs in irrigation**

Average annual cost of investment in irrigation, by level of public support and region, 2015–30

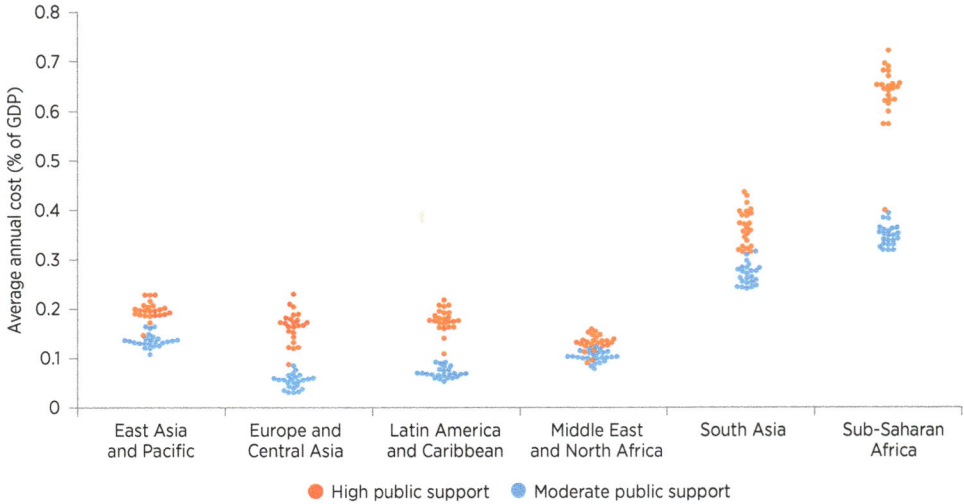

Source: Based on Palazzo and others 2019.
Note: Costs include replacement costs of existing capital, upgrade, efficiency, and new capital investments. High public support policies fully subsidize irrigation capital expenditures and water for farmers. Moderate public support policies cover only capital expenditures.

FIGURE 2.8 **Public support for irrigation increases food security in low- and middle-income countries**

Increase in food security, by level of public support for irrigation in various scenarios, 2030

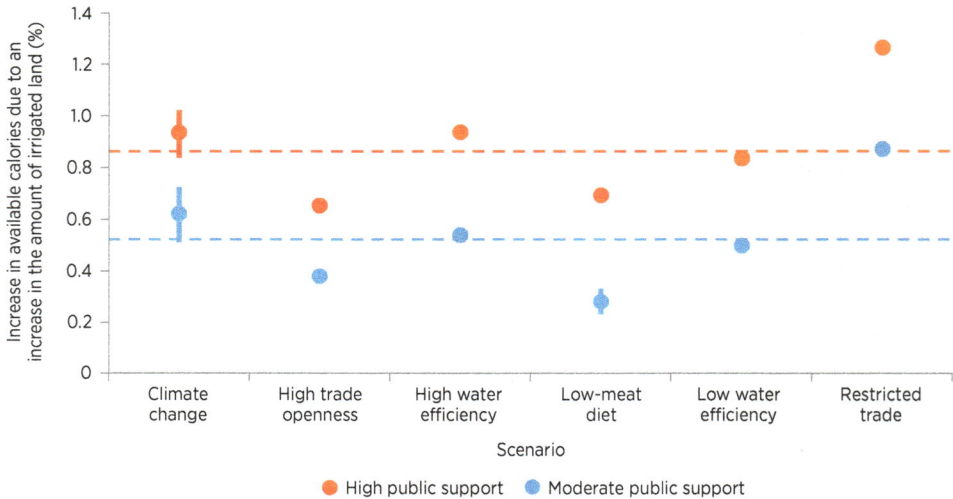

Source: Based on Palazzo and others 2019.
Note: For climate change, the dots represent the mean over several scenarios, and the vertical bars represent the range. The y-axis shows the percentage increase in total available calories in low- and middle-income countries in 2030. The calorie increase is measured relative to a strategy of no increase in irrigated land. The dashed lines show a business-as-usual scenario with unchanged climate, trade openness, water efficiency, and diets. High public support policies fully subsidize irrigation capital expenditures and water for farmers. Moderate public support policies cover only capital expenditures.

high trade openness, as food can easily be imported. Trade policies also imply a redistribution of production between regions—for example, trade restriction leads to agricultural expansion in the Middle East and North Africa and in South Asia, while trade openness results in expansion in regions where agricultural production is less costly than in the rest of the world (East Asia, Eastern Europe and Central Asia, and Latin America and the Caribbean).

Complementary Policies Are Needed to Prevent Negative Environmental Impacts

Support for irrigation, like many other policy instruments, affects more than one goal. In particular, it affects at least three SDGs: ending hunger (SDG 2), mitigating climate change (SDG 13), and protecting biodiversity (SDG 15). To understand how moderate versus high public support affects these areas, we conducted a multicriteria analysis. Our results, illustrated in table 2.5, show that developing irrigation is by no means a panacea for these SDGs. Thus, careful planning is needed to secure expected returns while minimizing negative impacts.

Ending Hunger

Investments in irrigation would lead to improved availability of food and hence contribute to food security in all of the regions considered. However, similar regional policies to increase irrigation to its full potential would lead to different regional increases in irrigated cropland and in food availability—varying from 10 kilocalories per capita per day in Europe and Central Asia to 51 kilocalories in South Asia. In South Asia this calorie increase requires expenses of 0.37 percent of GDP (US$10 billion per year), while in Sub-Saharan Africa, similar expenses of US$9 billion per year (0.68 percent of GDP) lead to an increase of 17 kilocalories per day.

Mitigating Climate Change

The effect of support for irrigation on greenhouse gas emissions is, in most cases, negative because of two factors: additional emissions from agricultural production and, in many regions, the conversion of natural areas, including forests, into cropland area. However, the effect is relatively modest compared with global greenhouse gas emissions. In 2050, emissions from agriculture, forestry, and other land use (AFOLU) would represent about 20 percent of global emissions under a business-as-usual or a 2°C scenario, so that a 2 percent increase in AFOLU emissions would represent 0.4 percent of global emissions.

Protecting Biodiversity

Supporting irrigation would also take a toll on biodiversity. In particular, even though irrigation is sometimes touted as a means to intensify agriculture and thereby reduce deforestation, we find that it could result in increased deforestation in all regions, except for Latin America and possibly Europe and Central Asia.

TABLE 2.5 Supporting irrigation helps to address hunger but is no panacea for climate change and biodiversity

Difference in impacts by indicator for the two public support strategies in 2030, by SDG scoring, in the business-as-usual scenario

Level of support and region	Investment cost (% of GDP)	Hunger		Climate change				Biodiversity	
		Crop prices (% change)	Food availability (kilocalories per capita per day)	AFOLU greenhouse gas (% change)	Cropland (hectares, millions)	Other natural land (hectares, millions)	Forest (hectares, millions)	Environmental flow requirement at risk (% change)	
Moderate public support									
East Asia and Pacific	0.13	−7.5	21.0	3.4	2.4	−3.2	−0.7	0.4	
Europe and Central Asia	0.04	−0.9	3.1	1.2	0	−0.1	0	0.3	
Latin America and Caribbean	0.08	−0.5	6.5	0.5	−0.7	1.6	−0.5	0.1	
Middle East and North Africa	0.10	−9.1	25.4	3.5	0.6	−0.7	0	3.6	
South Asia	0.27	−1.7	27.5	2.5	1.8	−0.7	0	3.4	
Sub-Saharan Africa	0.36	−3.5	14.9	0.6	1.2	−0.3	−0.4	0.3	
World	0.00	−3.3	17.3	1.6	5.5	−3.3	−1.6	0.4	
High public support									
East Asia and Pacific	0.20	−8.2	33.3	3.1	2.2	−4.0	−0.5	1.5	
Europe and Central Asia	0.17	−2.1	10.1	0.5	−0.9	0.5	0	1.4	
Latin America and Caribbean	0.19	−2.4	26.5	1.5	−1.4	2.5	−0.7	0.7	
Middle East and North Africa	0.13	−10.3	25.2	3.5	0.7	−0.7	0	4.0	
South Asia	0.37	−4.5	50.7	3.0	3.3	−1.3	0	8.3	
Sub-Saharan Africa	0.68	−4.0	16.6	0.1	0.6	−0.1	−0.2	0.7	
World	0.10	−4.5	28.7	1.6	4.1	−2.9	−1.4	1.2	

Source: Palazzo and others 2019.

Note: Results are for the business-as-usual scenario and are measured relative to a strategy of no increase in irrigated land. Environmental flow requirement at risk is the percentage change in the share of the environmental water flow requirement at risk of becoming unsustainable. Colors reflect SDG scoring. Dark red means a negative impact, while dark red means a negative impact, and light green and light red are in between. High public support policies fully subsidize irrigation capital expenditures and water for farmers. Moderate public support policies cover only capital expenditures. AFOLU = agriculture, forestry, and other land use; SDG = Sustainable Development Goal.

Expanding irrigation infrastructure could also substantially increase water withdrawals and compete with environmental water flows. Policies that support irrigation and provide subsidies for water may lead to unsustainable extraction from streams and threaten the biodiversity of wetlands and freshwater streams (Gerten and others 2013; Jägermeyr and others 2016; Verones and others 2013). In Europe and Central Asia, the Middle East and North Africa, and South Asia, about 10 percent of today's demand for surface water for agriculture could be classified as unsustainable. Although the share of water demand for agriculture in East Asia and Pacific may be less than 10 percent, there could be local impacts on locations in which the share of unsustainable extraction is significant.

Last but not least, while irrigation investments protect farmers against the adverse effects of variable rainfall, irrigated cropland may also paradoxically amplify the impacts of shocks (Damania and others 2017; Leclère and others 2014). In dry regions, free irrigation water creates an illusion of abundance and induces a shift toward more water-intensive crops (such as rice and sugarcane) that ultimately are not suited to these regions and lead to higher losses in case of drought (table 2.6). The high public support strategy might thus create maladaptation in dry regions, especially given the uncertainty pertaining to future climate change impacts.

Fortunately, complementary policies can be implemented to limit the negative impacts on biodiversity, while at the same time providing farmers with climate-smart practices and technologies—including for irrigation— to increase the productivity of cropland (Cervigni and Morris 2015). Crop improvement, smarter use of inputs, approaches to strengthen crop

TABLE 2.6 Public support for irrigation induces shifts toward more water-intensive crops

Effect of public support for irrigation on share of crops in production

Level of public support	Crops with a higher % of total production
Moderate public support	
East Asia and Pacific	Cassava
Europe and Central Asia	Corn, rapeseed
Latin America and Caribbean	Corn, soybean
Middle East and North Africa	Sugarcane, rice, cotton, sorghum
South Asia	Cotton, rapeseed, corn
Sub-Saharan Africa	Rice
High public support	
East Asia and Pacific	Sugarcane, cassava
Europe and Central Asia	Corn, rapeseed
Latin America and Caribbean	Corn, rice, wheat
Middle East and North Africa	Sugarcane, rice, cotton, sorghum
South Asia	Cotton, rapeseed, corn
Sub-Saharan Africa	Rice

Source: Palazzo and others 2019.
Note: High public support policies fully subsidize irrigation capital expenditures and water for farmers. Moderate public support policies cover only capital expenditures.

resistance to pests and diseases, and reduction of postharvest losses can contribute to the sustainable intensification of agriculture—thereby leading to greater food production (Beddington 2010; Tilman and others 2011). Even so, these policies and support will need to consider the local ecosystems carefully, and irrigation investments should be coupled with policies that protect biodiverse natural habitats (Byerlee and others 2014; Jägermeyr and others 2016).

IN SUM

Total investment costs in water and sanitation depend mostly on the ambition of the goal and the technology chosen. But there is no question that achieving SDG targets 6.1 and 6.2 will be significantly more expensive than simply providing basic access (as in the MDGs). Perhaps the most realistic scenario, given trade-offs and constraints, would be for LMICs to roll out safely managed water and sanitation gradually—using the higher-cost technology where most appropriate (high-density cities). Such a strategy would cost 0.55 percent of LMICs' GDP for capital costs, assuming no cost overrun, and 1.3 percent of GDP if O&M costs are included.

Future analyses for water and sanitation should consider the use of new technologies (described in chapter 6) to accelerate progress toward targets 6.1 and 6.2 at a relatively lower cost. Such technologies include ultraviolet rays and photocatalysts powered by solar panels, along with new trencher systems to make pipe laying much quicker and less expensive.

As for irrigation, the most desirable strategy in our analysis is perhaps the one that offers moderate public support, subsidizing irrigation equipment but not water, so that farmers have a sense of increased water scarcity when too much water is extracted. This strategy would cost LMICs 0.13 percent of GDP per year in a middle-of-the-road scenario, or between 0.12 percent and 0.19 percent of GDP per year, depending on diets, global markets, and climate change.

Future analyses for irrigation should consider more climate-smart practices and could explicitly model policies that reduce the negative impact of irrigation on biodiversity.

NOTES

1. In this chapter, we use service levels defined by the World Health Organization and United Nations Children's Fund Joint Monitoring Programme's investment ladder (https://washdata.org/monitoring/drinking-water).
2. The main limitations of the costing tool remain (a) uncertainties in the underlying data and (b) lack of consideration of the additional costs required to secure bulk water for drinking and household purposes, to provide wastewater drainage and sewerage systems, or to implement behavioral change programs to reach the hard to reach and sustain hygienic practices.

3. Key assumptions driving the replacement cost estimate are the following. The existing stock of assets is assumed to be halfway through its useful life in 2015 (some assets are likely to be close to new, but some are likely near the end of their useful life already), and assets are assumed to be replaced once they reach the end of their useful life. Useful life is estimated as follows: about 20 years for "safely managed" tier assets, 8–20 years for "basic" quality assets, and 2–10 years for hygiene and open defecation free–related assets. Hence, over the 2015–30 period, many assets are seeing at least one replacement cycle and, in some cases, more than one. On an annualized basis, this results in a high level of capital expenditure for existing assets.

4. The water available for irrigation is the estimated residual after household and industrial uses have been satisfied.

REFERENCES

Baldos, U. L. C., and T. W. Hertel. 2015. "The Role of International Trade in Managing Food Security Risks from Climate Change." *Food Security* 7 (2): 275–90.

Beddington, J. 2010. "Food Security: Contributions from Science to a New and Greener Revolution." *Philosophical Transactions of the Royal Society B: Biological Sciences* 365 (1537): 61–71.

Byerlee, D., J. Stevenson, and N. Villoria. 2014. "Does Intensification Slow Crop Land Expansion or Encourage Deforestation?" *Global Food Security* 3 (2): 92–98.

Cervigni, R., and M. Morris. 2015. *Enhancing Resilience in African Drylands: Toward a Shared Development Agenda*. Washington, DC: World Bank and Agence Française de Développement.

Damania, R., S. Desbureaux, M. Hyland, A. Islam, S. Moore, A.-S. Rodella, J. Russ, and E. Zaveri. 2017. *Uncharted Waters: The New Economics of Water Scarcity and Availability*. Washington, DC: World Bank.

Dellink, R., J. Chateau, E. Lanzi, and B. Magné. 2017. "Long-Term Economic Growth Projections in the Shared Socioeconomic Pathways." *Global Environmental Change* 42 (January): 200–14.

FAO (Food and Agriculture Organization). 2017. AQUASTAT database. Rome: FAO.

Frenken, K., ed. 2012. "Irrigation in Southern and Eastern Asia in Figures: AQUASTAT Survey—2011." FAO Water Report 37, Food and Agriculture Organization of the United Nations, Rome.

Gerten, D., H. Hoff, J. Rockström, J. Jägermeyr, M. Kummu, and A. V. Pastor. 2013. "Towards a Revised Planetary Boundary for Consumptive Freshwater Use: Role of Environmental Flow Requirements." *Current Opinion in Environmental Sustainability* 5 (6): 551–58.

Grubler, A., B. C. O'Neill, K. Riahi, V. Chirkov, A. Goujon, P. Kolp, I. Prommer, S. Scherbov, and E. Slentoe. 2007. "Regional, National, and Spatially Explicit Scenarios of Demographic and Economic Change Based on SRES." *Technological Forecasting and Social Change* 74 (7): 980–1029.

Havlík, P., U. A. Schneider, E. Schmid, H. Böttcher, S. Fritz, R. Skalský, K. Aoki, S. De Cara, G. Kindermann, and F. Kraxner. 2011. "Global Land-Use Implications of First and Second Generation Biofuel Targets." *Energy Policy* 39 (10): 5690–702.

Havlík, P., H. Valin, M. Herrero, M. Obersteiner, E. Schmid, M. C. Rufino, A. Mosnier, P. K. Thornton, H. Böttcher, and R. T. Conant. 2014. "Climate Change Mitigation through Livestock System Transitions." *Proceedings of the National Academy of Sciences* 111 (1): 3709–14.

Hutton, G., and M. C. Varughese. 2016. "The Costs of Meeting the 2030 Sustainable Development Goal Targets on Drinking Water, Sanitation, and Hygiene." Technical paper, Water and Sanitation Program. World Bank, Washington, DC.

Jägermeyr, J., D. Gerten, S. Schaphoff, J. Heinke, W. Lucht, and J. Rockström. 2016. "Integrated Crop Water Management Might Sustainably Halve the Global Food Gap." *Environmental Research Letters* 11 (2): 25002.

KC, S., and W. Lutz. 2014. "Demographic Scenarios by Age, Sex, and Education Corresponding to the SSP Narratives." *Population and Environment* 35 (3): 243–60.

Leclère, D., P. Havlík, S. Fuss, E. Schmid, A. Mosnier, B. Walsh, H. Valin, M. Herrero, N. Khabarov, and M. Obersteiner. 2014. "Climate Change Induced Transformations of Agricultural Systems: Insights from a Global Model." *Environmental Research Letters* 9 (12): 124018.

Mosnier, A., M. Obersteiner, P. Havlík, E. Schmid, N. Khabarov, M. Westphal, H. Valin, S. Frank, and F. Albrecht. 2014. "Global Food Markets, Trade, and the Cost of Climate Change Adaptation." *Food Security* 6 (1): 29–44.

Müller, C., W. Cramer, W. L. Hare, and H. Lotze-Campen. 2011. "Climate Change Risks for African Agriculture." *Proceedings of the National Academy of Sciences* 108 (11): 4313–15.

Mumssen, Y., G. Saltiel, and B. Kingdom. 2018. *Aligning Institutions and Incentives for Sustainable Water Supply and Sanitation Services.* Washington, DC: World Bank.

O'Neill, B. C., E. Kriegler, K. L. Ebi, E. Kemp-Benedict, K. Riahi, D. S. Rothman, B. J. van Ruijven, and others. 2017. "The Roads Ahead: Narratives for Shared Socioeconomic Pathways Describing World Futures in the 21st Century." *Global Environmental Change* 42 (January): 169–80.

Palazzo, A., H. Valin, M. Batka, and P. Havlík. 2019. "Investment Needs for Irrigation Infrastructure along Different Socio-Economic Pathways." Background paper prepared for this report, World Bank, Washington, DC.

Roudier, P., B. Sultan, P. Quirion, and A. Berg. 2011. "The Impact of Future Climate Change on West African Crop Yields: What Does the Recent Literature Say?" *Global Environmental Change* 21 (3): 1073–83.

Simson, R., and V. T. Tang. 2013. "Food Security in ECOWAS." In *Comparative Regionalisms for Development in the 21st Century: Insights from the Global South,* edited by E. Fanta, T. M. Shaw, and V. T. Tang, 159–77. Farnham, U.K.: Ashgate.

Tilman, D., C. Balzer, J. Hill, and B. L. Befort. 2011. "Global Food Demand and the Sustainable Intensification of Agriculture." *Proceedings of the National Academy of Sciences* 108 (5): 20260–64.

Toan, T. D. 2016. "Water Pricing Policy and Subsidies to Irrigation: A Review." *Environmental Processes* 3 (4): 1081–98.

van Dijk, M. 2011. "African Regional Integration: Implications for Food Security." Paper 101645, Wageningen University and Research Center, Agricultural Economics Research Institute.

Van Koppen, B., R. Namara, and C. Safilios-Rothschild. 2005. "Reducing Poverty and Gender Issues and Synthesis of Sub-Saharan Africa Case Study Reports." Working Paper 101, International Water Management Institute, Colombo, Sri Lanka.

Verones, F., D. Saner, S. Pfister, D. Baisero, C. Rondinini, and S. Hellweg. 2013. "Effects of Consumptive Water Use on Biodiversity in Wetlands of International Importance." *Environmental Science and Technology* 47 (21): 12248–57.

Whittington, D., W. M. Hanemann, C. Sadoff, and M. Jeuland. 2009. "The Challenge of Improving Water and Sanitation Services in Less Developed Countries." *Foundations and Trends in Microeconomics* 4 (6–7): 469–609.

WHO (World Health Organization) and UNICEF (United Nations Children's Fund). 2017. "Progress on Drinking Water, Sanitation and Hygiene: 2017 Update and SDG Baselines." World Health Organization, Geneva.

Wichelns, D. 2010. "Agricultural Water Pricing: United States." Background paper for the Organisation for Economic Co-operation and Development, Paris.

3

Power

CLAIRE NICOLAS, JULIE ROZENBERG, AND MARIANNE FAY

KEY MESSAGES

- Over 2015–30, investment needs for the power sector in low- and middle-income countries (LMICs) range from 0.9 percent to 3 percent of gross domestic product (GDP) annually, depending on the desired level and quality of service and the technologies deployed—with the deployment of new technologies and business models for the delivery of electricity a critical variable in potentially reducing costs.

- Investment costs are only one part of the access challenge: operations and maintenance (O&M) need to be budgeted for to ensure the reliability and affordability of electricity, two critical factors for uptake by yet unserved households.

- Taking climate change into account does not necessarily lead to higher investment costs. A low-emissions power sector can be achieved through three levers, each with very different impacts on cost: low-carbon technologies, demand management, and the early retirement of fossil fuel power plants. Financial instruments could help to promote the first two while minimizing the third, thereby limiting the amount of politically and financially costly stranded assets.

INTRODUCTION

Today, nearly 1 billion people—half of them in Africa—still do not have access to electricity.[1] Moreover, with electricity generation and heating contributing to 31 percent of carbon dioxide (CO_2) emissions, the power sector is central to decarbonization efforts (World Resources Institute 2018). Against this backdrop, it is vital for any analysis of investment needs to address both access to electricity and climate goals.

But estimating investment needs for electrification is difficult. Simply connecting households is not sufficient to realize the benefits of electrification: if service expansion comes at the expense of quality and affordability, it will compromise the benefits of electrification for existing users and depress demand from potential new users.

Over recent years, several attempts have been made to estimate the investments required to achieve universal access to electricity by 2030. One recent review underlines several limitations of these attempts, the main one being a lack of transparency regarding the underlying assumptions used in the estimation models (Bazilian and others 2014). Other limitations include the following: (a) most studies focus on capital costs and do not consider variable costs, (b) most models focus on generation, ignoring transmission and distribution, (c) decentralized energy investments are often omitted, and (d) the impact of geography and population density on costs is typically ignored.

Estimating the costs of decarbonizing electricity is no easier. Costs depend on how efficiently decarbonization is implemented and on uncertain factors, such as the evolution of technology costs, population, and economic growth. As a result, different models offer divergent results.

This chapter seeks to shed light on the drivers of investment costs in the power sector and to point to how a better understanding of these cost drivers could be used to inform the policy debate. Because a perfect model—one that could overcome the limitations of previous exercises to estimate investment needs as well as tackle both electrification and climate change—does not exist, we use a multipronged approach (see table 3.1 for a brief description of the models and parameters used in this chapter). We begin with an in-depth analysis of what it would take to electrify Africa and use this analysis to extrapolate to other countries with a large access deficit. Then, we turn to an ensemble of six integrated assessment models to explore the cost of reducing emissions from electricity generation. Finally, we bring together demand and climate challenges in a single optimization model, which unfortunately is limited to South America (where the access challenge is very small).

Our findings are threefold:

- *Power sector investment costs are driven mostly by policy choices regarding the strategy to increase access.* The amount of financing needed to achieve universal access while keeping up with industrial demand and maintaining the current quality of service for electrified households in 54 countries with a large access gap, is between US$45 billion and US$58 billion per year (0.9 percent to 1.2 percent of their GDP) to 2030. Whether governments

TABLE 3.1 **Overview of the assumptions and models used in this chapter**

Sector and objectives	Models	Source	Metrics	Policy scenarios	Uncertain parameters
Electricity infrastructure in South America					
Meet industrial and household demand (includes electric mobility); ensure reliable service; mitigate climate change (SDG 13)	Open-source energy modeling system—South America model base (least-cost optimization)	Moksnes and others 2019	Capital costs; variable costs; stranded assets	No constraint on emissions; 50% emissions reduction by 2050 versus 2013 for the electricity sector; zero emissions in 2050 for the electricity sector	Future cost of technologies; fuel price; future demand; future climate stress (availability of water for hydropower); cost of capital
Global power investment needs					
Meet industrial and household demand (includes electric mobility); mitigate climate change (SDG 13)	Six integrated assessment models: AIM/CGE, IMAGE, MESSAGEix-GLOBIOM, POLES, REMIND-MAgPIE, WITCH-GLOBIOM	McCollum and others 2018	Capital costs; maintenance costs; stranded assets; energy efficiency	Business as usual; implement the nationally determined contributions; limit global temperature increase to 2°C by 2100	Future cost of technologies; population and GDP growth; changes in consumption preferences; cost of capital; relationships between parameters (multiple models)
Electricity access in Sub-Saharan Africa					
Provide universal access to electricity (SDG 7)	World Bank access investment model	Jordan-Antoine and others, forthcoming; Nicolas and others 2019	Capital costs; operations and maintenance costs	Basic access; middle-range access; high-quality access; constant access	Future cost of technologies; population growth; industrial demand growth; urbanization; fuel price

Note: The structure of the table follows the framework developed in chapter 1. SDG = Sustainable Development Goal.

favor a strategy that can satisfy a high level of consumption or promote technologies that provide a more basic level of service (for example, simple solar home systems), drives this range in estimates. The recent development of new (and inexpensive) technologies for access, their evolution, and the regulation that will accompany these developments will have a significant impact on future power sector investment costs.

• *Increasing nominal access is not sufficient for the benefits of electrification to materialize.* In fact, an excessive focus on nominal rather than reliable and affordable access compromises the benefits of electrification for existing users, while depressing demand from potential new users. Thus, any analysis of the financial costs of achieving the access needed for development benefits to materialize has to factor in O&M costs, which nearly doubles the financing needed to achieve universal access, bringing it to between US$88 billion and US$118 billion (2.1 percent to 2.8 percent of GDP for 54 countries with low access) per year.

- *Taking climate change into account does not necessarily lead to higher investment costs.* A low-carbon power sector could cost anywhere between 1 percent and 3 percent of GDP per year, depending on how it is achieved and the assumptions made, while a business-as-usual system could cost between 0.9 percent and 2.4 percent. Keys to reducing the cost of a low-carbon power system are demand management and the early deployment of low-carbon technologies to reduce the need for early retirement of new fossil fuel power plants (which creates politically and financially costly stranded assets). Financial instruments that lower capital costs for low-carbon technologies are critical to this cost-efficient path.

UNIVERSAL ACCESS COSTS ARE DRIVEN BY POLICY CHOICES REGARDING THE STRATEGY TO INCREASE ACCESS

Access to electricity is a necessary condition for development. Electricity improves lives by extending the length of active days via lighting; frees up time, at least for households that can afford labor-saving household electric appliances; and can have positive health impacts, thanks to refrigeration and the replacement of kerosene lamps. Yet, if electrification is a necessary condition of development, it is not a sufficient one. When it comes to detailed examinations of the many possible economic and welfare impacts of power infrastructure and electricity access, the literature remains divided as to the benefits of electrification, especially in rural areas.

Two possible explanations may account for these varied findings. First, rural electrification may not necessarily be a priority for extremely poor households that may face other binding constraints, cannot afford appliances or machinery, have limited access to market centers, and may struggle to cover the cost (even subsidized) of electricity service. There is evidence that electrification has highly varied impacts on households, with poorer households benefiting less because their consumption is usually restricted to lighting (Khandker and others 2012, 2013). Second, rapid expansion may come at the cost of unreliable service in some countries.

These explanations bring up an important point: access is not binary and cannot be reduced to whether a household has a grid connection. If electricity supply is of poor quality or too expensive, its benefits will be limited, and consumers (households and businesses) will have constrained service. To reflect this situation better, the World Bank has developed the multitier framework (MTF) approach, which measures different levels of access, ranging from 0 (no service) to 5 (full service) (box 3.1). Conversely, if demand or consumers' willingness to pay are too low, electricity providers' businesses are not sustainable and the electrification effort is likely to suffer. Today, only 2 out of 39 electricity utilities in Africa are financially viable (Kojima and Trimble 2016).

BOX 3.1

THE MULTITIER FRAMEWORK

The multitier framework (MTF) approach measures access to household electricity as a multistep improvement (as opposed to a binary metric) by reflecting several attributes of electricity supply that affect the user's experience, while being technology- and fuel-neutral (figure B3.1.1). The approach attempts to provide insight into the types of policy reforms and project interventions that would drive higher levels of access to household electricity, while facilitating monitoring and evaluation.

The MTF has three distinct features:

- *The perspective of the user.* If a household receives a service, the MTF identifies six key attributes that determine its "usability": capacity, duration, quality or reliability, affordability, legality of service provision, and safety.

- *A tiered service classification.* Each attribute is assigned a score (based on the characteristics of the current service received), and the scores are combined to place each household into a tier of service ranging from tier 0 (no service) to tier 5 (full service). While achieving tier 5 for every household may be the ultimate objective, the MTF acknowledges the incremental benefits of advancing to higher tiers, leaving each country to set its access goal.

- *A technology-neutral approach.* The MTF does not consider how services are provided; it is only concerned with whether the service benchmarks for each tier are met. This allows for the aggregation of different technologies at each service level.

FIGURE B3.1.1 **Improving attributes of energy supply leads to higher tiers of access**

Attributes of electricity supply in the multitier framework

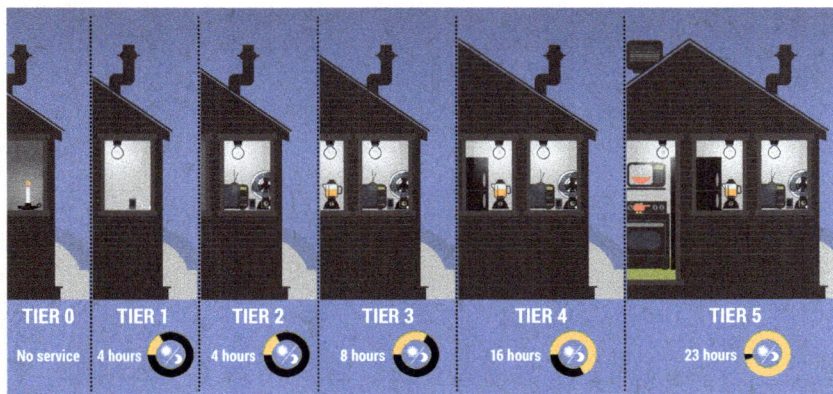

TIER 0	TIER 1	TIER 2	TIER 3	TIER 4	TIER 5
No service	4 hours	4 hours	8 hours	16 hours	23 hours

Source: Adapted from Bhatia and Angelou 2015.

A recent study in Kenya led by Lee and others (2016) found that households' willingness to pay was below the connection costs, leading the authors to conclude that electrification in the rural areas they studied resulted in a welfare loss of between US$510 and US$1,100 per household. Grimm and others (2016) found similar results for off-grid solutions in Rwanda: the average willingness to pay for solar kits was between 38 percent and 55 percent of the market price, implying that each connection generated social costs ranging from US$8 to US$83. These results may not hold for every rural household in Sub-Saharan Africa, but they help to explain why the access gap in Africa cannot be solved only by building new infrastructure.

Hence, bridging the access gap is not just a matter of extending the grid. Demand-side constraints must also be considered given that a significant share of households live near the grid but do not connect to it; these households account for nearly 40 percent of unconnected households in Africa (Blimpo and Cosgrove-Davies 2018). Reasons given for not connecting include high connection fees or inability to afford appliances that can deliver electricity services.

To understand the cost drivers of reaching universal access and how they relate to demand and supply constraints, we examine the situation in Sub-Saharan Africa—the region with the lowest rate of access to electricity (about 40 percent).[2] We do so by using the access investment model, a tool created by Jordan-Antoine and others (forthcoming) to estimate country-level funding requirements. The tool can assess (a) technology costs and diffusion associated with specific tiers of consumption (such as households with low consumption levels located far from the grid that are served through off-grid or mini-grid solutions) and (b) transmission and distribution investments.

Four policy choices are modeled, representing different ways of achieving universal access by 2030 across Sub-Saharan Africa. Three of them represent different paths to universal access (table 3.2): in the "high-quality" consumption policy, the government chooses to increase access mostly via the grid with a quality and level of service enabling productive use, while in the other two ("basic" or "middle range"), the government chooses to provide more basic electricity service to unserved households.

TABLE 3.2 **What should the new level of customer consumption of electricity be?**

Level of new consumption offered to newly connected consumers

Basic	Middle range	High quality	Constant access
50% of newly connected households are assigned to tier 1; the rest are assigned to tier 2.	Newly connected households are assigned to tier 3.	50% of newly connected households are assigned to tier 4; the rest are assigned to tier 5.	Newly connected households keep up with demographic growth; tier breakdown is business as usual.

Note. Industrial demand varies independently of the access scenarios.

TABLE 3.3 **Policy choices on tiers of service drive costs of electrification**

Average annual costs of investment in electrification, by tier of service provided, 2015–30

Costs	Basic	Middle range	High quality
Capital costs			
US$ (billions)	45–49	47–52	53–58
% of GDP	0.92–0.94	0.95–0.98	1.1–1.2
Total costs			
US$ (billions)	88–97	92–103	107–118
% of GDP	2.1–2.2	2.2–2.3	2.5–2.8

Note: Costs are for Sub-Saharan Africa, Afghanistan, Bangladesh, India, Myanmar, the Philippines, and the Republic of Yemen. "Basic" corresponds to tiers 1 and 2 of the multitier framework of the Sustainable Energy for All global tracking framework; "middle range" refers to tier 3; and "high quality" refers to tiers 4 and 5. Variations within tiers of service are driven by assumptions regarding population growth, urbanization rate, industrial demand growth, technology cost evolution, and fuel price. Total costs include fuel and operations and maintenance costs.

In the fourth policy choice ("constant access"), investments are made to maintain relative access at the current service level—thereby increasing absolute access to keep up with population growth—and to meet growing industrial demand.

We then assess these four policy choices under dozens of scenarios for 48 African countries by varying five parameters: population growth, urbanization rate, industrial demand growth, technology cost evolution, and fuel price. Finally, the study is replicated for 6 additional countries in other regions: Afghanistan, Bangladesh, India, Myanmar, the Philippines, and the Republic of Yemen. In 2015, these 54 countries together accounted for 95 percent of the population without access to electricity.

How great are power infrastructure investment costs? Capital costs vary between US$45 billion and US$58 billion (0.9 percent to 1.15 percent of GDP), while total costs vary between US$88 billion and US$118 billion (2.1 percent to 2.8 percent of GDP) (table 3.3). The main finding of our analysis is that what drives power sector investment costs in these 54 countries is the policy choice regarding the consumption level of newly connected households—that is, the targeted tier of service provision—followed, in decreasing order of importance, by the rate of growth of industrial demand, population growth, and urbanization rate. Hence, costs are driven primarily by policy choices. The second important finding is that the development and improved performance of new supply-side options could significantly affect the access gap and its bridging cost.

Demand Side: Policy Choices Drive the Cost of Electricity Access

The service tier targeted makes a significant difference in the cost of achieving universal access: the annual investment required for Sub-Saharan Africa by 2030 varies between US$14.5 billion, on average, for the basic scenario (representing 0.7 percent of the region's GDP per year

FIGURE 3.1 The cost of achieving universal access to electricity in Sub-Saharan Africa depends on the service tier targeted

Average annual cost for capital investment to achieve universal access to electricity in Sub-Saharan Africa by 2030, by targeted tier of service provision

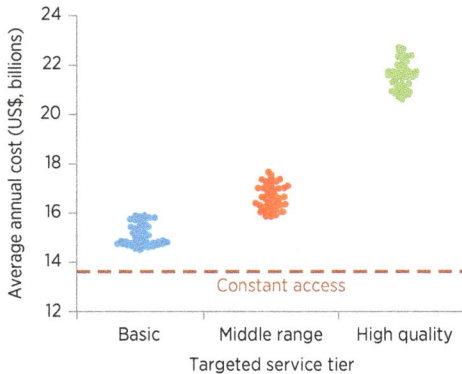

Note: Each dot represents one scenario summed over all Sub-Saharan African countries. The graph (like others in this chapter) is a "beeswarm" plot, which plots data points relative to a fixed reference axis (the x-axis) in a way that no two data points overlap, showing not only the range of values but also their distribution.

FIGURE 3.2 Within Sub-Saharan Africa, the financial burden of reaching universal electricity access varies significantly

Average annual cost of investment in electrification in Sub-Saharan Africa, by targeted tier of service provision, 2015–30

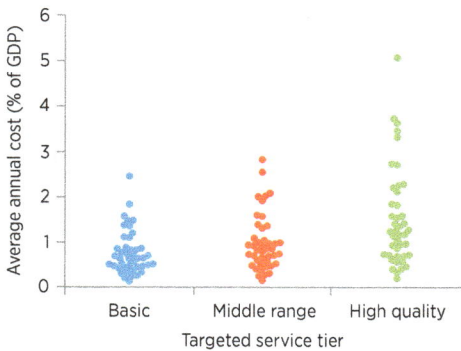

Note: Each dot represents one Sub-Saharan African country. All uncertain parameters are set to "reference scenario" values. See Nicolas and others (2019) for a presentation of the reference scenario (demography parameters: SSP 2; fossil fuel prices: medium; technology cost evolution: medium; industrial demand growth rate: growing with SSP 2 GDP). SSP = shared socioeconomic pathway.

over the period) and US$22.7 billion, on average, for the high-quality scenario (or 1 percent of GDP per year) (figure 3.1).

These regional averages hide significant variations across countries (figure 3.2). For some countries, reaching universal access by 2030 implies annual investment costs close to 2 percent of GDP per year (reaching 2.5 percent for Mozambique), even for the lowest-tier objective, while for others even the high-tier objective requires annual capital spending of just 0.5 percent of GDP (Angola, Botswana, and Gabon). These differences can be explained by a combination of factors, such as the initial access rate, population density, urbanization rate, income levels, and current structure of the energy system. As with other sectors, like water and transport, investment unit costs vary widely across countries, due to differences in efficiency, corruption, business environment, or the presence of conflict (see chapter 2 for more discussion of the unit cost spread across countries).

Furthermore, within-country differences are also large. It is cheaper and faster to connect people to the grid in urban areas, as little to no extension of transmission lines is needed. As a consequence, access rates are much higher in cities than in rural areas; the Democratic Republic of Congo is an extreme example, with a 42 percent access rate in urban areas and 0.2 percent in rural areas (Ministère du Plan and Ministère de la Santé Publique 2014). As expected, the high-quality consumption scenario based on grid connections is particularly sensitive to the rate of urbanization, with faster urbanization significantly reducing investment costs.

The finding that the tier(s) targeted has the largest impact on electrification investment costs has important policy implications. One option for tackling demand-side constraints and low willingness to pay from consumers could be to adapt the electrification offer to the socioeconomic situation of the countries or regions targeted. This does not mean that newly connected households would remain with low-tier access in the long run; rather, where appropriate, electrification could begin by delivering low levels of consumption using tailored technological solutions and upgrading service quality over time, rather than aiming to connect the whole population to the grid immediately.

Such an approach could help to achieve the SDG for energy access given the importance of demand-side constraints noted earlier.

Supply Side: A Paradigm Shift Based on New Technologies

New technologies and business models on the supply side could also help to tailor the electrification process to the population's needs and resources.

Between 2000 and 2012, 71 percent of the 62 million people who gained access to electricity did so with power generated from fossil fuels, mostly through grid connection (IEA 2017). But over 2012–15, the energy access landscape transformed: lower prices of renewables, efficient end-user appliances, and new business models to finance access led to an emergence of off-grid and mini-grid solutions. Decentralized renewables were the source of 6 percent of new electricity access, and this share is expected to grow rapidly (figure 3.3).

FIGURE 3.3 An increasing share of persons gaining access to electricity uses low-carbon options

Annual number of people worldwide gaining access to electricity, by type of fuel, 2000–15

percent

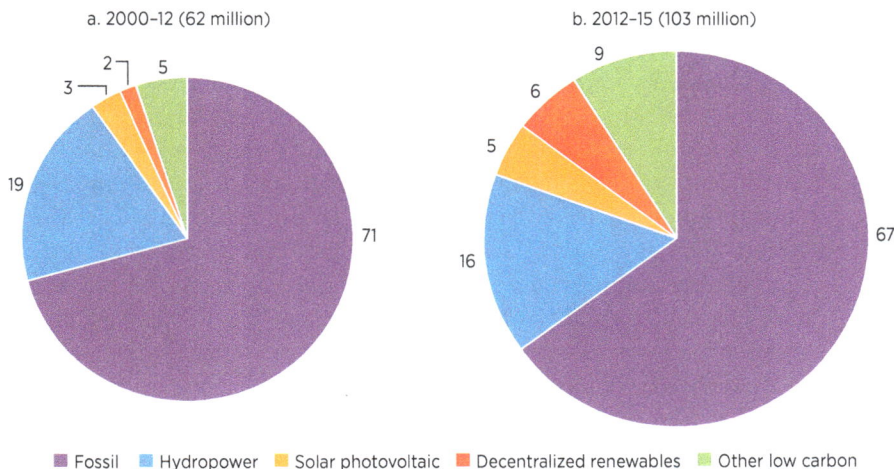

Source: IEA 2017.
Note: "Other low carbon" includes wind, geothermal, nuclear, bioenergy, concentrated solar power, marine, and waste.

FIGURE 3.4 The optimal mix of technology varies with the level of electricity service

Optimal mix of technology for the power sector in Sub-Saharan Africa, by targeted tier of service provision, 2015–30

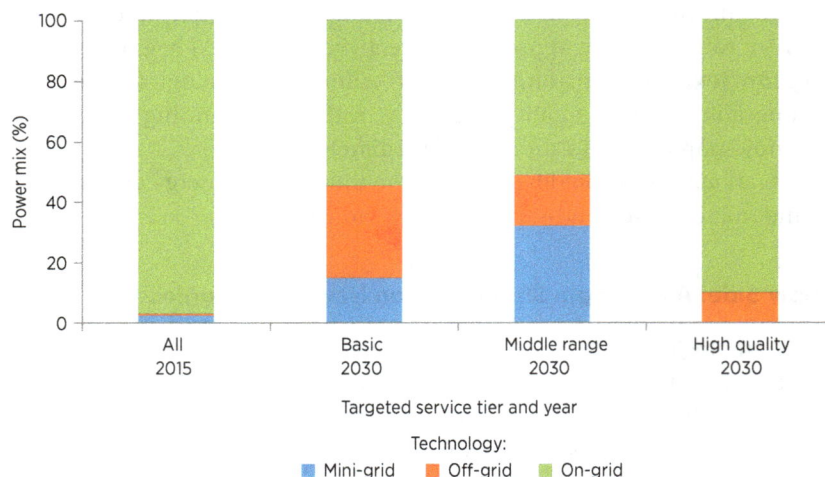

As the number of technologies and solutions for access increases, so does supply-side uncertainty. Indeed, different access scenarios will best be satisfied by different mixes of technology (figure 3.4). In particular, off-grid technologies are typically the most cost-effective way to serve households that are far from the grid and have low consumption. These different mixes of technology imply different cost structures that directly affect investment and total cost estimates.

In the Sub-Saharan Africa study, assumptions are made regarding which type of connection (on-grid, off-grid, or mini-grid) and technology are used to meet each service tier. These assumptions are country-specific and do not evolve over time (a limitation of this exercise). Yet, if prices for off-grid systems were to drop significantly or if improved technology were to allow off-grid systems to provide enough power for productive uses, their diffusion could accelerate. For example, Longe and others (2017) found that a renewable-energy-source hybrid micro-grid solution can be a viable option for electrifying far-from-the-grid unelectrified areas of the Eastern Cape Province of South Africa. Even though off-grid is generally a private investment and on-grid a public one, governments can still play a role in scaling up off-grid solutions by improving the business environment and enforcing clear regulations (see chapter 6 for more details).

These new solutions can alleviate some of the supply-side constraints that contribute to the electricity access gap. New smart-grid technologies (chapter 6) can also improve the availability and reliability of service—a challenge in many LMICs.

The Burden of High Variable Costs: A Challenge Everywhere, but Especially in Africa

The question of universal access cannot be restricted to capital investment needs; it has to encompass improvement of the existing service, maintenance of future infrastructure, and the financial implications of today's investment choices for tomorrow's variable costs.

- In most Sub-Saharan African countries, less than one-third of firms report having reliable access to electricity.

- On the household side, in 2014 more than 50 percent of connected households in Liberia reported that they never have power, as did around 30 percent in Sierra Leone and Uganda (Blimpo and Cosgrove-Davies 2018).

Variable costs play an important role in the poor quality and reliability of service experienced in many countries. Because fossil-fuel plants still produce most of the world's power, variable and fuel costs weigh heavily in the overall cost structure of the power sector. These recurrent costs can be a burden for LMICs that do not necessarily have the capacity to cover them, leading to heavily indebted utilities or a degraded level of service (or both). In Sub-Saharan Africa, recurrent costs represent two-thirds of the average annual costs of the power sector (figure 3.5).

But once again, differences between countries are quite high (figure 3.6). For some countries, the total cost of achieving universal access would represent more than 10 percent of GDP for the low-consumption scenario ("basic"), reaching up to 30 percent and 40 percent of GDP, respectively, for Eritrea and Liberia in the high-consumption scenario. For both countries, most of the energy is produced using diesel generators, which explains the very high variable costs.

To Maintain or Not to Maintain? That Should Not Be a Question

Maintenance is an often-forgotten component of the power sector industry in LMICs. In some countries, up to half of the installed capacity is unable to operate because of a lack of maintenance. In Madagascar, only 295 megawatts of the 500 megawatts of installed capacity were operating in 2017,

FIGURE 3.5 High variable power sector costs are a major challenge, especially in Sub-Saharan Africa

Average annual capital and variable costs of investment in the power sector in Sub-Saharan Africa, by targeted tier of service provision, 2015–30

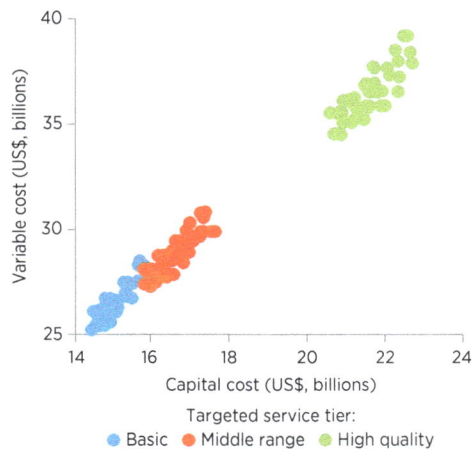

Note: Each dot represents a future scenario with varying combinations of consumption level for new households, industrial demand, technological costs, demography, and fuel costs. Average annual values are computed using a 6 percent discount rate over the 2015–30 period.

FIGURE 3.6 Electrification costs are much higher if the total cost of service is included

Average annual cost (capital investment and operations) of electrification in Sub-Saharan Africa, by targeted tier of service provision, 2015–30

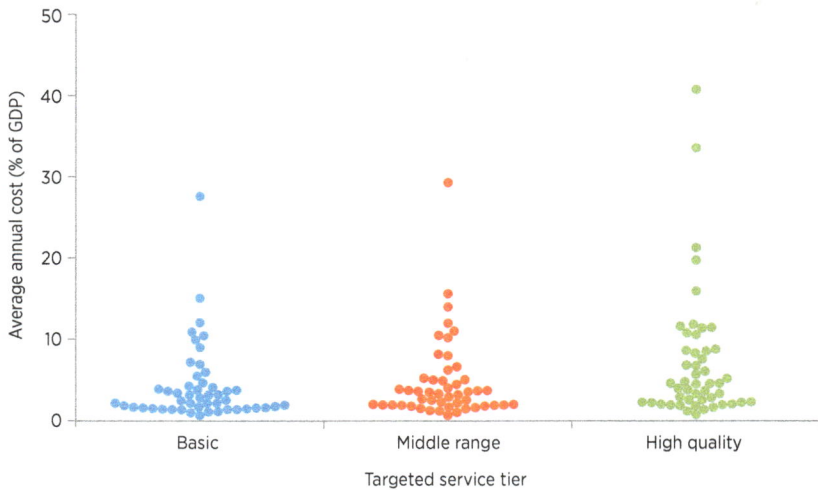

Note: Each dot represents one Sub-Saharan African country. Operating cost includes both maintenance and variable costs such as fuel. All uncertain parameters are set to reference scenario values.

while in the Democratic Republic of Congo, 29 percent of hydropower plants and 57 percent of thermal plants were not operational in 2018. The situation is even worse in Benin, the Comoros, Guinea-Bissau, and Sierra Leone, where less than 20 percent of installed generation capacity is used (United Nations 2015).

On the transmission and distribution side, regular maintenance improves reliability. Cutting the vegetation around distribution lines and maintaining distribution poles help to avoid outages. Maintenance in cities includes regularly checking the distribution network to detect illegal connections and limit power theft. Maintenance also helps to prevent idle capacity, lengthens the life of power plants, and ensures that the plant's initial performance is sustained throughout its operational life.

According to our estimates, annual maintenance cost averages around 3 percent of the cost of investment, which applies to all installed capacity, with the actual ratio varying between 1 percent and 6 percent, depending on the technology used (EIA 2016). These costs represent around US$136 billion in LMICs.[3] For Sub-Saharan Africa alone, maintenance costs are expected to run to between US$2.5 billion and US$3.6 billion per year, on average, over the 2015–30 period, on top of the US$14.5 billion to US$23 billion needed for capital costs (figure 3.7).

Thus, the pace of expansion must be balanced with the need to manage the existing network and maintain service levels. Failure to do so will reduce the value to existing customers and discourage others from taking up the service. Timely connection of new customers should occur when the electricity service is good enough to have a real impact on development.

Without taking maintenance costs into account, there is a high risk of ending up in a situation similar to the one identified by Gertler and others (2017) for some African cities, where the nominal access rate masks poor effective access (figure 3.8). Across a sample of 25 Sub-Saharan cities, most of which have close to a 100 percent nominal access rate, more than a quarter have a "reliable access rate" below 50 percent—where reliable access is defined as an electricity connection that works "most of the time" or "all of the time." Lagos is the most egregious

FIGURE 3.7 **Sub-Saharan Africa faces high annual fixed operations and maintenance costs for electricity**

Average annual fixed costs of operations and maintenance for electricity in Sub-Saharan Africa, by targeted tier of service provision, 2015–30

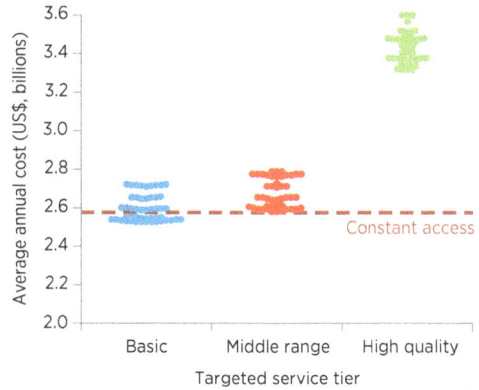

Note: Each dot represents one scenario summed over all Sub-Saharan African countries. Operations and maintenance costs includes both maintenance and variable costs such as fuel.

FIGURE 3.8 **High nominal access can mask low reliable access to electricity in major Sub-Saharan African cities**

Access to and reliability of electricity in major cities in Sub-Saharan Africa

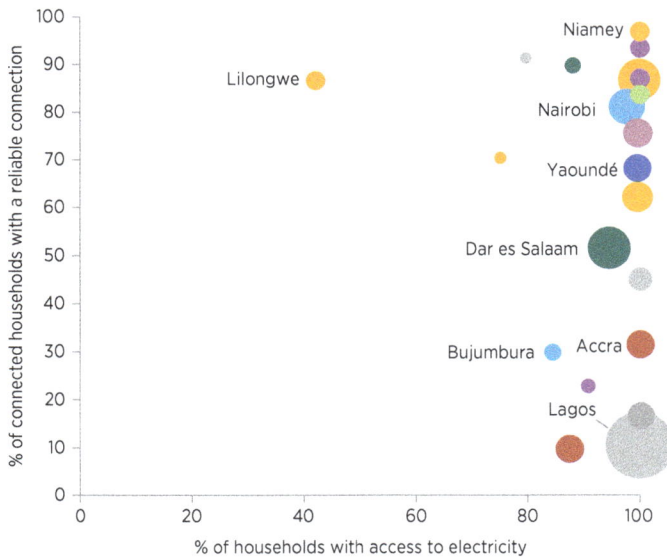

Source: Gertler and others 2017.
Note: Electricity access is defined as households located in areas with electricity lines nearby. Reliable connection is defined as an electricity connection that works "most of the time" or "all of the time." Dot size is proportional to a city's population size.

case, with a nominal access rate of 100 percent, but a reliable access rate of around 10 percent.

Improved reliability not only increases the impact of electrification but also improves uptake, as recent studies demonstrate (Chakravorty and others 2014; Mensah 2018; Samad and Zhang 2016). In addition, the provision of quality infrastructure services (such as reliable electricity) generates economic activities that can be tapped for tax revenues. Blimpo and others (2018) estimate that African countries could increase total tax revenues more than 4 percent solely by resolving issues related to electricity shortages.

FACTORING CLIMATE CHANGE INTO INVESTMENT NEEDS ESTIMATES

Transitioning to a more populous world where all or most of the population has access to electricity will lead to increased CO_2 emissions if the power system is not decarbonized. How much will it cost countries to transition to a lower-carbon world? Estimates vary according to the model used, the temperature objective, and the assumptions made about underlying socioeconomic scenarios and technological progress.

To understand the cost drivers behind these estimates, we commissioned a multimodel analysis to derive global electricity investment needs (box 3.2). This approach enabled us to compare the power sector results of six global energy-economy models that were used to derive investment needs under three futures: (a) a transformative pathway that constrains greenhouse gas emissions, resulting in warming of no more than 2°C by 2100 (2C scenario), (b) a business-as-usual scenario (BAU scenario), and (c) an in-between scenario in which countries implement their current nationally determined contributions to the Paris Agreement (NDC scenario). Although the behavior of the models is quite similar for the BAU and NDC scenarios, the models disagree as to whether aggressive climate policies (the 2°C pathway) will result in greater or lower investment costs.

The results show that investment costs depend more on the model used than on the climate objective. In the low- and middle-income world, annual power sector investments required per year for the 2015–30 period are between 0.9 percent and 2.4 percent of LMICs' GDP for the BAU scenario, 0.9 percent and 2.5 percent for the NDC scenario, and between 1 percent and 3 percent for the 2C scenario. The maximum cost difference between the BAU scenario and the 2C scenario is 0.89 percentage point of GDP, while the maximum cost difference between two models (for the same scenario) is 2 percentage points of GDP (figure 3.9). These variations come from different model structures, solution algorithms, and assumptions regarding the future cost of technologies (McCollum and others 2018).

BOX 3.2

PUTTING A PRICE TAG ON TRANSITIONING TO A CARBON-FREE WORLD

A report by McCollum and others (2018) was commissioned to shed light on the cost that society will have to bear to transform its energy system to meet international targets. A multimodel exercise was used to encompass a wide diversity of views of the future.

Methodology. The results of six global energy-economy models, or integrated assessment frameworks, were compared: AIM/CGE, IMAGE, MESSAGEix-GLOBIOM, POLES, REMIND-MAgPIE, and WITCH-GLOBIOM. Each of these models has its own perspective on how the future could unfold in light of varying assumptions for socioeconomic development, technological change, and policy choices. They also have different structures and solution algorithms: from least-cost optimization to computable general equilibrium models and from game-theoretic to recursive-dynamic simulation models. Such diversity is beneficial for shedding light on those model findings that are robust to diverging assumptions and on potential outliers deserving of further investigation. Of particular importance here, the six models have broad coverage of different types of energy technologies across the entire global energy system—including resource extraction, power generation, fuel conversion, pipelines and transmission, energy storage, and end-use and demand devices—and are therefore well-positioned to assess the evolving nature of the energy and climate mitigation investment portfolio over time.

Scenarios. Three scenarios were explored. A business-as-usual scenario serves as each model's reference case (or baseline). It accounts for those energy- and climate-related policies that were already "on the books" of countries as of 2015. The two other scenarios pursue low-carbon energy, energy efficiency, and climate change mitigation to varying degrees: (a) "nationally determined contributions" based on countries' submissions to the Paris Agreement and (b) "well below 2 degrees," a more ambitious scenario consistent with the decarbonization strategy needed to keep warming well below 2°C.

Assumptions regarding population and socioeconomic development across all scenarios are in line with the "middle-of-the-road" story line of the shared socioeconomic pathways (SSP 2) developed by the integrated assessment research community and used by the Intergovernmental Panel on Climate Change. The fact that the study does not vary the SSP could be construed as an oversight of this work. In practice, the findings are that varying the SSPs does not have a major impact on the insights derived from the study. In other words, the multimodel means and ranges for the energy investment needs reported are not expected to differ a great deal in those alternative cases.

FIGURE 3.9 A 2C world may cost less than the business-as-usual one—or a lot more

Average annual cost of investment in the power sector, by policy scenario and integrated assessment model used, 2015–30

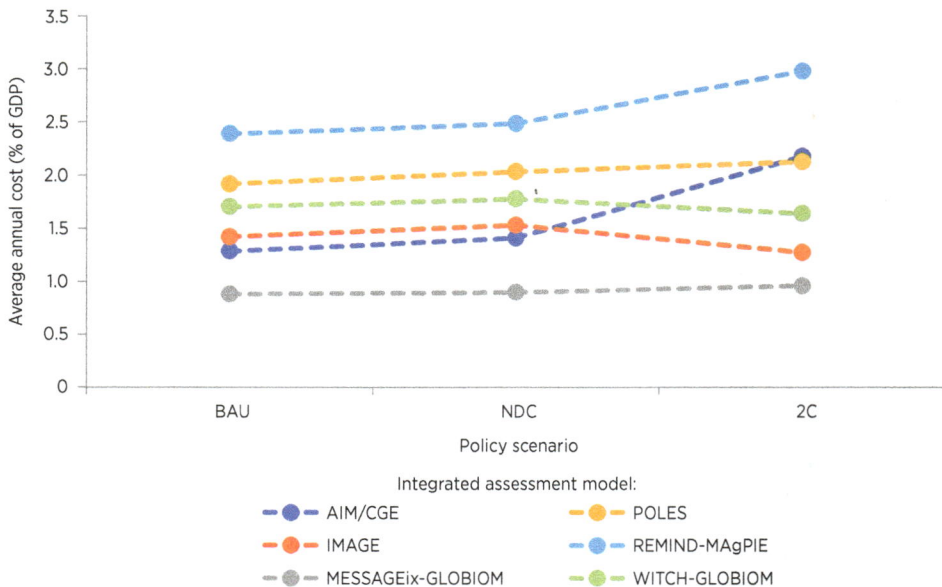

Source: Based on McCollum and others 2018.
Note: Results exclude high-income countries. BAU = business as usual; NDC = nationally determined contribution; 2C = 2°C.

Models also disagree as to which scenario is the most expensive. For 2C relative to BAU, two models anticipate higher investment costs, two models expect stable costs, and two models anticipate lower costs (figure 3.9). Such contrasting findings are often observed with other exercises to estimate investment needs: while the International Energy Agency estimated that the power sector investment consistent with a 2°C goal would be lower than under a BAU strategy, the International Renewable Energy Agency concluded that it would be higher (OECD/IEA and IRENA 2017).

Models disagree more in some regions than in others (figure 3.10). In the former Soviet Union, costs vary between 0.7 percent and 3.5 percent of GDP in the BAU scenario and between 0.7 percent and 5.3 percent of GDP in the 2C scenario, depending on the model used. In contrast, in Latin America and the Caribbean and in Africa and Middle East, costs are between 0.5 percent and 2 percent of GDP for all three scenarios.

The factors that explain these divergent views on the cost of the 2C scenario include (a) the assumed future costs of low-carbon technologies (renewables, nuclear, and carbon capture and storage), (b) the potential for improved energy efficiency and demand management (as captured by the elasticity of demand parameters in the models), and

FIGURE 3.10 **Models disagree more in some regions than in others**

Average annual cost of investment in the power sector, by policy scenario, region, and integrated assessment model used, 2015–30

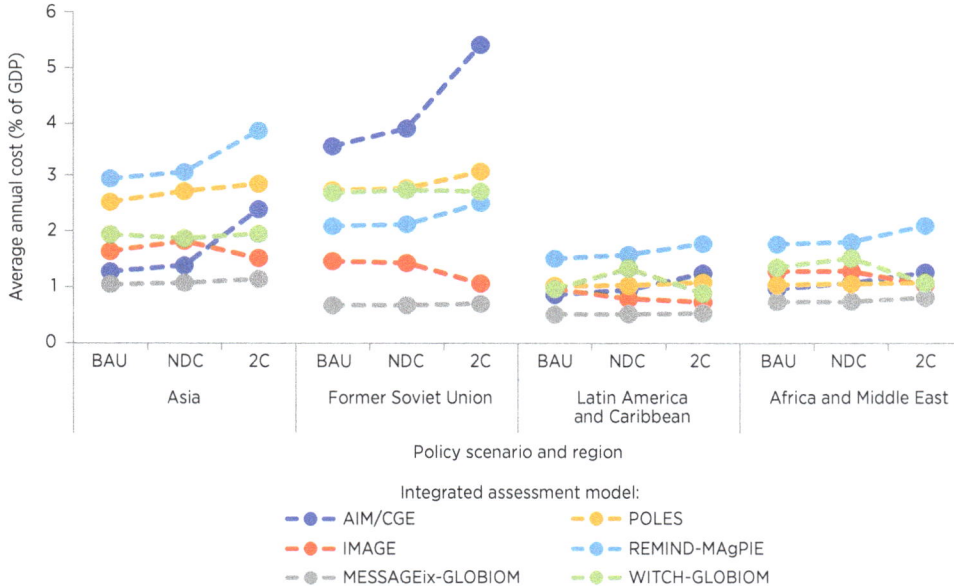

Source: Based on McCollum and others 2018.
Note: BAU = business as usual; NDC = nationally determined contribution; 2C = 2°C.

(c) the extent to which the transition results in stranded assets (such as thermal power plants that need to be retired early). Each model has a different way of employing these levers, leading to different possible futures. One notable trend identifiable across the models is that total costs increase with both stranded assets and consumption per capita.

Carbon-Constrained Power Sector: A Range of Solutions with Different Cost Implications

Accounting for the climate constraint when estimating power infrastructure needs leads to a sharp decrease of investments in fossil fuel power plants. In the low- and middle-income world, over the 2015–30 period, coal power plant investments decrease 51 percent for the transformative pathway (2C) and a bit less than 20 percent for the NDC scenario compared with the BAU scenario. Gas plant investments also decrease—by around 31 percent for the 2C scenario and 4 percent for the NDC scenario compared with the BAU scenario. While absolute investment numbers can vary, all models project a progressive scaling up of investments in low-carbon technology and energy efficiency as the climate constraint increases. By 2030,

FIGURE 3.11 The low-carbon share of investment rises progressively

Low-carbon share of investment in power generation, by policy scenario, 2015–30

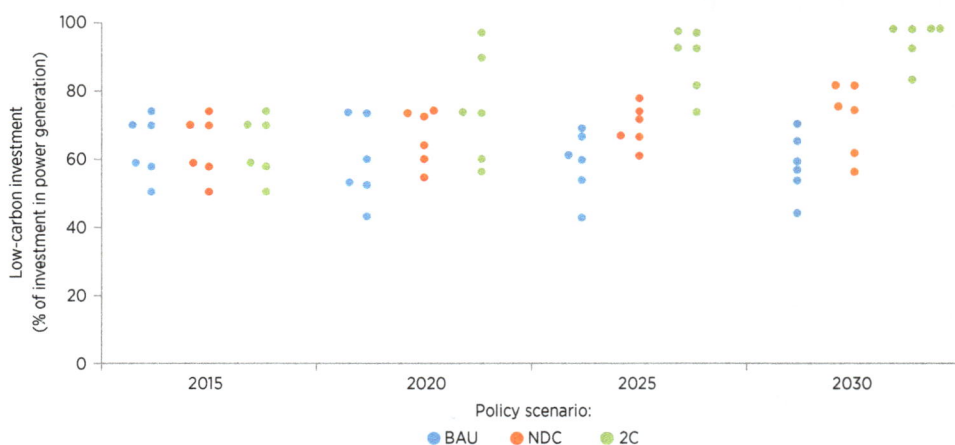

Source: Based on McCollum and others 2018.
Note: Each dot is one model and one scenario for LMICs. BAU = business as usual; LMICs = low- and middle-income countries; NDC = nationally determined contribution; 2C = 2°C.

in all models, most investments in power generation are low-carbon ones (figure 3.11).

Which strategies are favored for meeting the carbon constraint? While achieving a 2C scenario requires a step change in capital investments in most models, there are many ways of coping with a climate constraint on the supply side (figure 3.12). The intermodel variability in penetration rates of different technologies is quite high for low-carbon investments. As for the sums involved for the generation side of the power sector, the results show that low-carbon investments in 2030 vary from US$77 billion to US$414 billion across models for the BAU scenario and from US$145 billion to US$1,275 billion for the 2C scenario.

Policy makers can choose from a range of diverse, nonexclusive strategies to meet the climate constraint: (a) switch toward renewable energy generation and develop significant electricity storage, (b) drastically reduce demand, (c) keep fossil fuel technologies but add carbon capture and storage, or (d) pursue some combination of all three. The varying assumptions made in different models about the relative cost and deployment of these different options explain their varying results. For example, the REMIND-MAgPIE model assumes lower future capital costs for solar and wind than for other technologies and has the highest investments in the expansion of renewable electricity generation. But the IMAGE model forecasts a 25 percent decrease in power generation between the BAU and the 2C scenarios in 2030, with stable investments in renewable and nuclear energy and additional investments for the 2°C pathway. It assumes that

FIGURE 3.12 **Many models find many ways to meet the climate change constraint on the supply side**

Difference in investment and electricity consumption between the 2C scenario and the BAU scenario for each model in 2030

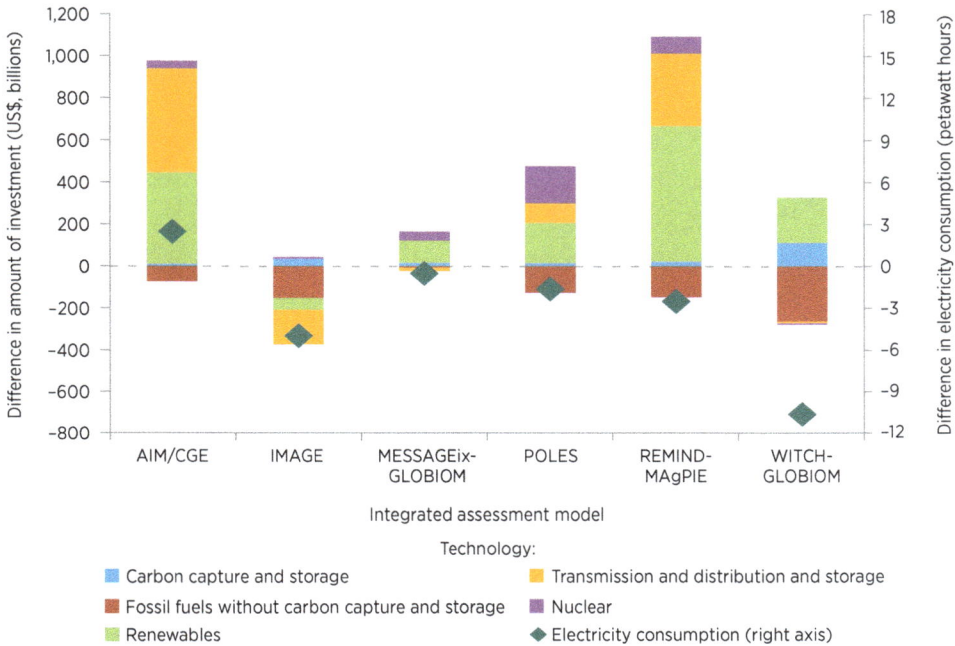

Source: Based on McCollum and others 2018.
Note: Dollar figures are constant 2015 U.S. dollars. BAU = business as usual; 2C = 2°C.

reducing the carbon intensity of the power sector is quite expensive, making it more cost-effective to cut demand.

Another driver of power sector investment cost is demand management and energy efficiency. For most models, per capita consumption decreases as the climate constraint becomes more stringent (figure 3.13). But some of the models—those in which energy efficiency is a key lever of the energy transition—see a particularly sharp decrease in per capita consumption and substantial investments in energy efficiency (40 percent of total investments in the WITCH-GLOBIOM model, as opposed to 5 percent in the POLES model).[4]

Stranded Assets: A Politically Unacceptable Solution?

The disruptive 2°C pathway not only means that all investments must be redirected toward low-carbon and energy efficient technologies but also that most high-emitting fossil fuel power plants have to be retired early. In fact, to stay on track for the 2C scenario, 60 percent of coal power plants,

FIGURE 3.13 **Electricity consumption falls as the climate constraint tightens**

Electricity consumption per capita in low- and middle-income countries in 2030,
by policy scenario and integrated assessment model used

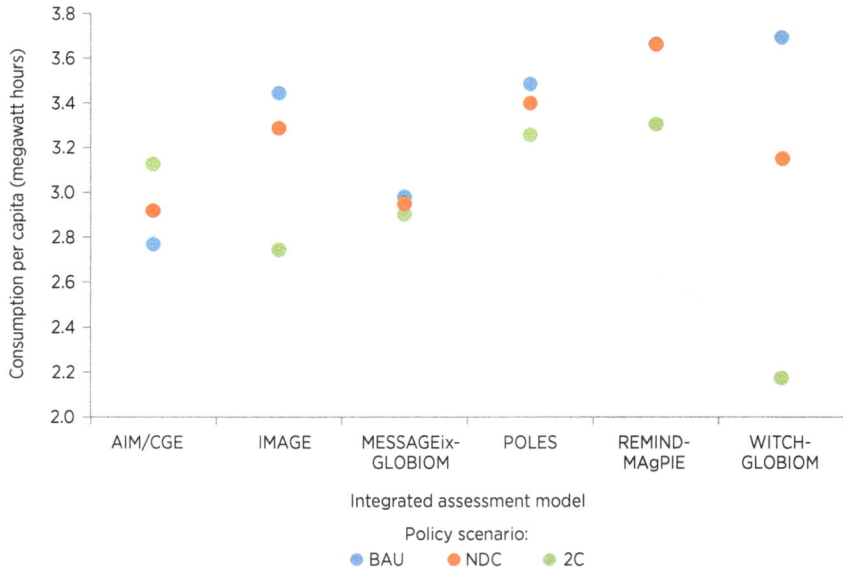

Source: Based on McCollum and others 2018.
Note: BAU = business as usual; NDC = nationally determined contribution; 2C = 2°C.

FIGURE 3.14 **Much of the coal-fired power infrastructure in the low- and middle-income world could become stranded assets by 2030**

Coal-fired power plants retired early or idled in 2030 as a share of 2020 capacity, by policy scenario and integrated assessment model used

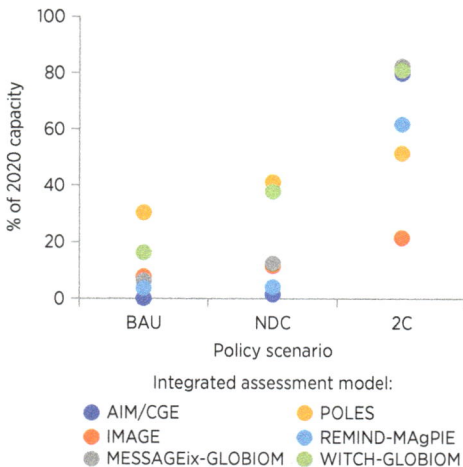

Source: Based on McCollum and others 2018.
Note: BAU = business as usual; NDC = nationally determined contribution; 2C = 2°C.

on average, have to become stranded assets by 2030, with the models showing a range of 20 percent to 80 percent (figure 3.14). When looking to stay on track for a 1.5C scenario, some models even find that 100 percent of coal power plants have to be stranded by 2030 (box 3.3).

For stringent climate targets, stranded assets are often part of the optimal decarbonization strategy (Johnson and others 2015; Rozenberg and others 2018). In the next section (which focuses on South America), we find that if the cost of capital is high, the most cost-effective option for achieving a climate-constrained scenario could be to keep investing in fossil fuel generation (gas in particular) in the medium term, but to retire these power plants early (Lecuyer and Vogt-Schilb 2014 found similar results). But this approach carries the risk of lock-in, whereby a country may find it politically difficult to retire costly

BOX 3.3

BY 2030, A 1.5C SCENARIO IS SIMILAR TO A 2C SCENARIO FOR ELECTRICITY GENERATION INVESTMENTS

According to the Intergovernmental Panel on Climate Change Special Report, *Global Warming of 1.5°C* (IPCC 2018), limiting global temperature increase to 1.5°C by the end of the century implies reaching net zero carbon dioxide (CO_2) emissions globally around 2050 and concurrent deep reductions in emissions of non-CO_2 forcers, particularly methane. As with the 2C scenario, a first step toward attaining full decarbonization is to decarbonize the electricity system as fast as possible. McCollum and others (2018) examined the electricity investments required for both 1.5°C and 2°C (figure B3.3.1).

By 2030, the 1.5C scenario is very similar to the 2C scenario but brings somewhat greater variability across model results. Some models find that investments required for the 1.5C scenario are lower than for the business-as-usual scenario (down to 1.1 percent of low- and middle-income countries' [LMICs'] GDP on average for the model that reduces demand most aggressively), while some models find that investment costs are higher (up to 3.2 percent of LMICs' GDP, on average). Here again, models rely differently on demand reduction and stranded assets, with some models requiring that almost 100 percent of installed coal capacity in 2020 in LMICs be stranded by 2030, while other models retire "only" 40 percent of 2020 capacity early. But for both the 2C and the 1.5C scenarios, all models agree that in 2030, almost 100 percent of electricity generation investments should be low carbon.

FIGURE B3.3.1 **Between 2015 and 2030, the 1.5C and the 2C investment paths for the power sector are very similar**

Average annual cost of investment in the power sector, by policy scenario and integrated assessment model used, 2015–30

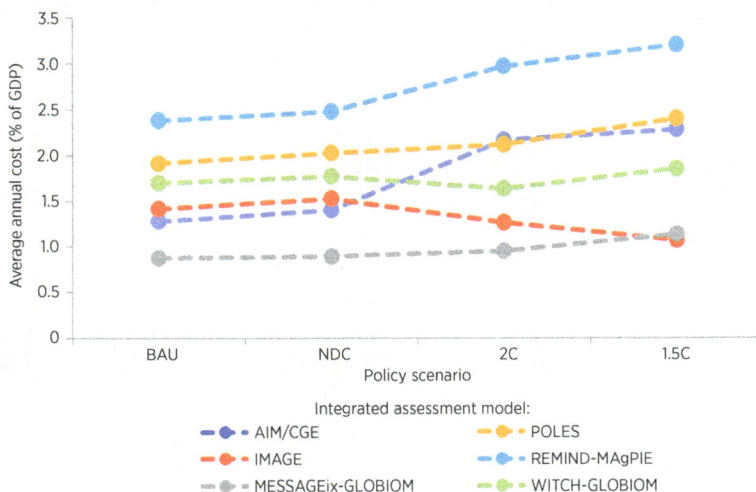

Source: Based on McCollum and others 2018.
Note: Results exclude high-income countries. BAU = business as usual; NDC = nationally determined contribution; 2C = 2°C; 1.5C = 1.5°C.

power plants early. Indeed, stranded assets are a visible loss of wealth concentrated in a few vested interests (such as the coal industry), who may oppose the reform and, in some cases, even have the power to veto it (Olson 2009; Trebilcock 2014). To avoid this kind of lock-in, one solution could be to use financial incentives today to lower the capital costs of low-carbon solutions (Rozenberg and others 2018).

SOUTH AMERICA: BRINGING CLIMATE AND DEMAND CONSTRAINTS TOGETHER

South America has almost closed its access gap, with 90 percent of the population connected to the grid in Bolivia and Peru and almost 100 percent elsewhere (World Bank 2016). The carbon intensity of the electricity sector in South America is the lowest in the world, with 100 percent of electricity produced from hydropower in Paraguay and more than 60 percent in Brazil, Colombia, Uruguay, and República Bolivariana de Venezuela (World Bank 2016).

But the energy sector in South America could be at a turning point for several reasons (Elizondo-Azuela and others 2017):

- Demand is rising due to rapid urbanization and a growing middle class, and the share of electricity produced from hydropower has declined in recent years due to droughts and poor water resource management.

- Hydropower expansion in the region may be difficult due to mounting opposition to large hydroelectric projects (Fay and others 2017).

- Future demand is uncertain, and some climate change scenarios imply lower hydropower production with lower availability of water.

On the one hand, high learning rates and falling costs of renewable energy technologies, together with climate policies and institutional, behavioral, and social factors, will stimulate the penetration of carbon-free technologies (Iyer and others 2015). On the other hand, the high cost of capital in LMICs makes capital-intensive power plants harder to finance (Schmidt 2014).

Under what conditions will capital and O&M costs be the highest or lowest? To shed light on this, we commissioned an additional study focused on South America (Moksnes and others 2019). Using an open-source model, hundreds of scenarios were generated by introducing uncertainty into parameters for the cost of technologies, fossil fuel prices, demand, financial discount rate (or cost of capital), climate change impacts on hydropower production, and CO_2 constraints (table 3.1).

The results show that the costs of capital investment in electricity could range between US$16 billion and US$29 billion per year, on average, with variable costs between US$15 billion and US$19 billion per year (figure 3.15). The variable costs are lower than capital investment costs, because of the high share of hydropower production—unlike in Africa. Total costs (capital and variable) for power infrastructure range between US$33 billion and US$47 billion per year between 2013 and 2030 (representing 1 percent to 1.4 percent of South America's GDP) and are driven by a combination of cost of capital, demand, and CO_2 constraints.

The combination of high capital costs and a strong CO_2 constraint leads to high total infrastructure costs (above 1.2 percent of GDP when demand is medium or high), because the high cost of capital favors fossil fuel technologies (which have a lower capital intensity), while the CO_2 constraint favors renewable electricity. This results in a trajectory characterized by investments in fossil fuel generation until 2020, followed by stranded fossil fuel capacity and high penetration of renewable energy capacity after 2020 (figure 3.16).

However, low demand and low capital costs lead to low system costs (less than 1.05 percent of GDP). Low capital costs favor renewable energy even before 2020, and low demand allows the investment to be limited to just what is needed to meet

FIGURE 3.15 **Variable costs are lower than capital costs for power infrastructure in South America**

Average annual variable and capital costs of investment in power infrastructure in South America, 2013–30

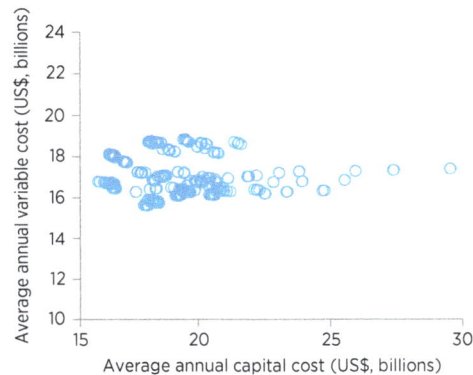

Source: Based on Moksnes and others 2019.
Note: Average annual costs are calculated over 2013–30 using a 6 percent discount rate.

FIGURE 3.16 **Total costs of electricity in South America are driven by cost of capital, demand, and CO_2 constraint**

Average annual cost of electricity, by climate scenario and level of demand, 2013–30

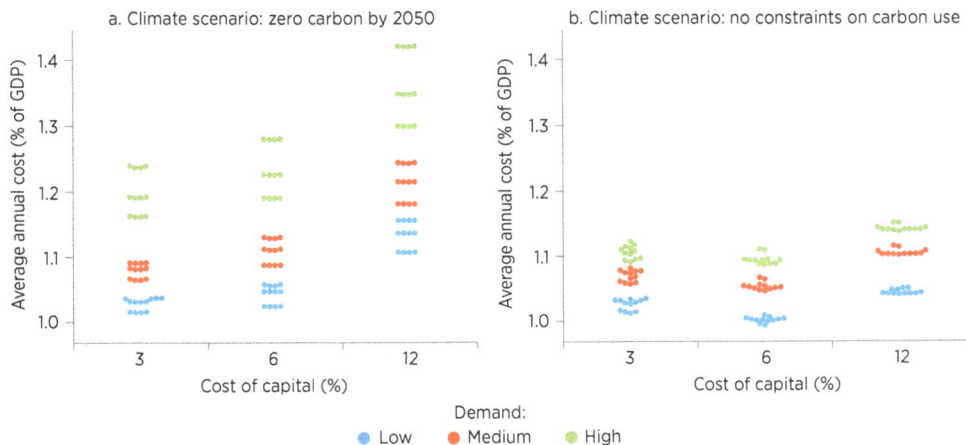

Source: Adapted from Moksnes and others 2019.

the reserve margin. Indeed, providing a reserve margin for peak demand with renewable energy can be very expensive in the absence of storage, as it requires significant excess capacity because of the intermittent nature of wind and solar. Thus, demand management is key to reducing infrastructure investment costs in low-carbon scenarios. Some of the new technologies presented in chapter 6 (smart grids, smart meters, and batteries) are very promising in this regard.

Unlike in Africa, in South America, changing demand does not change technological choices, which are driven instead by the cost of capital and CO_2 constraints. This occurs because all investments are assumed to be on-grid and because South America has large interconnection potential, which allows hydropower resources to be traded between countries.

In South America, relatively abundant hydropower resources and good integration of electricity markets favor a low-cost, low-carbon electricity system. With demand management and low financial costs for renewable energy investments, the electricity system can be zero carbon by 2050, while requiring spending less than 1.1 percent of GDP annually on new capital investments and variable costs before 2030 (numbers are of the same order of magnitude by 2050).

These results suggest that concessionary finance and policies that would effectively lower interest rates for low-carbon technologies would make renewable energy technologies more competitive, which would avoid burdening LMICs with high variable costs and prevent stranded fossil fuel capacities over the coming decades if there is a need to comply with stringent climate targets.

IN SUM

Investment costs to reach universal access to power depend on the ambition of policy makers. Yet, in addition to providing access to the millions without it, the goal is also to continue providing the world with reliable and affordable electricity and to do so while moving toward a decarbonized power system consistent with the 2°C global warming target.

By creating adequate incentives, policy makers could enable the early adoption of low-carbon technologies and the diffusion of demand management practices, while limiting stranded assets. Early adoption of low-carbon technologies would also benefit LMICs by lowering their fuel costs. The most desirable pathway for the power sector in our analysis is one that limits stranded assets and invests mostly in renewable energy and storage. It would result in total costs of 2.2 percent of GDP per year, on average, for LMICs and would enable the world to stay on a 2°C pathway.

How difficult will it be to reconcile social and economic goals with the environmental goal? Certainly, some new technologies like micro-grids and mini-grids (see chapter 6), as well as the likely continued decline in the cost of renewables, will make it easier. However, this reconciliation will not be without challenges. For example, greater use of wind and solar will pose problems of intermittency, require sophisticated management of the network, and necessitate a rethinking of the traditional pricing and cost-recovery model. In addition, while these technologies and the increased prevalence of decentralized generation open up opportunities for LMICs to leapfrog in the energy sector—as they have for telecommunications—progress will depend on governments' ability to put in place the needed regulatory framework and core supporting infrastructure.

NOTES

1. The number of people without access to electricity is 940 million. See https://trackingsdg7.esmap.org/data/files/download-documents/chapter_2 _electrification.pdf.
2. Sub-Saharan Africa is also the only region where the number of people without access to electricity has increased, as population growth has outstripped progress in electrification (Lucas and others 2017).
3. Using a World Bank estimate of total operating capital installed in the world today.
4. To calculate energy efficiency investments, we compare total final electricity demand in each of the model's tightened policy scenarios (NDC and 2C) to that model's demand in the BAU case (CPol). We then assume that, in equilibrium, investments made to reduce power demand could be equated with the investments that have been simultaneously offset on the supply side. For a single model and region, we calculate the ratio of supply-side investments in the policy scenario to total final electricity demand in that same scenario and then multiply this ratio (which is in units of U.S. dollars per 67 exajoules) by the final reduction in energy demand calculated separately for that policy scenario (relative to the reference case; units in exajoules). That investment value (in U.S. dollars) is then weighted by the ratio share of total GDP in the policy scenario to GDP in the reference case (in percent) for each time period and summed over the entire time frame of interest (2015–30).

REFERENCES

Bazilian, M., R. Economy, P. Nussbaumer, E. Haites, K. K. Yumkella, M. Howells, M. Takada, D. S. Rothman, and M. Levi. 2014. *Beyond Basic Access: The Scale of Investment Required for Universal Energy Access*. New York: Oxford University Press.

Bhatia, M., and N. Angelou. 2015. *Beyond Connections: Energy Access Redefined*. Washington, DC: World Bank.

Blimpo, M., and M. Cosgrove-Davies. 2018. *Electricity Uptake for Economic Transformation in Sub-Saharan Africa*. Washington, DC: World Bank.

Blimpo, M. P., J. T. Mensah, K. O. Opalo, and R. Shi. 2018. *Electricity Provision and Tax Mobilization in Africa*. Washington, DC: World Bank.

Chakravorty, U., M. Pelli, and B. Ural Marchand. 2014. "Does the Quality of Electricity Matter? Evidence from Rural India." *Journal of Economic Behavior and Organization* 107 (pt. A): 228–47.

EIA (Energy Information Administration). 2016. "How Much Does It Cost to Generate Electricity with Different Types of Power Plants?" Frequently Asked Questions, U.S. Energy Information Administration, Washington, DC. https://www.eia.gov/tools/faqs/faq.php?id=19&t=3.

Elizondo-Azuela, G., A. A. Barbalho, L. Maurer, S. Moreira, C. Garcia-Kilroy, C. de Gouvello, J. Benavidez, D. Reinstein, and J. Liu. 2017. *Energy Markets in Latin America and the Caribbean: Emerging Disruptions and the Next Frontier.* Washington, DC: World Bank.

Fay, M., L. A. Andres, C. J. E. Fox, U. G. Narloch, S. Straub, and M. A. Slawson. 2017. *Rethinking Infrastructure in Latin America and the Caribbean: Spending Better to Achieve More.* Washington, DC: World Bank.

Gertler, P. J., K. Lee, and A. M. Mobarak. 2017. "Electricity Reliability and Economic Development in Cities: A Microeconomic Perspective." Working paper, Department for International Development, London.

Grimm, M., L. Lenz, J. Peters, and M. Sievert. 2016. "Demand for Off-Grid Solar Electricity: Experimental Evidence from Rwanda." Ruhr Economic Paper, RWI, Essen, Germany.

IEA (International Energy Agency). 2017. *World Energy Outlook 2017.* Paris: OECD Publishing. https://doi.org/10.1787/weo-2017-en.

IPCC (Intergovernmental Panel on Climate Change). 2018. *Global Warming of 1.5°C.* Special Report. Nairobi: United Nations Environment Programme; Geneva: World Meteorological Organization.

Iyer, G., N. Hultman, J. Eom, H. McJeon, P. Patel, and L. Clarke. 2015. "Diffusion of Low-Carbon Technologies and the Feasibility of Long-Term Climate Targets." *Technological Forecasting and Social Change* 90 (pt. A): 103–18.

Johnson, N., V. Krey, D. L. McCollum, S. Rao, K. Riahi, and J. Rogelj. 2015. "Stranded on a Low-Carbon Planet: Implications of Climate Policy for the Phase-Out of Coal-Based Power Plants." *Technological Forecasting and Social Change* 90 (pt. A): 89–102.

Jordan-Antoine, R., S. Banerjee, W. Blyth, and M. Bazilian. Forthcoming. "Estimates of the Cost of Reaching Universal Access to Electricity." Working paper, World Bank, Washington, DC.

Khandker, S. R., D. F. Barnes, and H. A. Samad. 2012. "The Welfare Impacts of Rural Electrification in Bangladesh." *Energy Journal* 33 (1): 187–206.

———. 2013. "Welfare Impacts of Rural Electrification: A Panel Data Analysis from Vietnam." *Economic Development and Cultural Change* 61 (3): 659–92.

Kojima, M., and C. Trimble. 2016. *Making Power Affordable for Africa and Viable for Its Utilities.* Washington, DC: World Bank.

Lecuyer, O., and A. Vogt-Schilb. 2014. *Optimal Transition from Coal to Gas and Renewable Power under Capacity Constraints and Adjustment Costs.* Washington, DC: World Bank.

Lee, K., E. Miguel, and C. Wolfram. 2016. "Experimental Evidence on the Demand for and Costs of Rural Electrification." NBER Working Paper 22292, National Bureau of Economic Research, Cambridge, MA.

Longe, O. M., N. Rao, F. Omowole, A. S. Oluwalami, and O. T. Oni. 2017. "A Case Study on Off-Grid Microgrid for Universal Electricity Access in the Eastern Cape of South Africa." *International Journal of Energy Engineering* 7 (2): 55–63.

Lucas, P. L., A. G. Dagnachew, and A. F. Hof. 2017. *Towards Universal Electricity Access in Sub-Saharan Africa: A Quantitative Analysis of Technology and Investment Requirements.* The Hague: PBL Netherlands Environmental Assessment Agency.

McCollum, D. L., W. Zhou, C. Bertram, H.-S. de Boer, V. Bosetti, S. Busch, J. Després, and others. 2018. "Energy Investment Needs for Fulfilling the Paris Agreement and Achieving the Sustainable Development Goals." *Nature Energy* 3 (7): 589–99.

Mensah, J. T. 2018. *Jobs! Electricity Shortages and Unemployment in Africa.* Washington, DC: World Bank.

Ministère du Plan et Suivi de la Mise en Oeuvre de la Révolution and Ministère de la Santé Publique. 2014. *Deuxième enquête démographique et de santé.* EDS-RDC II 2013–2014. Rockville, MD: MEASURE DHS, ICF International.

Moksnes, N., J. Rozenberg, O. Broad, C. Taliotis, M. Howells, and H. Rogner. 2019. "Determinants of Energy Futures—A Scenario Discovery Method Applied to Cost and Carbon Emissions Futures for South American Electricity Infrastructure." Background paper prepared for this report, World Bank, Washington, DC.

Nicolas, C., J. Rozenberg, and B. Samson. 2019. "Meeting the SDGs for Electricity Access—Using a Multi Scenario Approach to Understand the Cost Drivers of Power Infrastructure in Sub-Saharan Africa." Background paper prepared for this report, World Bank, Washington, DC.

OECD/IEA (Organisation for Economic Co-operation and Development/ International Energy Agency) and IRENA (International Renewable Energy Agency). 2017. "Perspectives for the Energy Transition: Investment Needs for a Low-Carbon Energy System." OECD/IEA and IRENA, Paris. https://www.irena .org/publications/2017/Mar/Perspectives-for-the-energy-transition-Investment -needs-for-a-low-carbon-energy-system.

Olson, M. 2009. *The Logic of Collective Action: Public Goods and the Theory of Groups.* Cambridge, MA: Harvard University Press.

Rozenberg, J., A. Vogt-Schilb, and S. Hallegatte. 2018. "Instrument Choice and Stranded Assets in the Transition to Clean Capital." *Journal of Environmental Economics and Management.* In press.

Samad, H. A., and F. Zhang. 2016. *Benefits of Electrification and the Role of Reliability: Evidence from India.* Washington, DC: World Bank.

Schmidt, T. S. 2014. "Low-Carbon Investment Risks and De-Risking." *Nature Climate Change* 4 (4): 237–39.

Trebilcock, M. J. 2014. *Dealing with Losers: The Political Economy of Policy Transitions.* New York: Oxford University Press.

United Nations. 2015. *United Nations Energy Statistics Yearbook.* New York: United Nations.

World Bank. 2016. World Development Indicators database. Washington, DC: World Bank.

World Resources Institute. 2018. CAIT Climate Data Explorer. Washington, DC: World Resources Institute.

4

Transport

JULIE ROZENBERG AND MARIANNE FAY

KEY MESSAGES

- For many countries, universal access to paved roads by 2030 is not a realistic goal given costs. But indicators of access can help to prioritize investments, and other solutions exist to improve integration in low-density areas.

- Investment costs for the transport sector in low- and middle-income countries (LMICs) for 2015–30 range between 0.5 percent and 3.3 percent of gross domestic product (GDP) per year depending on modal choice and the success of policies to influence occupancy. Future demand for mobility can be satisfied at relatively low infrastructure investment costs (1.3 percent of GDP) and low carbon dioxide (CO_2) emissions via a shift toward more rail and urban public transport if policies are in place that ensure high rail occupancy and urban densification.

- The maintenance of existing and new transport infrastructure costs as much as new transport capital investment—and even more in regions that have already built the bulk of their infrastructure. Failure to perform routine maintenance would increase total capital and rehabilitation costs by 50 percent over the 2015–30 period.

INTRODUCTION

Transport infrastructure investments have economic characteristics that call for careful long-term planning before making investment decisions. But in practice, the decisions are often political and do not necessarily prioritize investments based on economic or environmental impacts (Burgess and others 2015; Cadot and others 2006).

These characteristics include immobile capital with a long lifetime (Prud'homme 2004), investments that are often "lumpy" and arrive in waves (Lecocq and Shalizi 2014), increasing returns to scale through network effects (Driscoll 2014), and the creation of path dependence (Bleakley and Lin 2012). The transport sector is also one of the fastest-growing greenhouse gas (GHG)–emitting sectors, representing 28 percent of final energy use in 2008 (IEA 2012). Hence significant emissions cuts from the transport sector will be needed to limit the rise in global temperature to below 2°C, or even "well below 2°C," as targeted in the Paris Agreement.

Complicating matters, transport is the most difficult sector for which to estimate infrastructure investment needs. One reason is the absence of a single universal goal equivalent to universal access for water and sanitation or for electricity. The Sustainable Development Goals (SDGs) identify an indicator for only one subsector of transport (rural accessibility) and do not set a target; the associated Sustainable Mobility for All agenda calls for broad, but difficult to measure, "equitable, green, efficient, and safe mobility." Another reason is the fact that transport infrastructure is composed of different, highly heterogeneous, subsectors. At the very least, there is a need to distinguish between urban mobility, rural accessibility, and interurban transport as well as between freight and passenger transport.

Data are also a constraint. At the local scale, transport investment needs can be assessed using spatially explicit data that measure access to jobs, services, and markets (He and others 2018) or network resilience and redundancy (Briceño-Garmendia and others 2015). Spatial computable general equilibrium and spatial econometric models can also be used to assess the impact of investments (Asian Development Bank and others 2018).

Unfortunately, such detailed spatial information does not exist at the global level. Thus, for this global study, we use the following three approaches (table 4.1):

- A spatially explicit study on rural access that is carried out in 166 countries, with a detailed analysis of the affordability of increasing rural access in 20 countries (Mikou and others 2019).

- A global urban passenger model—representing the 1,692 urban agglomerations in the world with populations above 300,000—that assesses urban transport investment needs under multiple scenarios of incentives for modal choice and land-use planning (ITF 2018a).

- A global energy-economy-environment model that estimates mobility needs (rural, urban, and interurban for passengers and freight) in different regions over the next 30 years under various macroeconomic conditions

TABLE 4.1 **Overview of the assumptions and models used in this chapter**

Sector and objectives	Models and source	Metrics	Policy scenarios	Uncertain parameters
Rural access				
Increase rural access to all-season roads (SDG 9.1)	World Bank rural road investments model (Mikou and others 2019)	Number of people within 2 kilometers of an all-season road; capital costs; maintenance costs	Pave all tertiary roads that provide connectivity with main network; spend 1% of GDP per year in paving rural roads; provide basic supplies with drones	Road construction cost; population growth and urbanization; GDP growth; drones cost
Urban passengers				
Meet mobility demand; mitigate climate change (SDG 13)	ITF urban passenger model (ITF 2018a)	Capital costs; O&M costs; local pollutants; CO_2 emissions; passenger surplus	Business as usual; robust governance (demand management, higher investment in public transport, stringent fuel standards); land-use and transport planning (robust governance scenario combined with land-use planning); shared-mobility scenario	Not explored
Global freight and passengers				
Meet mobility demand; mitigate climate change (SDG 13)	Energy-economy-environment model IMACLIM-R (Fisch-Romito and Guivarch 2019; Waisman and others 2012)	Passenger and freight demand; capital costs; maintenance costs	Global climate mitigation: business as usual; 2°C–3°C temperature increase by 2100 Transport sector: shift to rail and bus rapid transit; constant shares	Transport activity; transport structure (for example, car occupancy); technology costs (car and truck technologies); fuel costs; population and GDP growth; climate change mitigation challenges (technical change, fossil fuel reserves, energy demand); rail and road occupancy; infrastructure construction costs

Note: Categories follow the framework developed in chapter 1. CO_2 = carbon dioxide; ITF = International Transport Forum; O&M = operations and maintenance; SDG = Sustainable Development Goal.

(labor productivity growth, technical change, trade patterns, and climate change mitigation objectives) (Fisch-Romito and Guivarch 2019). These mobility needs are then translated into transport infrastructure investment costs, using various assumptions on costs, terrestrial modes for interurban transport, and utilization rates.

The last two models allow us to explore the influence of climate change mitigation objectives on transport investment needs. Climate mitigation policies radically change the transport modes and technologies that must be used and require transport planning to be better integrated with land-use planning. Absent this integration, the long-lived nature and path dependence of transport investment can lock the sector into emissions-intensive pathways centered around personal vehicles, which could then be very expensive to decarbonize (Guivarch and Hallegatte 2011).

Our study estimates that total future infrastructure investment costs for the transport sector in LMICs for 2015–30 range between US$157 billion and US$1,060 billion per year, on average—or about 0.9 percent to 3.3 percent of GDP per year—depending on the choice of modal share (rail for terrestrial transport can increase costs significantly) and the success of policies to influence occupancy level (high rail occupancy decreases costs significantly).

This chapter begins with a discussion of rural accessibility and what it would cost to improve, before turning to urban transport and global transport. It has three key findings:

- *First, universal access to all-weather roads—defined here as paved roads—may not be affordable in the short or medium term for many countries.* Even if countries spent 1 percent of their GDP per year on paving rural roads by 2030, rural accessibility would only increase from 39 to 52 percent, on average, across LMICs under an optimistic growth scenario. However, other solutions exist to increase social integration at a lower cost—including waterways, gravel roads, smaller roads designed for bikes or motorcycles, and drones to deliver basic supplies on a weekly basis.

- *Second, future total demand for mobility (for both freight and passengers) can be supplied at relatively low infrastructure investment costs (1.3 percent of GDP per year) and low CO_2 emissions.* But this requires a shift toward more rail, urban public transport, and low-emissions vehicles, combined with policies to ensure high rail occupancy and encourage land uses that make cities denser. In the absence of these policies, the costs of responding to mobility demand through low-carbon infrastructure would be 26 percent more in urban areas and 90 percent more for the overall transport sector.

- *Third, the stakes pertaining to maintenance are high: maintenance is expensive to do (it will cost as much as new transport investment) but expensive to neglect (failure to perform adequate maintenance will increase overall investment needs by 50 percent).* Over the next 15 years, the maintenance of existing and new transport infrastructure will cost as much as new transport capital investment—and even more in the regions that have already built the bulk of their transport infrastructure. But failure to perform routine maintenance will result in poor service and cost 50 percent more overall because of additional rehabilitation needs. Maintenance costs need to be factored in at the infrastructure planning stage.

RURAL ACCESSIBILITY

Rural accessibility is the only goal regarding transport infrastructure that can be found in the SDGs. Specifically, SDG target 9.1.1 refers to the proportion of the rural population who live within 2 kilometers of an all-season road. One measure of rural accessibility is the rural access index (RAI), defined as "the number of rural people who live within 2 kilometers (typically equivalent to a walk of 20–25 minutes) of an all-season road as a proportion of the total rural population" (Roberts and others 2006). An "all-season road" refers to "a road that is motorable all year round by the prevailing means of rural transport." In countries with a strong rainy season, all-season roads mean paved roads, but in drier countries, all-season roads can also be interpreted as gravel roads.

Recent econometric studies have found that access to all-weather roads has a significant impact on households' welfare. In Bangladesh, a road-paving project implemented from 1997 to 2001 increased household expenditure by 9 percent to 10 percent, on average (Khandker and Koolwal 2011). Similarly, in Ethiopia, access to an all-season road reduces poverty 7 percent and increases household consumption 16 percent (Dercon and others 2008). However, a road may bring few economic benefits in areas with no market to sustain nonagricultural jobs.

For this report, we calculate the RAI in 166 countries using open-source geospatial data, but without information on road quality and thus transitability.[1] The analysis assumes that all roads in the primary and secondary networks are all-season roads in good condition, which is an optimistic assumption but gives comparable results with previous estimates based on surveys (see Mikou and others 2019 for methods and caveats). Although the RAI is close to 100 percent in most European countries, it is below 60 percent in most LMICs, below 51 percent in every Sub-Saharan country, and below 20 percent in 24 countries (map 4.1).

We also find that some countries could more than double their RAI by paving their tertiary roads (Bolivia could increase its RAI from 20 percent to 70 percent, while Sierra Leone could increase its RAI from 27 percent to 90 percent)—but many others would not see a significant benefit (the RAI in Mauritania and Turkmenistan would stay below 30 percent), because their countries are too vast, their population too scattered, or their existing tertiary road network too scant.

MAP 4.1 Sub-Saharan Africa stands out for rural accessibility issues

Rural access index, by region

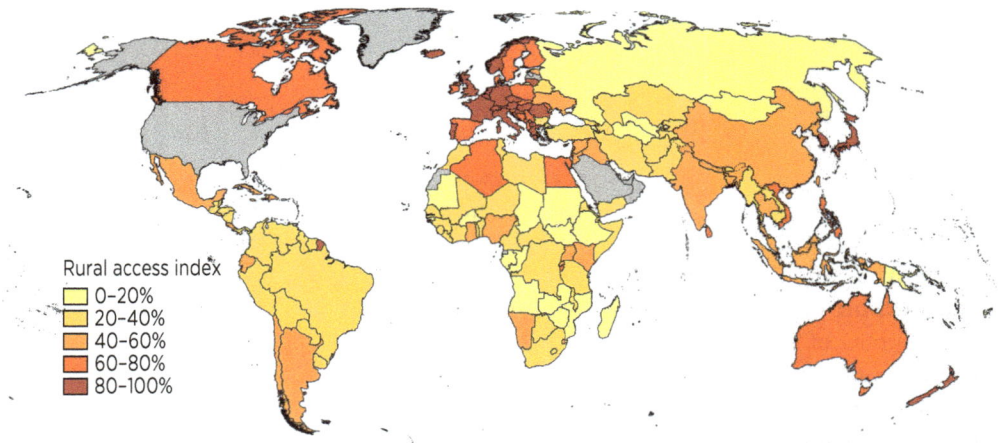

Rural access index
- 0–20%
- 20–40%
- 40–60%
- 60–80%
- 80–100%

Source: See Mikou and others 2019 for details.

Prioritizing Rural Investments Based on Rural Accessibility and Connectivity

Besides, paving rural roads does not guarantee connectivity with the rest of the network. This means that the RAI alone cannot be used in the absence of a broader network model to prioritize investments. To gain more insight, we built a model to prioritize rural road investments based on two simple criteria: (a) maximizing the RAI and (b) providing connectivity with the primary and secondary network. The only investment option available in our model is to upgrade existing tertiary roads or tracks to all-season roads. The analysis is done in 20 countries in which the potential for increasing the RAI is high and for which the data are complete enough (Mikou and others 2019).[2]

The results show not only that costs balloon quickly, but also that they depend on geography, road network connectivity, population distribution, and road unit costs.

- In Sierra Leone, paving tertiary roads would increase the RAI from 28 percent to 70 percent but cost US$4 billion—more than the country's GDP in 2017 (figure 4.1). Marginal costs increase quickly: improving the RAI by 1 percentage point would cost US$30 million (about 1 percent of GDP) when the RAI is 30 percent, but US$200 million when the RAI is 70 percent.

- While Bolivia has the same distribution of rural population as Morocco and a similar one as Togo, mountainous Bolivia would need to spend US$2 billion to increase the RAI from 20 percent to 30 percent, Morocco could increase it from 30 percent to 47 percent with the same amount, while smaller Togo could increase it from 30 percent to 65 percent (figure 4.2).

FIGURE 4.1 Upgrading rural roads in Sierra Leone becomes costly—fast

Cumulative and marginal costs of increasing access, and maps of initial and final road networks in Sierra Leone

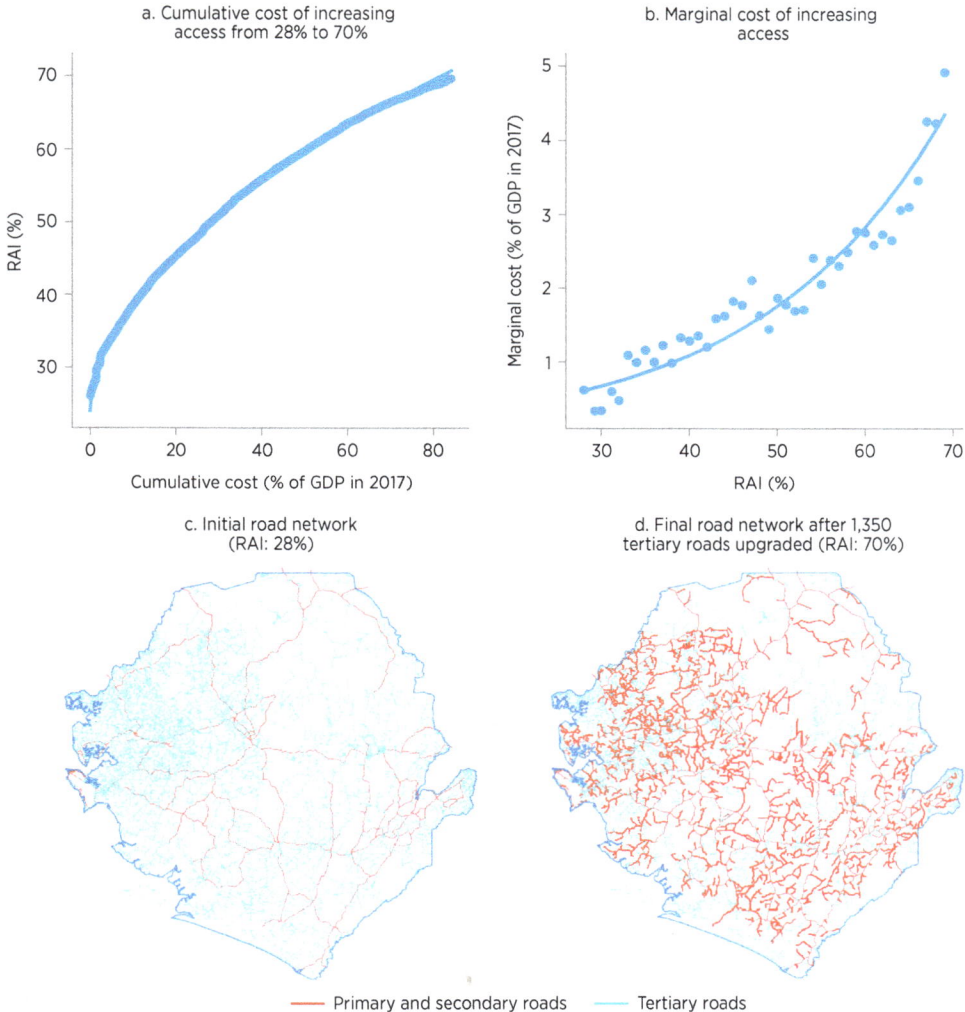

a. Cumulative cost of increasing access from 28% to 70%

b. Marginal cost of increasing access

c. Initial road network (RAI: 28%)

d. Final road network after 1,350 tertiary roads upgraded (RAI: 70%)

—— Primary and secondary roads   —— Tertiary roads

Note: Tertiary roads are upgraded in the most efficient order while increasing connectivity. In panels a and b, each road addition is represented by a dot, and a solid line represents an estimation of the relation between RAI and cost. RAI = rural access index.

As with all infrastructure sectors, road unit costs vary greatly across countries. A single surface treatment can cost anywhere from US$10,000 per kilometer in the Lao People's Democratic Republic to US$65,000 per kilometer in Armenia.[3] Many factors could explain the spread in road costs, including varying labor and material costs, spending efficiency, corruption, and conflict (Collier and others 2016). See chapter 2 for a discussion.

FIGURE 4.2 The cost of greater accessibility depends on many country-related factors

Distribution of rural population and corresponding cost of greater accessibility in select countries

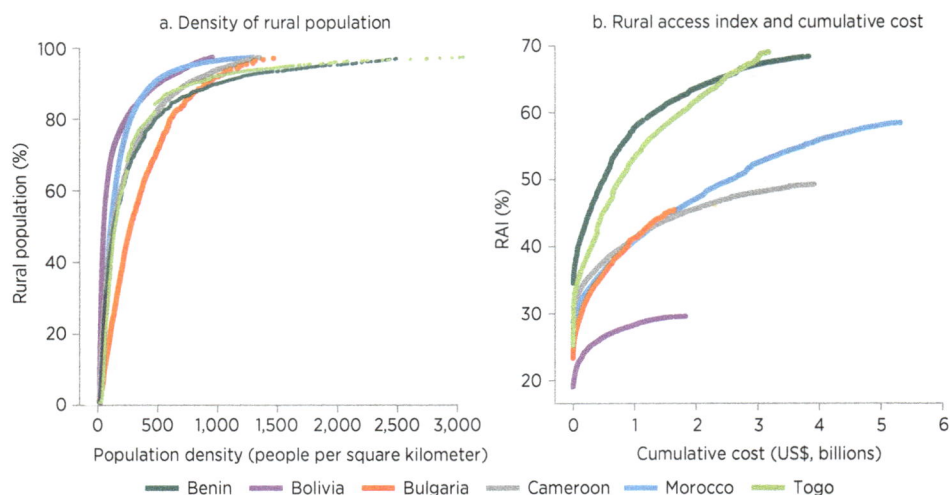

a. Density of rural population

b. Rural access index and cumulative cost

Benin · Bolivia · Bulgaria · Cameroon · Morocco · Togo

Note: Rural population (panel a) excludes people who live within 2 kilometers of a primary or secondary road. RAI = rural access index.

Moreover, many countries will not be able to achieve universal access to all-weather roads any time soon. In the Kyrgyz Republic, where the road network is very sparse and small pockets of population are scattered throughout the country, the cost of increasing the RAI by 1 percentage point goes from US$10 million when the RAI is 28 percent to US$120 million (about 2 percent of the country's GDP) when the RAI is 32 percent. In the Kyrgyz Republic, increasing the RAI to 100 percent might not be a viable objective. Similarly, in Burkina Faso, the cost of improving the RAI from 32 to 33 percent goes up to US$500 million because hundreds of kilometers of roads need to be paved to reach remaining populations.

Countries aiming to improve social integration through improved rural access might find that they cannot afford to build a large rural road network, let alone maintain it. In Sierra Leone and Togo, maintenance of a network that provides access to about 70 percent of the rural population would cost about 2.5 percent of their current GDP annually (table 4.2).

Given that goals and costs are so country specific that it is impossible to cost overall rural access, we reverse the question: how much access could countries achieve by 2030 if each spent 1 percent of its GDP on new rural roads every year? Our results show that, with optimistic assumptions on GDP growth, access could increase between 9 percentage points, on average, in East Asia to 17 percentage points, on average, in Sub-Saharan Africa (table 4.3).

Table 4.3 also shows that most of the gains can be obtained by spending only 0.5 percent of GDP every year, since the cost of access quickly escalates as ambition increases.

TABLE 4.2 **High road maintenance costs pose a hurdle in Sub-Saharan Africa**

Capital and maintenance costs of reaching a given RAI objective in select Sub-Saharan African countries

Country	RAI objective (%)	Total cost of upgrading tertiary roads (% of current GDP)	Total annual cost of maintaining rural paved roads (% of GDP)
Burkina Faso	24	15	1.6
	33	50	2.1
Guinea	40	20	1.0
	48	55	2.0
Sierra Leone	51	40	1.5
	70	121	2.6
Togo	56	25	1.8
	72	73	2.5

Note: The two RAI objectives are a mid-point and the maximum that countries can reach by upgrading tertiary roads. RAI = rural access index.

TABLE 4.3 **Universal access to paved roads is not within countries' reach by 2030**

Ability to achieve universal access to paved roads by 2030, by level of spending and region

% of rural population within 2 kilometers of a primary or secondary road

Region	2017	If all countries in the region spend 0.5% of their GDP per year by 2030	If all countries in the region spend 1% of their GDP per year by 2030
East Asia and Pacific	52	59	61
Europe and Central Asia	29	37	40
Latin America and Caribbean	34	42	45
Middle East and North Africa	39	49	51
South Asia	43	54	57
Sub-Saharan Africa	29	42	46

Note: GDP for each country grows following the shared socioeconomic pathway 5, which has the highest growth rate.

Environmental Impact of Rural Roads

A growing body of literature is sounding the alarm on the potential negative impacts of roads on forest cover and biodiversity, although impacts strongly depend on the local context and type of road. Asher and others (2018) found that rural roads have a significant impact on forests in India, while Damania and others (2018) and Pfaff and others (2018) found that impacts can be significant in the Amazon forest and in Africa.

To understand the possible order of magnitude of the impact, we run three scenarios based on this literature: (a) newly paved rural roads lead to deforestation in an area of 25 meters on each side of the road, (b) the impact spreads to 2 kilometers on each side of the road, and (c) the blast of the impact is 10 kilometers on each side of the road. If the impact is 2 kilometers

FIGURE 4.3 **Road paving can have a major impact on forest cover**

Extent of deforestation due to construction of paved roads in select countries

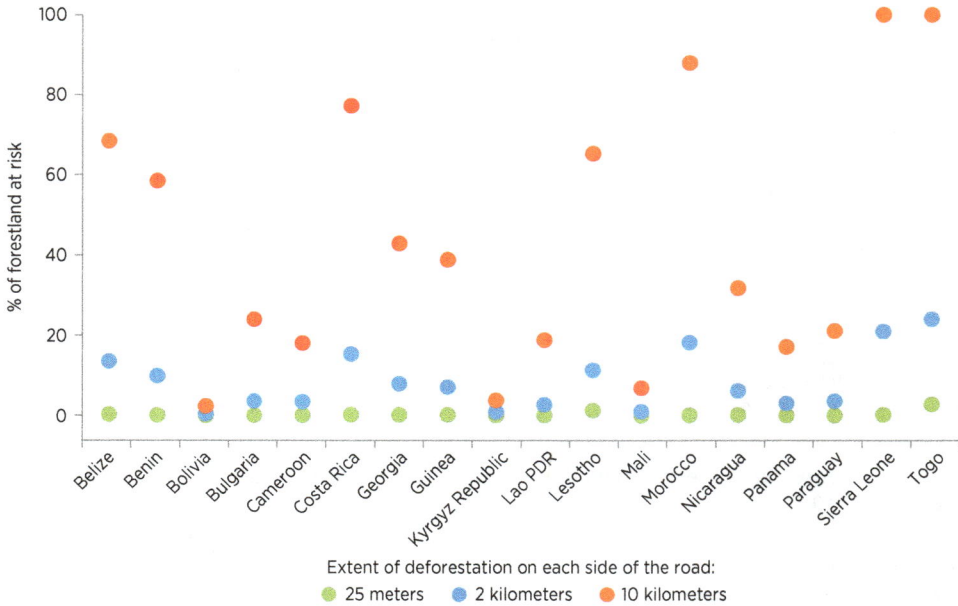

Extent of deforestation on each side of the road:
● 25 meters ● 2 kilometers ● 10 kilometers

or more of deforestation, as figure 4.3 shows, the consequences for biodiversity could be dramatic in countries like Belize, Morocco, Sierra Leone, and Togo. What can be done to minimize the damage? Two recent studies suggest that new types of analysis can prioritize rural roads based on both their economic and social benefits and their potential negative environmental impact (Damania and others 2018; Laurance and others 2014).

The Cost of Making Roads Safer

Another transport issue is unsafe roads. Indeed, traffic accidents represent one of the main causes of death globally and the leading cause of death for people ages 15 to 29, according to the World Health Organization. The United Nations explicitly refers to road safety in the SDGs: as part of SDG 3 on health and well-being, target 3.6 seeks to "halve the number of global deaths and injuries from road traffic accidents" by 2020. While road safety needs to be addressed with many instruments, including safer vehicles, lower speeds, improved driver education, and better institutional capacity, roads can also be made safer via better designs and protection. World Bank experts estimate that the cost of making roads safer is about 10 percent more than the cost of constructing a "basic" road, which should be added in as part of the total cost when planning to boost rural access.

Solutions for Rural Integration if Paved Roads Are Not Affordable

Even though many countries cannot achieve universal rural access by 2030, in the meantime other solutions exist to improve social integration. When rural paved roads are not affordable, other options could include investing in cabotage in coastal areas (Iimi and Rao 2018) or smaller roads better suited for bicycles and motorcycle traffic (Raballand and others 2010). In countries with a dry climate and no rainy season, gravel roads can be sufficient for rural access at a significantly lower cost than paved roads. In Morocco, for example, the RAI can be increased from 32 percent to 65 percent using gravel roads for less than 0.5 percent of GDP (figure 4.4). In practice, investment costs for rural roads can be somewhere between the cost of paved roads and the cost of gravel roads, if drainage structures (like culverts) are put in place but the surface of the road is not paved.

More recently, some countries have been experimenting with the use of drones for delivering medical supplies in remote rural areas (USAID 2017). Although drones do not generate access to economic opportunities in the same way that transport infrastructure does, they can significantly improve people's lives by carrying medical and school supplies, especially if people have access to the Internet for consulting doctors.

As a thought experiment, we estimated the cost of using drones to deliver weekly supplies to low-density rural areas in Sierra Leone. New commercial drones can now fly 40–60 kilometers, but cheaper ones, like the ones used by nongovernmental organizations, can fly 20 kilometers (Raptopoulos 2013; USAID 2017). In Sierra Leone, 75 percent of the rural population who live more than 2 kilometers from a primary or secondary road are within 10 kilometers of a primary or secondary road, 16 percent are within 10–20 kilometers, and 8 percent are within 20–40 kilometers (only 1 percent live farther than 40 kilometers from a primary or secondary road). If drone deliveries target only low-density areas (fewer than 150 people per square kilometer), the cost of delivering 1 kilogram of supplies for 10 people every week would be between US$1 per person per year and US$26 per person per year, depending on their distance to the closest all-season road and the drone technology used. The total cost would be US$5 million to US$9 million per year (table 4.4).

FIGURE 4.4 **The cost of greater accessibility is much lower using gravel rather than paved roads in dry climates**

Cumulative cost of increasing rural access with gravel and paved roads in Morocco

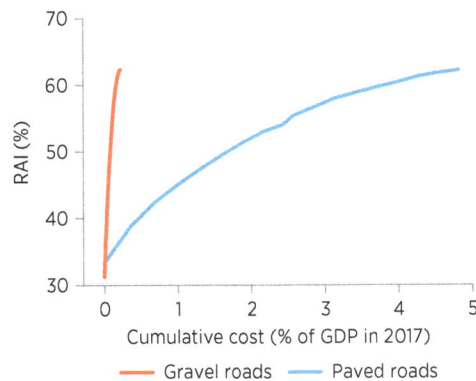

Note: RAI = rural access index.

TABLE 4.4 **Drone delivery helps to increase social integration in rural areas**

Annual cost of delivering weekly supplies to low-density areas in Sierra Leone, by different maximum population densities and different drone technologies

Maximum density served (population per square kilometer)	% of isolated rural population served	Total annual cost, 5-year average (US$, millions)	
		US$3,000 drones	US$50,000 drones
150	69	5	9
100	51	4	7
75	37	3	5

Note: A US$3,000 drone flies at 40 kilometers per hour, can carry 1 kilogram of goods, and can fly for 8 hours. A US$50,000 drone flies at 100 kilometers per hour, can carry 2 kilograms of goods, and can fly for 8 hours. Costs include the capital cost of the drones plus operating costs (including labor). Isolated population means farther than 2 kilometers from an all-season road.

Based on the most conservative assumptions in this analysis, bringing weekly supplies to remote areas by drone costs three times less every year than increasing rural accessibility from 30 percent to 31 percent and 22 times less than increasing accessibility from 69 percent to 70 percent. Moreover, these costs are likely to decline quickly, as drone markets mature and the number of service providers increases. Thus, at least in the short term, drone delivery could help to increase social integration in remote rural areas.

URBAN TRANSPORT

Although urban areas are much denser than rural areas, accessibility can still be very low in many cities in the low- and middle-income world. Formal public transportation is simply not available in most cities in the world: 75 percent of world cities have no subway, tramway, light rail system, or bus rapid transit. Mass transit systems are more common in high-income countries, and there are no subways in cities in low-income countries. A few cities in LMICs have mass transit infrastructure, but the networks are usually very limited (table 4.5). The length of subway per inhabitant is twice as high in high-income cities as in middle-income ones. And the extent of light systems (tramway, light rail systems, and bus rapid transit) per inhabitant is almost four times higher in high-income cities than in middle-income ones.

LMICs, instead, have vast informal (paratransit) public transport networks in many cities (*tro-tros* in Accra, *dala dalas* in Dar es Salaam, *ndiaga ndiayes* in Dakar, and *matatus* in Nairobi). The challenge is to improve this existing service, make it safer, and ultimately integrate it within any new formal system of mass transit.

TABLE 4.5 **Major gaps remain in the availability of mass transit infrastructure**

Availability of mass transit infrastructure, by country income group

Income group	% of cities with subway	% of cities with light rail system	Kilometers of subway per million inhabitants (for cities with subway)	Kilometers of light rail system per million inhabitants (for cities with light rail system)
High income	25	63	1.86	3.70
Upper middle income	13	27	0.93	0.93
Lower middle income	7	14	0.17	0.51
Low income	0	3	0.0	0.17

Source: ITF 2018a based on OpenStreetMap.

An Urban Passenger Model

What can governments do to improve urban transport? We seek to answer this question by examining transport investment needs in urban areas globally and testing the impact of several urban transport policies. To do this, we use an urban passenger model developed by the Organisation for Economic Co-operation and Development's International Transport Forum (ITF) that covers the 1,692 urban agglomerations in the world with population above 300,000 (United Nations 2014). The model, described in detail by ITF (2018a), is structured around the following modules:

- Urban population projections based on United Nations Habitat

- Projected city GDP growth rates in which the relationship between the national share of urban population and the national share of urban GDP follows an S-shaped curve

- Regression models for urban transport supply, including road provision and public transport supply

- A discrete choice model to estimate the modal split in each city

- A model to forecast passenger car ownership and assumptions to infer the share of other types of vehicles

- CO_2 intensities and technological pathways by mode for converting vehicle activities into CO_2 emissions from the International Energy Agency's mobility model.

Total transport demand is thus mostly exogenous, but the total number of passenger-kilometers can vary slightly with transport costs and length of trip.

Here we analyze three policy scenarios developed by ITF, looking at the following metrics: mobility, passenger surplus (the benefit from greater accessibility), infrastructure investment costs (including vehicles for public transport), operations and maintenance (O&M) costs, and environmental impact (CO_2 emissions and local pollutants emissions).

In the *business-as-usual (BAU) scenario*, the combined effects of urban extension, population, and income growth result in a surge in demand for motorized mobility. Global urban road traffic, measured as the sum of cars and motorcycles per kilometer, doubles by 2050. In absolute value, most of the increase comes from upper-middle-income countries, with 3.7 billion additional vehicles per kilometer out of a total of 7.6 billion. However, car use per capita remains lower in LMICs than in high-income countries.

The *robust governance (ROG) scenario* assumes that local and national governments deploy three levers to promote low-carbon mobility. First, they use demand management instruments, mainly pricing and regulatory policies (gasoline taxes, road taxes, and car efficiency standards) to slow down the ownership and use of personal vehicles from 2020 onward. The existing literature provides evidence on the effectiveness of rigorous pricing strategies to shift households away from the use of personal cars and toward the use of modes with lower carbon intensities (Greening 2004). Second, higher investment effort in public transport infrastructure is assumed everywhere, comparable to the one estimated for European cities. Third, more stringent fuel standards are set, and policies are implemented to encourage higher market penetration of alternative-fuel vehicles.

The *integrated land-use and transport planning (LUT) scenario* assumes that, on top of the policies introduced in the ROG scenario, a joint land-use and transport policy is implemented. To be effective, this approach, which is known as "transit-oriented development," requires that local governments have the ability to coordinate and integrate land-use and transport planning decisions (Geerlings and Stead 2003). Higher density of both population and the public transit network can trigger an increase in the public transit share of overall transport and lower average trip distances—changes that help to reduce CO_2 emissions. But modeling policies that mix land-use and transport instruments is challenging, partly because transit-oriented development policies typically are designed at the local level. The shortcut in the ITF model is to assume that urban sprawl is controlled from 2020 onward. In practical terms, this means that the size of urban area remains constant for every city.

Land-Use Planning Allows for Higher Passenger Surplus at Lower Infrastructure Investment Costs

Our results show that there is a shift toward public transport in the ROG and LUT scenarios, reflecting more stringent pricing policies and expanded public transport. In the BAU scenario, private motorized vehicles represent 57 percent of all passenger-kilometers in LMICs by 2030, while public transport represents 47 percent (figure 4.5). But in the ROG and LUT scenarios, almost 60 percent of all passenger-kilometers are made by public transportation by 2030. This reduction in the share of cars happens everywhere in these two scenarios by 2030, except in China and India, where rapid income growth causes the mode share of cars to continue to increase.

While the total number of passenger-kilometers is similar in all three scenarios in 2030, in 2050, it is 10 percent higher in ROG than in BAU. This occurs thanks to greater accessibility provided by better public transport—for example, people switch from walking or cycling to taking public transportation and thus go farther, on average. But mobility levels, measured as passenger-kilometers, are largely the same in the LUT scenario as in the BAU scenario in 2050. While the number of trips is higher thanks to better public transportation, trips tend to be shorter because urban forms are more compact. ITF (2018a) estimated that the gain in passenger surplus compared with the BAU scenario amounts to US$5.5 trillion in the ROG scenario and US$7.6 trillion in the LUT scenario, globally over the period 2015–50.[4]

Better planning is critical to containing costs. Between 2015 and 2030, investment costs in urban transport infrastructure range from US$195 billion per year in the LUT scenario to US$245 billion per year in the ROG scenario in LMICs—or between 0.37 percent and 0.47 percent of total LMICs' GDP per year, on average (figure 4.6) (ITF 2018a).[5] At the regional level, about US$100 billion will need to be invested in Asia, and about US$40 billion to US$50 billion will need to be invested in Latin America.

The burden is highest for the more urbanized upper-middle-income countries. While low- and lower-middle-income regions would have to spend between 0.1 percent and 0.2 percent of GDP to

FIGURE 4.5 A growing role exists for public transport

Mode share of public transport in LMICs in 2030, by planning scenario

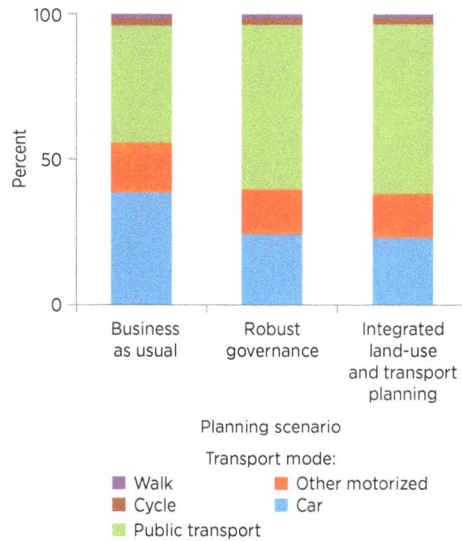

Source: Based on ITF 2018a.
Note: LMICs = low- and middle-income countries.

FIGURE 4.6 Better planning lowers urban transport needs by 20 percent

Average annual cost of investment in roads and public transport, by planning scenario, 2015–30

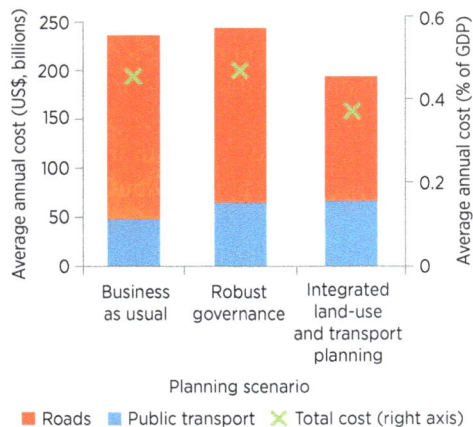

Source: Based on ITF 2018a.
Note: These numbers exclude Organisation for Economic Co-operation and Development countries. Investments in U.S. dollars include a 6 percent discount rate.

FIGURE 4.7 **The biggest burden in urban transport investment is on upper-middle-income countries**

Average annual cost of investment in urban transport, by region and planning scenario, 2015–30

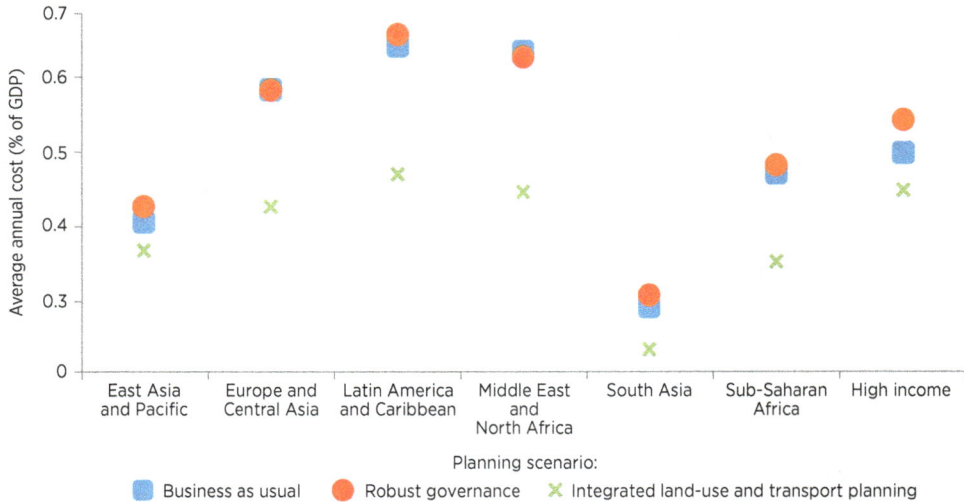

Source: Based on ITF 2018a.

accommodate projected mobility growth, upper-middle-income regions (Eastern Europe and Central Asia, Latin America and the Caribbean, and Middle East and North Africa) would need to spend between 0.4 percent and 0.6 percent of their GDP annually on investments for their urban transport systems (figure 4.7).

In the ROG scenario, investments in public transportation infrastructure are greater than in the BAU scenario, but road investment needs are comparable because cities grow quickly and sprawl. Overall, infrastructure investment needs increase by 3 percent compared with the BAU scenario. In upper-middle-income cities, this is driven by more mass transit infrastructure. For example, the size of Asian tramway networks is multiplied by six between 2015 and 2050. But in lower-income cities, investments are targeted to the acquisition of new buses.

In the LUT scenario, investments in public transportation increase, but they are accompanied by land-use policies that restrict urban sprawl and favor density. Under these conditions, total investment costs between 2015 and 2030 are 20 percent lower than in the BAU scenario. The increase in public transport supply is similar to the one in the ROG, but investments in roads are kept to a minimum—mainly large maintenance works for major roads. The lower cost of the LUT scenario is particularly noticeable in Eastern Europe and Central Asia, Latin America and the Caribbean, and the Middle East and North Africa—regions that spend 1 percentage point of GDP less each year for their urban transport systems than in the BAU scenario.

Land-use policies that increase urban density can thus reduce the investment cost of improved mobility services by 20 percent by 2030. For example, between 2015 and 2030, the density of the Nairobi metropolitan area would rise from 6,000 people per square kilometer to 9,000 people per square kilometer in the LUT scenario, while it would decrease to 5,600 people per square kilometer in the BAU scenario. However, some cities might not want to densify further, given how dense they are. For example, Karachi would rise from 19,000 people per square kilometer in 2015 to 25,000 people per square kilometer in 2030 in the LUT scenario (figure 4.8).

A big part of the urban transport challenge are the trade-offs associated with urban density. On the one hand, denser cities reduce infrastructure investment costs and municipal service spending (Libertun de Duren and Guerrero Compeán 2016), increase accessibility to jobs and services,

FIGURE 4.8 Large differences in urban density around the world are maintained in the planning scenarios

Urban density in select metropolitan areas in 2030, by planning scenario

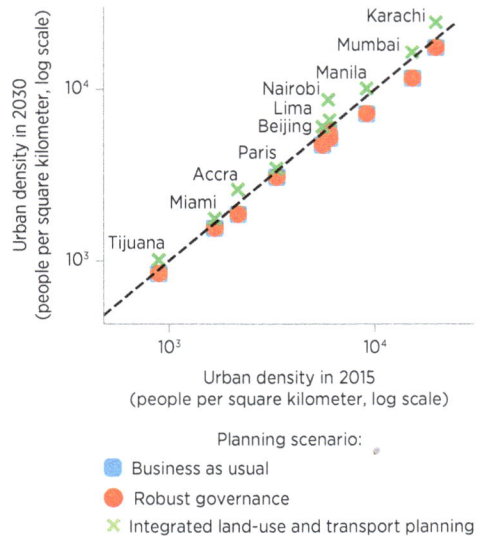

Source: Based on ITF 2018a.

and reduce pollution associated with long commutes by car. On the other hand, densification can result in higher housing and land prices, thereby harming the poorest urban populations. It can also increase the number of people exposed to local pollution and affect the local climate with the "heat island effect," although the direction of the effect is unclear.[6]

Bringing in Multiple Objectives

Further complicating matters, urban transport planners must also consider GHG emissions and local pollution when they explore ways to provide mobility services with low capital expenditures.

Indeed, the results from the ROG scenario show that improved fuel efficiency and increased investments in public transportation are not sufficient to reduce future emissions significantly in LMICs without restrictions on automobile use and coordination with urban planning (figure 4.9). Avoided emissions attributable to public transport development are 45 percent smaller in the ROG scenario than in the LUT scenario. The increase in the number of trips and the average distance traveled, as well as the modal shift from walking and cycling to public transport, limit the impact of public transport investments on CO_2 emissions. In addition, in LMICs, many of the buses are diesel-powered and thus do not contribute significantly to lower emissions.

FIGURE 4.9 **Urban planning and climate change mitigation must be coordinated**

Mitigation potential of two alternative planning scenarios, by categories of measures (difference with the BAU scenario), 2015–50

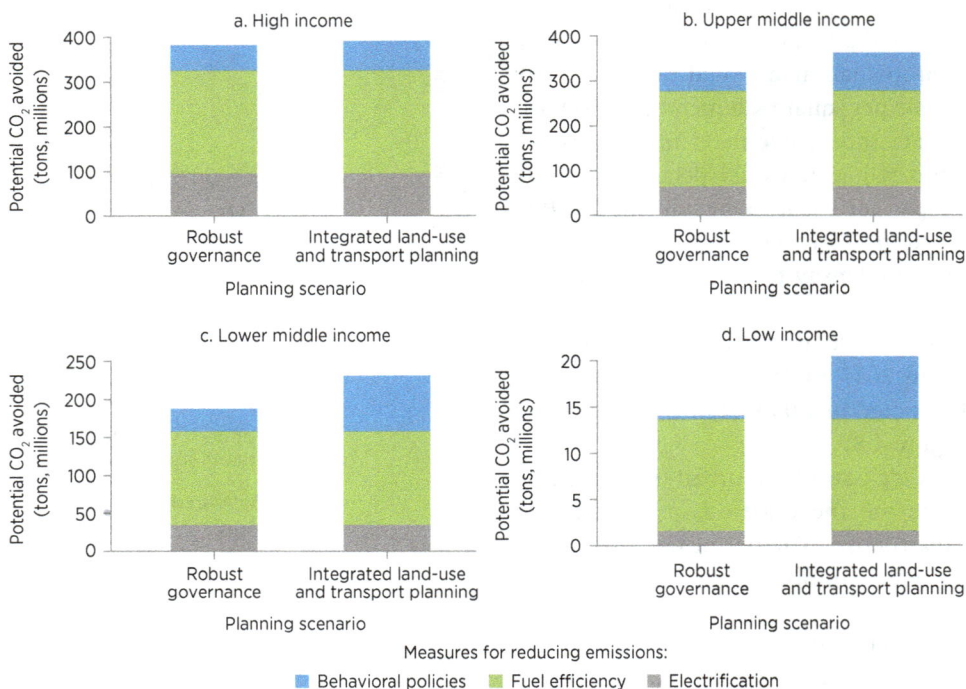

Measures for reducing emissions:
- Behavioral policies
- Fuel efficiency
- Electrification

Source: ITF 2018a.
Note: BAU = business as usual.

Only the LUT scenario, which combines land-use policies with investments in public transport, mode shift, and efficiency incentives, is consistent with the mitigation effort required to limit global warming to 2°C (ITF 2017). Compared with 2015 levels, CO_2 emissions decrease 35 percent in the LUT, while they increase 20 percent in the BAU scenario. Fuel efficiency and electrification of the fleet contribute to 75 percent of the CO_2 emissions avoided, while the remaining 25 percent come from behavioral changes—that is, from reductions in trip length and modal shifts. Electrification of the fleet needs to be paired with decarbonization of electricity production, otherwise these reductions in tank-to-wheel emissions could be offset by increased emissions from electricity production (Fay and others 2015). See chapter 3 for a discussion of costs.

Local pollutants like nitrogen oxides (NOx) also have detrimental impacts on health (Seaton and others 1995). NOx emissions resulting from the three scenarios are calculated based on the road map of the International Council on Clean Transportation, which includes expected improvements in vehicle standards and their probable penetration in the vehicle fleet until 2030. In both LUT and ROG, NOx emissions increase faster than in the BAU scenario because diesel buses replace private cars. Diesel buses indeed form the majority of bus fleets in the low- and middle-income world and have higher emissions factors per passenger-kilometer than cars. Thus, reducing local pollution while improving access and reducing CO_2 emissions requires additional policies regarding bus standards and possibly the electrification of bus fleets.

Budgeting for High O&M Costs for Urban Transport

How do O&M costs fit in? Our results show that, in urban areas, total maintenance costs range from US$84 billion per year, on average, over 2015–30 in the LUT scenario to US$90 billion per year in the BAU scenario—due to longer road networks. These costs represent about 0.07 percent of GDP, on average, every year in South Asia but 0.42 percent of GDP in Latin America (figure 4.10).

But the highest costs come from the operation of public transport infrastructure, which adds up to between US$427 billion and US$548 billion per year, on average, in LMICs (twice as much as infrastructure investment costs). These costs amount to 1 percent of South Asian countries' GDP per year,

FIGURE 4.10 **Operating costs for urban transport are high**

Average annual cost of operations and maintenance in urban public transport and roads, by region and investment type, 2015–30

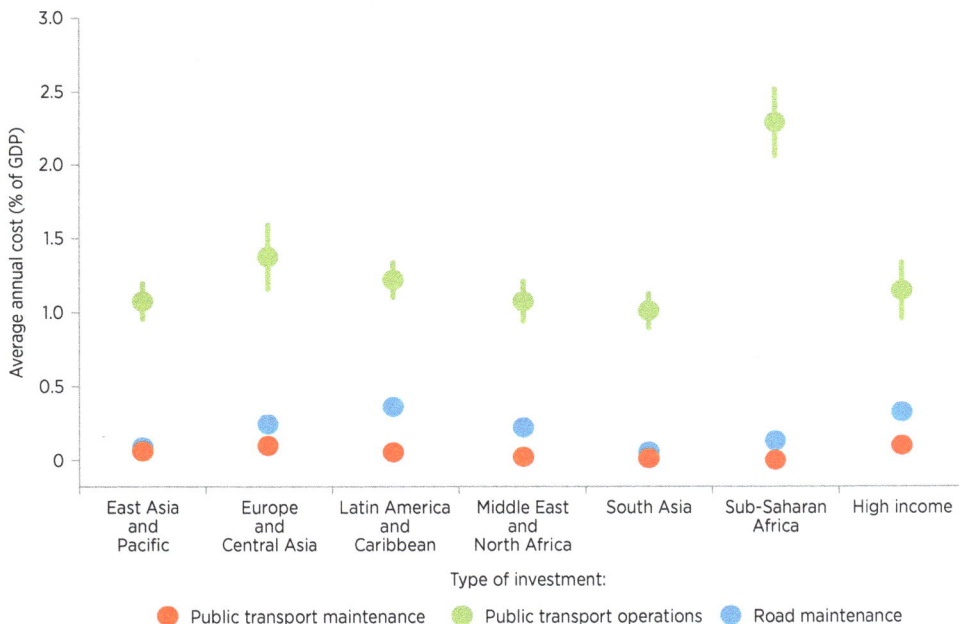

Source: Based on ITF 2018a.
Note: GDP is country-level, not city-level, GDP. Dots represent the average over the three planning scenarios (business as usual, robust governance, and integrated land-use and transport planning), and the vertical bars represent the range across the three scenarios.

on average, but 2.3 percent of Sub-Saharan African countries' GDP. While some of these costs can be paid for by users, even in European countries, subsidies for public transport represent up to 60 percent of total operation costs. The bottom line is that cities should be prepared to spend at least as much on the operation of their public transport systems as they spend on the construction of new infrastructure.

A Preliminary Exploration of the Impact of Shared Low-Carbon Mobility

Many observers foresee that urban mobility will go through a dramatic transition in the next decades. The convergence of electrification, car sharing, and autonomous driving offers the promise of a more efficient, cleaner, and more inclusive mobility system—provided that policies enable these potential disruptions to work efficiently together and benefit everyone. The key element of this transition is undoubtedly the sharing aspect, because automation alone (that is, a scenario where self-driving cars would be owned privately) would result in greater car use (ITF 2018a) and possibly more sprawl, given lower perceived costs of inconvenience and time.

Using Lisbon as an illustration, an ITF study demonstrates that an electrified, shared, and self-driving fleet of vehicles can significantly reduce the number of cars on city streets, while offering the same level of mobility as today, with transfer-free rides at a price comparable to that of public transport (ITF 2015). Such a fleet would also bring about significant reductions in distances traveled, congestion, and pollution. These results have been confirmed in other high-income cities (ITF 2018a). However, to materialize, these benefits require shared mobility penetration rates of at least 30 percent.

Building on these ITF studies, we consider a fourth "SHARED" scenario with a simple shared-mobility service (see ITF 2018a for details) and the following, simplified, assumptions on top of the LUT scenario:

- The market penetration of shared services increases from 2020 to 2030, with users switching from their main mode to the shared services. However, the service is implemented only if the resulting demand is at least 30 percent of total passenger-kilometers.

- Global transport demand remains stable—that is, the new mobility services do not induce additional trips or increase the length of existing ones. Here, the assumption is that demand management policies are implemented. Otherwise, the wider range of mobility options offered by shared-mobility services would lead to a surge in demand, due to conventional rebound effects.

- The detour ratio is assumed to be 1.5, meaning that transporting a single passenger for 1 kilometer would require 1.5 vehicle-kilometers, due to the distance traveled to pick up extra passengers and make empty journeys back to the depots. The average occupancy rate is assumed to be 8 passengers per vehicle.

Our results show that the impact of the SHARED scenario on GHG emissions is significant, with a 50 percent decrease in emissions in 2050 compared with today. But the impact on traffic is relatively small compared with the LUT scenario, and thus investment needs for roads remain almost the same as in the LUT scenario (mostly because not all cities obtain the minimum adoption rate for shared systems to be viable [ITF 2018a]). However, those results should be taken with caution, as they are built on strong and questionable assumptions. For example, they highlight that the transition to a shared transport system might be hampered in cities where the willingness to share is too low. In these cases, alternative pathways would probably require some disincentives against private car use, at least temporarily, to support growth of the service.

The SHARED policies would also sharply reduce the need for parking spaces. Currently, there are 2–3 parking spaces per car in cities, because parking in residential areas tends to be vacant during the workday, while parking at work is vacant at night. Shared-mobility services would lead to reduced car ownership, with 5–15 cars removed for each shared car added to the fleet (ITF 2018a). Using conservative assumptions, the decrease in vehicle stock resulting from the SHARED scenario would lead to 600 million parking spaces saved, accounting for US$1.4 trillion globally.[7] This area also represents more than 9,000 square kilometers—about the area of Beijing, Paris, and Washington, D.C., combined.

Besides the financial aspect, shared-mobility policies represent an opportunity to reshape cities by providing additional public spaces. Large amounts of space could be converted to other uses, including bicycle lanes, public parks, broader sidewalks, and commercial activities (such as restaurants or kiosks). This conversion might be costly, but it would contribute to citizens' well-being and improve cities' livability. At the same time, with the rise of shared-mobility services and the growth of urban goods delivery, road curbs will be used more and more for pick-up and drop-off. Rather than just the road itself, the complete street design might evolve to accommodate new uses (ITF 2018b).

GLOBAL TRANSPORT NEEDS

At the global level, debates about future transport needs need to factor in the impact of global shifts and trends—like technological change or climate change mitigation policies. This can be done using global models, as we do below.

An Energy-Economy-Environment Model to Explore Mobility Pathways and a Costing Model

We use the IMACLIM-R model to simulate the evolution of the transport sector within the global economy (Waisman and others 2012; Waisman and others 2013). IMACLIM-R is a multiregion and multisector model (including transport) that was built to simulate decarbonization pathways—and thus represents the intertwined evolution of technical systems, energy demand behavior, and economic growth. It combines a computable general equilibrium framework with bottom-up sectoral modules that model technologies explicitly.

Future mobility needs for both freight and passengers are simulated in hundreds of scenarios that explore the uncertainty regarding growth drivers (demography, labor productivity, and trade), consumer preferences, spatial organization, climate change mitigation policies, and technical challenges to mitigation policies (availability of low-carbon technologies in the electricity and transport sectors, availability of fossil fuels, and energy efficiency). Socioeconomic conditions are derived from the Intergovernmental Panel on Climate Change's shared socioeconomic pathways (Dellink and others 2017; KC and Lutz 2014; O'Neill and others 2013; O'Neill and others 2017). Climate change mitigation policies are modeled as carbon prices, calculated to follow a global emissions pathway consistent with a 2°C temperature increase by the end of the century (Fisch-Romito and Guivarch 2019).

The investment needs that would be required to satisfy such mobility demand are assessed ex post with a costing model. Hence, the potential feedback loops between supply and demand are not considered (like limited infrastructure capacity creating congestion and thus reducing expressed demand or increased road traffic following the building of new roads). However, further uncertainty is considered in the costing model:

- *Future infrastructure cost.* Three scenarios for infrastructure costs are explored: (a) constant cost over time, (b) linear increase over time (because material and labor costs increase and infrastructure becomes more complex over time), and (c) linear decrease over time (because learning-by-doing effects dominate).

- *Mode switch.* Two strategies are explored for future choice of terrestrial transport mode: (a) mode shares remain constant over time between rail and trucks for freight and constant between buses, bus rapid transit, rail and high-speed rail for passengers; and (b) shares evolve toward more low-carbon modes in 2050 (rail instead of trucks and bus rapid transit instead of buses; see Fisch-Romito and Guivarch 2019 for detailed shares).

- *Operational efficiency of the infrastructure (measured by occupancy rate).* The uncertainty regarding rail occupancy rates comes from the variations in current rail occupancy (a combination of traffic density and average load), which range from less than 350,000 passenger-kilometers and ton-kilometers per kilometer of track in Eastern Europe to more than 30 million passenger-kilometers and ton-kilometers in China, Mexico, and the Republic of Korea (Dulac 2013). This important heterogeneity in rail occupancy could be the result of geography, service quality, government policies, or operational models (Harris 1977; Jain and others 2008; Oum and Yu 1994). For roads, the current use rate varies from 150,000 vehicle-kilometers per kilometer of paved lane in India to more than 1 million vehicle-kilometers per kilometer of paved lane in Latin America (Dulac 2013). As in the case of rail, many factors can explain the heterogeneity in road occupancy rates, including road quality and efficiency of trucking markets (Foster and Briceño-Garmendia 2010).

The scenarios are assessed in terms of mobility, infrastructure investment costs, maintenance costs, and environmental impacts (CO_2 emissions). The model was initially built to analyze the cost of climate mitigation policies, allowing it to create an extensive set of scenarios to analyze the impact of climate objectives on future mobility needs under different "mitigation challenges": (a) ability to implement energy efficiency measures, (b) lower costs for low-carbon electricity generation, and (c) technological progress in the car manufacturing sector.

Carbon Prices Slow the Growth in Transport Demand in Most Scenarios

The study finds that in all low- and middle-income regions, carbon prices—calculated to follow a global emissions pathway consistent with a 2°C temperature increase by the end of the century—are important drivers of future transport demand, along with patterns of economic growth. In all scenarios, carbon prices slow the growth in transport demand by 2030 compared with a business-as-usual scenario, especially for freight but also for passenger transport in some regions.

But the magnitude of the resulting deceleration depends greatly on the region and the difficulty of reducing GHG emissions in other sectors. In Asia, the Middle East and North Africa, and Sub-Saharan Africa, carbon prices have a strong impact on mobility demand, especially when technical challenges are high for reducing emissions (low-carbon electricity and electric mobility technologies have slow learning rates so their cost remains high). This is because slow technical change requires higher carbon prices to reach the same emissions objective and thus affects demand for transport more. With pessimistic assumptions about technology, freight transport in Asia grows 46 percent slower than in a business-as-usual scenario between 2018 and 2030 due to carbon prices (compared with 29 percent slower with optimistic technologies). In contrast, in Latin America, where decarbonization of the electricity sector is easier, carbon prices have a relatively modest impact on transport demand—which is driven instead by assumptions regarding economic growth and supply chain organization for freight and on motorization and road capacity for passengers.

It is possible to reduce GHG emissions in transport without impairing demand—but only if pricing policies are paired with innovation policies to decrease the cost of decarbonized electricity and low-carbon mobility, infrastructure spending in low-carbon modes to induce mode shifts (Hamdi-Cherif and O'Broin, forthcoming), and land-use policies (ITF 2018a).

However, the impact of climate mitigation policies on infrastructure investment costs is not as straightforward and depends on policies to boost rail occupancy rates: even if carbon prices reduce transport demand, climate mitigation requires a shift from road to rail investments, which can increase infrastructure investment costs if occupancy rates are low.

Future Investment Costs Are Driven by Choice of Terrestrial Mode and Occupancy Rates

Future investment costs for the transport sector vary significantly across regions, driven by differences in current infrastructure endowment and population densities. Investment costs amount to between 0.5 percent and 1 percent of GDP annually between 2015 and 2030 in Asia and the former Soviet Union, while Latin American countries would have to spend between 1 percent and 3.6 percent of their annual GDP, and African countries would have to spend between 1 percent and 6 percent of their GDP (figure 4.11). The bulk of these costs come from terrestrial (road and rail) transport, with air transport and bus rapid transit negligible in comparison.[8] In Asia, most investment needs come from rail, while in Africa most needs come from roads.

For all LMICs taken together, total future infrastructure investment costs for the entire transport sector range between 0.5 percent and 3.3 percent of LMICs' GDP per year, on average, between 2015 and 2030. The two main uncertainties that drive this wide range in global investment estimates come from the costing model and are rail occupancy levels and modal share choices between rail and road for terrestrial transport. Uncertainties from the IMACLIM-R model (which pertain to future mobility demand) are secondary compared with these two factors.

FIGURE 4.11 **Global transport infrastructure investment needs are highest for road and rail**

Average annual cost of capital investment in global transport infrastructure, by region and transport mode, 2015–30

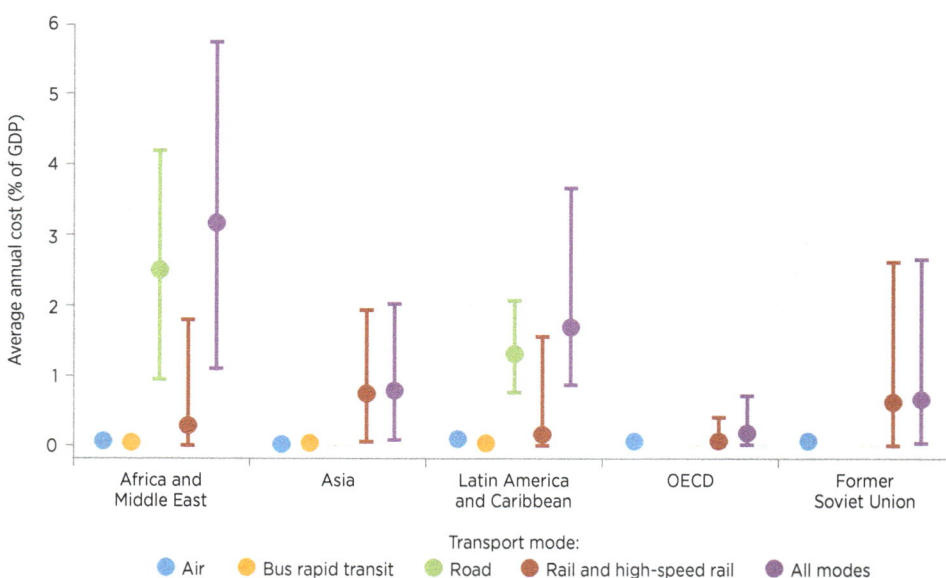

Source: Based on Fisch-Romito and Guivarch 2019.
Note: The bars represent the range of estimates, generated by hundreds of scenarios, while the central dots represent the median value across estimates. The regional breakdown is that of the IMACLIM-R model and is more aggregated than the usual World Bank regional breakdown. OECD = Organisation for Economic Co-operation and Development.

Scenarios with the highest investment costs—above 2 percent of LMICs' GDP per year between 2015 and 2030—are scenarios with higher rail share for terrestrial transport as well as low rail occupancy rates, so that the length of the rail network corresponding to a given mobility demand is higher (figure 4.12). But when rail occupancy rates are high, part of the increase in rail mobility can be accommodated with existing infrastructure, and new investment costs depend primarily on the uncertainty of mobility, especially economic growth and the structure of road transport demand (car occupancy, motorization rates, and road capacity).

In scenarios with high occupancy, transport investment costs would amount to less than 1.3 percent of GDP per year between 2015 and 2030 for all LMICs. The occupancy parameter is especially important in Asia and in Europe and Central Asia, where most new investments by 2030 are expected to be in rail, given that the model follows current mode shares.[9]

FIGURE 4.12 The choice of terrestrial mode and rail occupancy drive transport investment costs

Average annual cost of capital investment in transport, by choice of terrestrial mode and rail occupancy, 2015–30

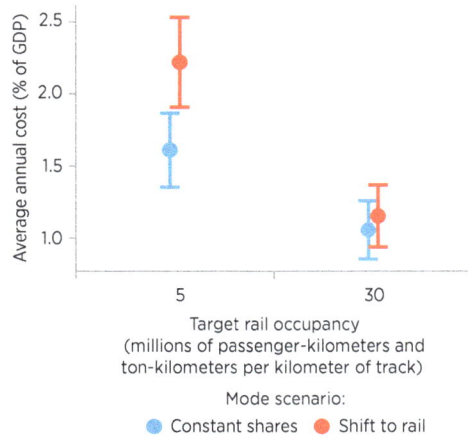

Source: Based on Fisch-Romito and Guivarch 2019.
Note: Numbers exclude Organisation for Economic Co-operation and Development countries. The bars represent the range of estimates, generated by hundreds of scenarios, while the central dots represent the median value across estimates.

These results highlight the importance of rail traffic density to ensure that investments deliver mobility supply at a reasonable cost. The potential to increase rail infrastructure occupancy (and thus benefits) will depend strongly on local conditions with respect to geography, local governance, and operational models—and the levers to trigger this increase may be institutional or technical. In Africa, one study found that the decline in traffic on many railway systems over the last decade often had little to do with changes in the underlying demand (Foster and Briceño-Garmendia 2010). Instead, in some countries, it was driven by war or natural disasters, while in others the shortage of locomotives or weak interconnections with other modes—in ports, in particular—were to blame. Given the cost of rail investments and the role that railways can play in decarbonizing transport, it is crucial for decision makers to take these elements into account when deciding to switch to rail for terrestrial transport.

Through similar mechanisms, road utilization rates have an impact on transport investment costs, especially in Africa, where most of the needs are in road transport. If a road utilization target of 600,000 vehicle-kilometers per kilometer of paved lane is used, investment costs are 3.6 percent of GDP per year for Africa and Middle East (on average across all scenarios), while they are 2.5 percent of GDP if a target of 900,000 vehicle-kilometers per kilometer of paved lane is used.

But determining the "optimal" road utilization rate is complex given that high utilization means greater congestion—which, in turn, implies financial costs and welfare losses due to vehicle delays, increased depreciation of vehicles, accidents, and negative impacts of congestion on the location of economic activities in urban areas (Bilbao-Ubillos 2008). In Africa in particular, road safety is a major issue and should be a priority for government if traffic density is to increase. Possible solutions include measures other than infrastructure, such as eliminating corruption in licensing, enforcing good on-road behavior, and inspecting and controlling vehicle conditions (Foster and Briceño-Garmendia 2010).

Maintenance Costs Are as Important as New Infrastructure Costs

When looking at future infrastructure investment needs, the cost of maintaining current and future infrastructure often receives less attention. And yet, maintenance costs in LMICs for all transport infrastructure (existing and future for all transport sectors) would amount to between 1.1 percent and 2.1 percent of GDP per year, on average, between 2015 and 2030, which is almost as much as what is needed for new capital investment. Maintenance costs are even higher than new investment costs in countries that already have large transport networks, such as those in Asia or the former Soviet Union (figure 4.13).

FIGURE 4.13 Maintenance may cost as much as or more than new investments in transport

Average annual cost of investment in maintenance and new transport infrastructure, by region, 2015–30

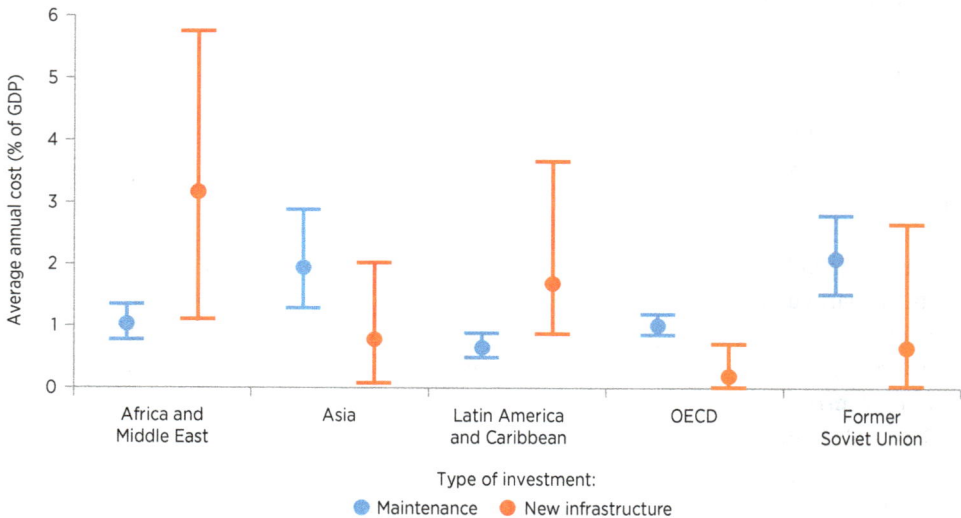

Source: Based on Fisch-Romito and Guivarch 2019.
Note: The bars represent the range of estimates, generated by hundreds of scenarios, while the central dots represent the median value across estimates. The regional breakdown is that of the IMACLIM-R model and is more aggregated than the usual World Bank regional breakdown. OECD = Organisation for Economic Co-operation and Development.

IN SUM

Our results offer general guidance, but in practice transport infrastructure needs must be determined locally based on population density, proximity to opportunities and services, and affordability. In cities, a goal may be to improve accessibility to employment—say, by increasing the number of jobs that can be reached within one hour of transport (Boisjoly and El-Geneidy 2017; He and others 2018). In rural areas, new tools like rural accessibility maps that look at market, service, or agricultural potential can be used to prioritize investments that increase access to economic opportunities or services for the largest number of individuals.[10]

In addition, any investment in transport infrastructure should be accompanied by a careful assessment of the investment's impact on different groups of actors and by the inclusion of mitigating measures for identified losers. Much attention should also be given to complementary policies that improve the market structure of service delivery, along with measures that mitigate environmental degradation and biodiversity loss.

That said, insights useful for policy design can be extracted from our work.

First, *future mobility demand can be supplied at relatively low infrastructure investment costs and low CO_2 emissions with a shift toward more rail and urban public transport (or shared mobility), if accompanied by policies that ensure high rail occupancy and land-use policies that densify cities.* For the entire transport sector, our "preferred scenario"—which allows for a low-cost shift to low-carbon infrastructure thanks to smart policies—would cost 1.3 percent of LMICs' GDP (table 4.6). For urban areas, our preferred scenario is the LUT scenario (or LUT+SHARED), which integrates land-use and transport policies to deliver low-carbon infrastructure at a relatively modest 0.37 percent of LMICs' GDP.

Absent accompanying policies, responding to demand with low-carbon infrastructure like rail and bus rapid transit systems can cost 26 percent more in urban areas and 80 percent more overall, on average. In urban

TABLE 4.6 **The preferred scenario uses low-carbon modes and accompanying policies for rail and public transport**

Average annual cost of investment in transport infrastructure, by scenario, 2015–30
% of GDP

Mode	Entire transport sector		Urban transport sector only	
	Accompanying policy for high rail occupancy	No accompanying policy	Land-use planning	No land-use planning
Low carbon (rail, bus rapid transit)	**1.3**	2.3	**0.37**	0.47
Business as usual (roads)	n.a.	1.7	n.a.	0.45

Note: The preferred scenario is in bold. n.a. = not applicable.

areas, responding to the same demand with roads (the business-as-usual option) would cost 22 percent more than responding with public transportation and land-use policies. For transport as a whole, responding to demand with more roads would cost 30 percent more than in the preferred scenario in the absence of policies to increase rail occupancy. It would also lock transport into emissions-intensive pathways that would be very costly to decarbonize later.

Second, *maintenance needs in transport are of the same order of magnitude as new capital investments and should be budgeted for at the same time as capital investments.* In our preferred scenario, maintenance costs amount to 1.3 percent of LMICs' GDP per year between 2015 and 2030, which brings total spending needs to 2.6 percent of GDP. If routine maintenance is not performed annually, the total cost of the system increases 50 percent due to rehabilitation costs and reaches 3.9 percent of GDP.

In urban areas, the operation of public transport infrastructure can be expensive for local authorities. In our preferred scenario, the operation of public transport costs 1.3 percent of LMICs' GDP per year. Even if part of this cost is borne by users, sustainable cost models should be evaluated carefully before making the investment.

Third, *careful planning before making decisions is essential for transport investments.* The long-term environmental and distributional impacts of current choices should be assessed, and solutions that prevent future lock-ins into unsustainable pathways should be preferred. In addition, more attention should be given to the future costs of the system under unexpected future conditions—including less optimistic traffic than initially planned for or higher costs (Bain 2009; Flyvbjerg and others 2003, 2006). If the analysis shows that the transport system would not be affordable if traffic is lower than projected, then the system should be designed differently or complementary policies should be adopted, before implementation.

ANNEX 4A: TRANSPORT INVESTMENT CAN HAVE POSITIVE IMPACTS ON WELFARE BUT HIDE NEGATIVE IMPACTS FOR SOME ACTORS AND FOR THE ENVIRONMENT

Transport infrastructure has a wide range of impacts on the economy at the micro level (Andres and others 2013). Better transportation infrastructure can reduce travel times and transport costs (BenYishay and Tunstall 2011), improving people's access to schools and hospitals in rural areas (Levy 2004) and potentially raising productivity and income. Lower transport time and costs also give workers access to employment opportunities over a wider area (Gannon and Liu 1997) and increase regional and interregional trade (Roberts and others 2018; Volpe Martincus and Blyde 2012). However, these positive impacts are moderated by endowments of human capital, existing market development, and complementary infrastructure (van de Walle 2009). In rural areas, people with higher education levels are more likely to access nonagricultural job opportunities provided by a new road. In urban areas, women tend to take shorter but more frequent trips than men, which means that they are discouraged from using public transport service that has a flat-fare structure, even if it provides excellent connectivity (Mehndiratta 2014).

At the macro level, the impacts of transport investments are not always clear. A meta-analysis of 776 estimates of elasticity of production with respect to transport infrastructure—in both high-income countries as well as LMICs—found that the estimated effect of investing in transport infrastructure varies from −0.06 to 0.52, with the effect depending on the type of infrastructure and the economic sectors in which the impact is measured (Holmgren and Merkel 2017).

Transport infrastructure can create winners and losers (figure 4A.1). In a meta-analysis of 78 studies, Roberts and others (2018) found that, although transport corridor investments always have a positive impact on aggregate or average income and poverty, some investments have negative impacts on equality (with some regions winning and others losing from the investments)—including sometimes absolute negative impacts on the income of some groups. In China, while construction of the National Expressway Network increased real income across prefectures by about 4 percent, on average, in many prefectures, it had a negative impact on real wages in either the urban or the rural sector, because it removed the effective trade

FIGURE 4A.1 **Investments in transport corridors can create both winners and losers**

Economic impacts of investments in transport corridors

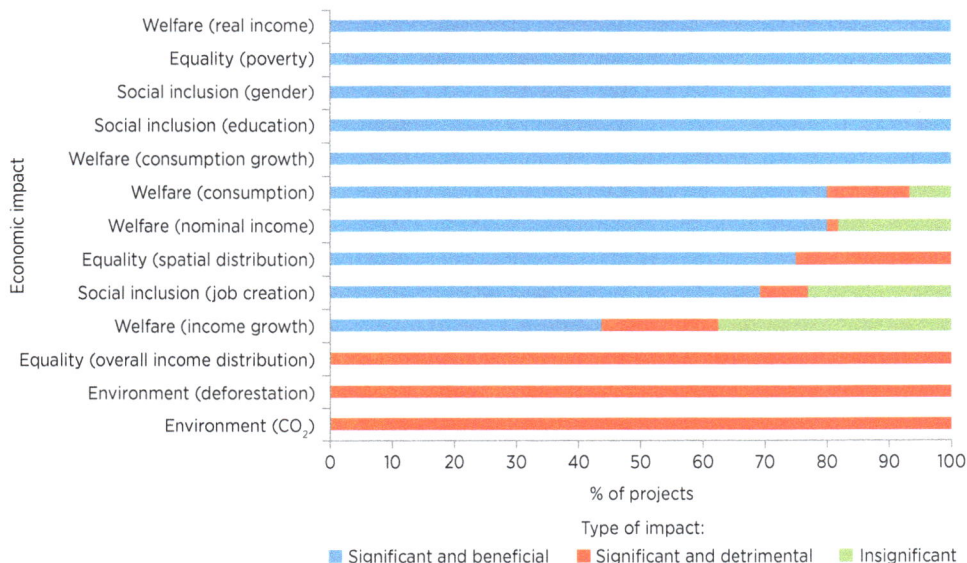

Source: Roberts and others 2018.
Note: Covers 78 papers with 234 results (analyzed outcomes) tagged by April 2017.

protection offered by poor transport (Roberts and others 2012). The National Expressway Network appears to have caused hinterland prefectures to specialize more in agriculture and to lose economic activity, when the intention was to promote growth in these areas (Baum-Snow and others 2018). In addition, large-scale transport projects can also have spillover effects in other countries, which may benefit more from the investment than the country that did the investing.

Roberts and others (2018) also found that all transport corridor projects studied had a negative impact on the environment through deforestation and increased greenhouse gas emissions (figure 4A.1).

Finally, improved transport services are fundamental to making transport infrastructure investments worthwhile (Foster and Briceño-Garmendia 2010). Many investments in roads in West Africa, for example, have not resulted in the expected price reductions because the trucking market remains cartelized, with informal intermediaries capturing the rents (Bove and others 2018).

These results suggest that, while transport investments can be desirable, it is important to acknowledge the nature and extent of trade-offs regarding the impact of transport corridors on various development outcomes—including on the environment—and the varied impacts across multiple economic actors. Much more attention should also be given to complementary policies to improve the market structure of service delivery, along with mitigating measures to lessen the negative effects of transport infrastructure investments on identified losers or for environmental degradation and biodiversity loss. As for CO_2 emissions, research shows that it is possible to increase mobility without increasing emissions, by electrifying the transport sector (with more rail and electric vehicles) while decarbonizing electricity production (Fay and others 2015).

NOTES

1. The code and documentation are available at http://rai-wb.readthedocs.io /readme.html. The WorldPop data set was used for population distribution, which spreads the population out more than other population data sets. The RAI might thus be underestimated in some countries.
2. Data are considered good enough if the completeness score on OpenStreetMap is higher than 75 percent.
3. World Bank ROCKS database (Doing Business 2018 update).
4. The analysis of consumer surplus includes high-income countries.
5. If high-income countries are included, the numbers increase to between US$5.3 trillion and US$6.5 trillion globally.
6. Stone and others (2010) found that in Atlanta the heat island effect is higher in low-density areas, while Streutker (2003) found that the heat island effect in Houston increases with densification. Lemonsu and others (2015) found that in Paris, densification happens in areas more exposed to heat waves and therefore increases the heat island risk. Lohrey and Creutzig (2016) found a "sustainability window" for urban density between 5,000 and 15,000 people per square

kilometer, considering transport costs and emissions, local pollution, and the social impacts through housing costs. Metropolitan areas like Karachi or Mumbai might thus prefer the ROG scenario to the LUT scenario.

7. The cost of building and providing parking spaces is difficult to assess; it typically varies from several orders of magnitude depending on whether it is street, surface, multistory, or underground parking. A conservative value for surface-level parking is US$150 per square meter (Dulac 2013).

8. Maritime transport infrastructure needs are not assessed because data on port infrastructure capacity and costs are not available.

9. A scenario in which Central Asia would keep investing in rail, despite persistently low rail occupancy levels, may be inconsistent and could be removed from the analysis. This comes from modeling design, which does not represent feedback loops between infrastructure investments and mobility demand.

10. See http://ruralaccess.info/.

REFERENCES

Andres, L. A., A. Iimi, A. Orfei, and H. Samad. 2013. *Impact Evaluation for Infrastructure: General Guidance and Existing Evidence*. Washington, DC: World Bank.

Asher, S. E., T. Garg, and P. M. Novosad. 2018. *The Ecological Impact of Transportation Infrastructure*. Washington, DC: World Bank.

Asian Development Bank, U.K. Department for International Development, Japan International Cooperation Agency, and World Bank Group. 2018. *The WEB of Transport Corridors in South Asia*. Washington, DC: World Bank.

Bain, R. 2009. "Error and Optimism Bias in Toll Road Traffic Forecasts." *Transportation* 36 (5): 469–82.

Baum-Snow, N., J. V. Henderson, M. A. Turner, Q. Zhang, and L. Brandt. 2018. "Does Investment in National Highways Help or Hurt Hinterland City Growth?" NBER Working Paper 24596, National Bureau of Economic Research, Cambridge, MA.

BenYishay, A., and R. Tunstall. 2011. "Impact Evaluation of Infrastructure Investments: The Experience of the Millennium Challenge Corporation." *Journal of Development Effectiveness* 3 (1): 103–30.

Bilbao-Ubillos, J. 2008. "The Costs of Urban Congestion: Estimation of Welfare Losses Arising from Congestion on Cross-Town Link Roads." *Transportation Research Part A: Policy and Practice* 42 (8): 1098–1108.

Bleakley, H., and J. Lin. 2012. "Portage and Path Dependence." *Quarterly Journal of Economics* 127 (2): 587–644.

Boisjoly, G., and G. B. El-Geneidy. 2017. "Measuring Performance: Accessibility Metrics in Metropolitan Regions around the World." Moving to Access Report, Brookings Institution, Washington, DC.

Bove, A. P. B., O. Hartmann, A. Stokenberga, V. Vesin, and Y. Yedan. 2018. *West and Central Africa Trucking Competitiveness*. Washington, DC: World Bank.

Briceño-Garmendia, C., H. Moroz, and J. Rozenberg. 2015. *Road Networks, Accessibility, and Resilience: The Cases of Colombia, Ecuador, and Peru*. Washington, DC: World Bank.

Burgess, R., R. Jedwab, E. Miguel, A. Morjaria, and G. Padró i Miquel. 2015. "The Value of Democracy: Evidence from Road Building in Kenya." *American Economic Review* 105 (6): 1817–51.

Cadot, O., L.-H. Röller, and A. Stephan. 2006. "Contribution to Productivity or Pork Barrel? The Two Faces of Infrastructure Investment." *Journal of Public Economics* 90 (6–7): 1133–53.

Collier, P., M. Kirchberger, and M. Söderbom. 2016. "The Cost of Road Infrastructure in Low- and Middle-Income Countries." *World Bank Economic Review* 30 (3): 522–48.

Damania, R., J. Russ, D. Wheeler, and A. F. Barra. 2018. "The Road to Growth: Measuring the Tradeoffs between Economic Growth and Ecological Destruction." *World Development* 101 (January): 351–76.

Dellink, R., J. Chateau, E. Lanzi, and B. Magné. 2017. "Long-Term Economic Growth Projections in the Shared Socioeconomic Pathways." *Global Environmental Change* 42 (January): 200–14.

Dercon, S., D. Gilligan, J. Hoddinott, and T. Woldehanna. 2008. "The Impact of Agricultural Extension and Roads on Poverty and Consumption Growth in Fifteen Ethiopian Villages." *American Journal of Agricultural Economics* 91 (4): 1007–21.

Driscoll, P. A. 2014. "Breaking Carbon Lock-In: Path Dependencies in Large-Scale Transportation Infrastructure Projects." *Planning Practice and Research* 29 (3): 317–30.

Dulac, J. 2013. "Global Land Transport Infrastructure Requirements." Informational paper, International Energy Agency, Paris.

Fay, M., S. Hallegatte, A. Vogt-Schilb, J. Rozenberg, U. Narloch, and T. Kerr. 2015. *Decarbonizing Development: Three Steps to a Zero-Carbon Future.* Washington, DC: World Bank.

Fisch-Romito, V., and C. Guivarch. 2019. "Investment Needs for Transport Infrastructures along Low Carbon Pathways." Background paper prepared for this report, World Bank, Washington, DC.

Flyvbjerg, B., M. K. Skamris Holm, and S. L. Buhl. 2003. "How Common and How Large Are Cost Overruns in Transport Infrastructure Projects?" *Transport Reviews* 23 (1): 71–88.

———. 2006. "Inaccuracy in Traffic Forecasts." *Transport Reviews* 26 (1): 1–24.

Foster, V., and C. M. Briceño-Garmendia. 2010. *Africa's Infrastructure: A Time for Transformation.* Washington, DC: World Bank.

Gannon, C. A., and Z. Liu. 1997. *Poverty and Transport.* Washington, DC: World Bank.

Geerlings, H., and D. Stead. 2003. "The Integration of Land Use Planning, Transport, and Environment in European Policy and Research." *Transport Policy* 10 (3): 187–96.

Greening, L. A. 2004. "Effects of Human Behavior on Aggregate Carbon Intensity of Personal Transportation: Comparison of 10 OECD Countries for the Period 1970–1993." *Energy Economics* 26 (1): 1–30.

Guivarch, C., and S. Hallegatte. 2011. "Existing Infrastructure and the 2°C Target." *Climatic Change* 109 (3–4): 801–05.

Hamdi-Cherif, M., and E. O'Broin. Forthcoming. "The Transportation Sector as a Lever for Reducing Long-Term Mitigation Costs in China." Paper submitted to *China Economic Review.*

Harris, R. G. 1977. "Economies of Traffic Density in the Rail Freight Industry." *Bell Journal of Economics* 8 (2): 556–64.

He, H., T. P. Quirós, N. Lozano-Gracia, P. Avner, G. A. Zagatti, L. Bengtsson, and M. Gonzalez. 2018. "Accessibility-Based Assessment of Transit Improvements in Data-Poor Environments: Case Study of Port-au-Prince, Haiti." World Bank, Washington DC.

Holmgren, J., and A. Merkel. 2017. "Much Ado about Nothing? A Meta-Analysis of the Relationship between Infrastructure and Economic Growth." *Research in Transportation Economics* 63 (August): 13–26.

IEA (International Energy Agency). 2012. *Energy Technology Perspectives.* Paris: Organisation for Economic Co-operation and Development.

Iimi, A., and K. Rao. 2018. *Spatial Analysis of Liberia's Transport Connectivity and Potential Growth.* Washington, DC: World Bank.

ITF (International Transport Forum). 2015. *Urban Mobility System Upgrade: How Shared Self-Driving Cars Could Change City Traffic.* Corporate Partnership Board Report. Chicago: American Planning Association.

———. 2017. *Transport Outlook.* Paris: International Transport Forum.

———. 2018a. "The Billion Dollar Question: How Much Will It Cost to Decarbonise Cities' Transport Systems?" Background paper prepared for this report, World Bank, Washington, DC.

———. 2018b. *The Shared-Use City: Managing the Curb.* Corporate Partnership Board Report. Paris: OECD.

Jain, P., S. Cullinane, and K. Cullinane. 2008. "The Impact of Governance Development Models on Urban Rail Efficiency." *Transportation Research Part A: Policy and Practice* 42 (9): 1238–50.

KC, S., and W. Lutz. 2014. "Demographic Scenarios by Age, Sex, and Education Corresponding to the SSP Narratives." *Population and Environment* 35 (3): 243–60.

Khandker, S. R., and G. B. Koolwal. 2011. "Estimating the Long-Term Impacts of Rural Roads: A Dynamic Panel Approach." Policy Research Working Paper 5867, World Bank, Washington, DC.

Laurance, W. F., G. R. Clements, S. Sloan, C. S. O'Connell, N. D. Mueller, M. Goosem, O. Venter, and others. 2014. "A Global Strategy for Road Building." *Nature* 513 (7517): 229–32.

Lecocq, F., and Z. Shalizi. 2014. "The Economics of Targeted Mitigation in Infrastructure." *Climate Policy* 14 (2): 187–208.

Lemonsu, A., V. Viguié, M. Daniel, and V. Masson. 2015. "Vulnerability to Heat Waves: Impact of Urban Expansion Scenarios on Urban Heat Island and Heat Stress in Paris (France)." *Urban Climate* 14 (pt. 4): 586–605.

Levy, H. 2004. *Rural Roads and Poverty Alleviation in Morocco.* Washington, DC: World Bank.

Libertun de Duren, N., and R. Guerrero Compeán. 2016. "Growing Resources for Growing Cities: Density and the Cost of Municipal Public Services in Latin America." *Urban Studies* 53 (14): 3082–107.

Lohrey, S., and F. Creutzig. 2016. "A 'Sustainability Window' of Urban Form." *Transportation Research Part D: Transport and Environment* 45 (June): 96–111.

Mehndiratta, S. 2014. "Are Women 'Forced' to Work Closer to Home due to Other Responsibilities? Does This Contribute to Gender Wage Differentials?" World Bank Transport for Development blog, February 20.

Mikou, M., J. Rozenberg, E. Koks, C. Fox, and T. Peralta-Quiros. 2019. "Assessing Rural Accessibility and Rural Roads Investment Needs Using Open Source Data." Background paper prepared for this report, World Bank, Washington, DC.

O'Neill, B. C., E. Kriegler, K. L. Ebi, E. Kemp-Benedict, K. Riahi, D. S. Rothman, B. J. van Ruijven, D. P. van Vuuren, J. Birkmann, and K. Kok. 2017. "The Roads Ahead: Narratives for Shared Socioeconomic Pathways Describing World Futures in the 21st Century." *Global Environmental Change* 42 (January): 169–80.

O'Neill, B. C., E. Kriegler, K. Riahi, K. Ebi, S. Hallegatte, T. R. Carter, R. Mathur, and D. P. van Vuuren. 2013. "A New Scenario Framework for Climate Change Research: The Concept of Shared Socio-Economic Pathways." *Climatic Change* 122 (3): 387–400.

Oum, T. H., and C. Yu. 1994. "Economic Efficiency of Railways and Implications for Public Policy: A Comparative Study of the OECD Countries' Railways." *Journal of Transport Economics and Policy* 28 (2): 121–38.

Pfaff, A. S. P., J. Robalino, E. J. Reis, R. Walker, S. Perz, W. Laurance, C. Bohrer, and others. 2018. "Roads & SDGs, Tradeoffs and Synergies: Learning from Brazil's Amazon in Distinguishing Frontiers." *Economics: The Open-Access, Open-Assessment E-Journal* 12 (2018–11): 1–26.

Prud'homme, R. 2004. *Infrastructure and Development.* Washington, DC: World Bank.

Raballand, G., P. Macchi, and C. Petracco. 2010. *Rural Road Investment Efficiency: Lessons from Burkina Faso, Cameroon, and Uganda*. Washington, DC: World Bank.

Raptopoulos, A. 2013. "No Roads? There's a Drone for That." TEDGlobal, June.

Roberts, M., U. Deichmann, B. Fingleton, and T. Shi. 2012. "Evaluating China's Road to Prosperity: A New Economic Geography Approach." *Regional Science and Urban Economics* 42 (4): 580–94.

Roberts, M., M. Melecky, T. Bougna, and Y. Xu. 2018. *Transport Corridors and Their Wider Economic Benefits: A Critical Review of the Literature*. Washington, DC: World Bank.

Roberts, P., S. KC, and C. Rastogi. 2006. "Rural Access Index: A Key Development Indicator." Transport Paper TP-10, World Bank, Washington, DC.

Seaton, A., D. Godden, W. MacNee, and K. Donaldson. 1995. "Particulate Air Pollution and Acute Health Effects." *The Lancet* 345 (8943): 176–78.

Stone, B., J. J. Hess, and H. Frumkin. 2010. "Urban Form and Extreme Heat Events: Are Sprawling Cities More Vulnerable to Climate Change Than Compact Cities?" *Environmental Health Perspectives* 118 (10): 1425–28.

Streutker, D. R. 2003. "Satellite-Measured Growth of the Urban Heat Island of Houston, Texas." *Remote Sensing of Environment* 85 (3): 282–89.

United Nations. 2014. *World Population Prospects: The 2014 Revision*. New York: United Nations Population Division.

USAID (U.S. Agency for International Development) Global Health Supply Chain Program—Procurement and Supply Management. 2017. *Unmanned Aerial Vehicles Landscape Analysis: Applications in the Development Context*. Washington, DC: Chemonics International.

van de Walle, D. 2009. "Impact Evaluation of Rural Road Projects." *Journal of Development Effectiveness* 1 (1): 15–36.

Volpe Martincus, C., and J. S. Blyde. 2012. *Shaky Roads and Trembling Exports: Assessing the Trade Effects of Domestic Infrastructure Using a Natural Experiment*. Washington, DC: Inter-American Development Bank.

Waisman, H., C. Guivarch, F. Grazi, and J. C. Hourcade. 2012. "The IMACLIM-R Model: Infrastructures, Technical Inertia, and the Costs of Low Carbon Futures under Imperfect Foresight." *Climatic Change* 114 (1): 101–20.

Waisman, H.-D., C. Guivarch, and F. Lecocq. 2013. "The Transportation Sector and Low-Carbon Growth Pathways: Modelling Urban, Infrastructure, and Spatial Determinants of Mobility." *Climate Policy* 13 (Suppl. 01): 106–29.

5

Flood Protection

JULIE ROZENBERG AND MARIANNE FAY

KEY MESSAGES

- Investment costs for protection against both coastal and river floods depend primarily on the level of risk that is acceptable to local populations and the uncertainty pertaining to construction costs.

- The economically optimal investment trajectory would cost low- and middle-income countries (LMICs) between 0.1 percent and 0.5 percent of their gross domestic product (GDP) annually by 2030 for both new capital and maintenance, depending on construction costs, economic growth, urbanization, and climate change.

- Failure to secure the appropriate financial tools, institutions, and governance mechanisms to ensure maintenance—and thus continuous protection over time—would increase risk and could result in catastrophic failures. Absent a firm commitment to reliable maintenance, a combination of nature-based protection, land-use planning, and retreat should be favored.

INTRODUCTION

Flood damages are expected to increase significantly over the 21st century as sea-level rise, more intense precipitation, extreme weather events, and socioeconomic developments result in an ever-rising number of people and an ever-more-expensive value of assets at risk in coastal and riverine floodplains. While these increased damages and corresponding adaptation costs might well be the most costly impacts of climate change (World Bank 2010), little attention has been paid so far to the investments needed in flood protection.

To shed more light on this issue, this chapter examines one of the most comprehensive quantifications to date of future investment needs in infrastructure for coastal and river flood protection (table 5.1). It does so by considering (a) different *levels* of protection (reflecting different levels of risk aversion), (b) different *means* of providing that protection (like surge barriers and river dikes), and (c) uncertainties regarding the cost of protection, future socioeconomic changes, and climate change. It uses the state-of-the-art DIVA model and new estimates of coastal protection construction costs (Nicholls and others 2019). For river floods, it uses investment costs from Ward and others (2017).

Our results suggest that, for both coastal and river floods, key cost drivers are construction costs and protection strategy (or level of risk tolerance). The protection strategy determines which coastal and inland areas invest in hard protection and the level of protection (such as the return period of floods that the protection can manage). Communities not protected by hard infrastructure would need to cope with floods and their impacts or retreat. For both coastal and river floods, uncertainty surrounding climate change or socioeconomic change affects the amount of investment needed for protection much less than construction costs and risk tolerance—even though climate change and socioeconomic change are critical in determining which areas to protect and how to protect them.

Overall, LMICs would have to spend between 0.10 percent and 0.52 percent of their GDP annually in capital and maintenance for coastal and river flood protection by 2030 if they followed a strategy that minimizes overall costs (that is, the sum of protection costs and residual flood damages).[1]

TABLE 5.1 Overview of the assumptions and models used in this chapter

Sector	Objectives	Models	Metrics	Policy scenarios	Uncertain parameters
Coastal flood protection	Limit coastal flood risk (SDG 13)	DIVA model	Capital costs; maintenance costs; residual risk	Maintain current absolute losses; maintain current relative losses; keep relative average annual losses below 0.01% of local GDP; minimize total costs and residual risk	Sea-level rise; population and GDP growth; construction costs; technology choice
River flood protection	Limit river flood risk (SDG 13)	GLOFRIS global food risk model	Capital costs; maintenance costs	Maintain current absolute losses; maintain current relative losses; minimize total cost and residual risk	Climate change; population and GDP growth; construction costs

Sources: For coastal flood protection, Hinkel and others 2014; Nicholls and others 2019. For river flood protection, Ward and others 2017.
Note: Categories follow the framework developed in chapter 1. SDG = Sustainable Development Goal.

Although these estimates appear relatively modest, actual investment costs might be higher in practice if protection strategies are to be made robust to the many different and possible futures associated with uncertain climate and patterns of urbanization. In addition, investments will need to be accompanied by complementary policies such as land-use planning to prevent people from settling in flood-prone areas, nature-based solutions to increase water storage and decrease runoff (hence the need for hard infrastructure), and early-warning systems and communication about residual risk.

Moreover, a key message of this chapter is the central importance of maintenance—in terms of both cost-effectiveness and its role in delivering effective protection. Without the needed maintenance, neither existing nor new infrastructure can deliver on their promise of protection and instead will put people's lives at risk by creating a false sense of protection.

The implication is that the development of appropriate institutions and governance mechanisms to deliver maintenance is as necessary as the funding stream for an effective protection-based adaptation strategy. Absent a solid commitment to maintaining protective infrastructure and the necessary financial instruments, alternative adaptation approaches (such as accommodation or retreat) are recommended to avoid catastrophic events. A strategy that builds dikes but fails to maintain them would actually increase the number and value of lives and assets at risk.

In sum, investment needs in "hard" flood protection (such as dikes and pumping stations) are highly dependent on many policy choices, including the level of risk considered acceptable by the population, the protection of ecosystems (and the nature-based solutions they offer), and the implementation of restrictive land-use plans to limit new development in flood-prone areas.

COSTING COASTAL AND RIVER FLOOD PROTECTION STRATEGIES

Investment needs in flood protection depend on the level of protection that is considered appropriate. This differs across countries and cultures and even within countries. In the Netherlands, for example, the Delta Committee determines an acceptable level of flood risk based on a cost-benefit analysis and, from it, derives an optimum level of protection. Areas with high population density and high asset values are provided with better protection than lower-density areas. Few countries, however, have adopted such a rule-based approach to determining the level of protection to be provided.

Coastal Protection

For coastal protection, Nicholls and others (2019) assess the costs of four different coastal protection strategies until the end of the 21st century in different socioeconomic pathways (that is, varying economic and demographic futures) for different sea-level-rise scenarios. Here, protection standards represent the return period of the worst event against which the infrastructure can protect. There are four strategies:

- *Constant absolute flood risk.* This strategy maintains the current (2015) average annual losses constant in monetary terms for protected areas as defined in table 5.2. This strategy raises protection levels with both rising sea levels and socioeconomic development (population, GDP).

- *Constant relative flood risk.* This strategy maintains relative average annual losses constant in terms of percentage of local GDP for protected areas as defined in table 5.2. This strategy raises protection levels given rising sea levels and socioeconomic development.

- *Low risk tolerance.* This strategy keeps average annual losses below 0.01 percent of local GDP for protected areas. The GDP threshold of 0.01 percent is based on the residual risk implied by the protection infrastructure of Amsterdam and Rotterdam in 2005, as calculated by Hallegatte and others (2013). We take this (high) Dutch standard as the acceptable risk standard in a low-risk-tolerance world.

- *Optimal protection.* This strategy pursues the economically optimal level of protection, defined as the level that minimizes the sum of protection costs (capital and maintenance) and residual flood damage (to assets) to 2100. It follows the methods of Lincke and Hinkel (2018).

TABLE 5.2 **Protection standards vary with wealth and location**

Protection standards (expressed in return period) adopted in this analysis

Wealth class (annual income per capita)[a]	Urban (>1,000 people per square kilometer)	Rural (30–1,000 people per square kilometer)	Uninhabited (<30 people per square kilometer)
136 largest coastal cities	Following the rule described in Hallegatte and others 2013	Following the rule described in Hallegatte and others 2013	Following the rule described in Hallegatte and others 2013
Other cities			
Low income (<US$1,035)	1:10	No protection	No protection
Lower middle income (US$1,035–US$4,085)	1:25	No protection	No protection
Upper middle income (US$4,086–US$12,615)	1:100	1:20	No protection
High income (>US$12,615)	1:200	1:50	No protection
Special case: the Netherlands	1:10,000	n.a.	n.a.

Source: Sadoff and others 2015.
Note: Protection standards represent the return period of the maximum event against which the infrastructure can protect. 1:10 means that the infrastructure protects against an event that happens every 10 years, on average. Current protection levels are taken from Sadoff and others (2015), which complement current protection levels for the biggest 136 coastal cities from Hallegatte and others (2013) with expert judgment for other coastal areas. n.a. = not applicable.
a. GDP per capita (2014 US$, purchasing power parity).

We define our optimal protection strategy as the one that minimizes investment costs and flood risks to assets in coastal communities rather than risks to welfare. The limitations of this approach have been discussed in Hallegatte and others (2017), which proposes complementing measures of risks to assets with measures of risks to welfare—given that US$1 lost by a poor community has a much bigger impact on people's welfare than US$1 lost by a rich community. Prioritizing investments based on welfare rather than asset losses can lead to different investment strategies, at least if it is assumed that rich communities can pay for protecting the poorest (Hallegatte and others 2017; World Bank 2017).

In addition to these protection strategies, different technologies can be used to deliver the desired level of protection. Protection on the open coast is always provided by sea dikes. But river protection can be provided either by river dikes to the upstream limit of coastal effects (open protection, map 5.1, panel a) or by storm surge barriers (closed protection, panel b). Our analysis considers both options.

Furthermore, there is significant uncertainty around the construction costs of protection infrastructure. Previous estimates relied on rather dated unit costs of Dutch dikes that are now thought to be an underestimate. Besides, costs might increase in the future if demand for hard protection increases faster than the capacity of construction companies. Our analysis thus offers both a low and a high estimate for sea dikes, river dikes, and surge barriers, drawing on more recent studies. Maintenance costs are assumed

MAP 5.1 Using open or closed riverine coastal protection in the Netherlands

a. Open protection   b. Closed protection

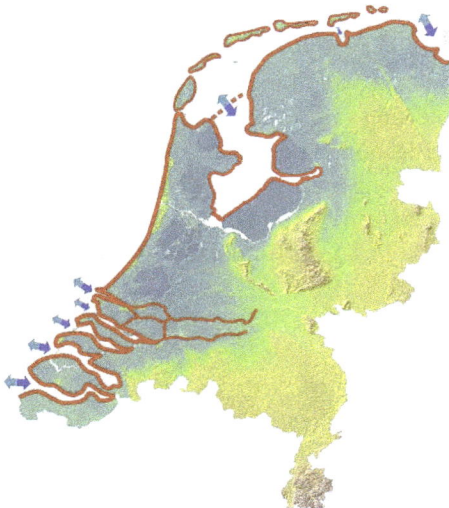

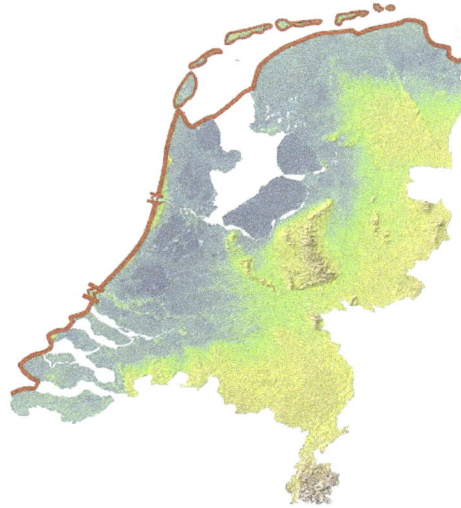

Source: Nicholls and others 2019.

TABLE 5.3 **A wide range of sea-level rise scenarios**

*Global coastal average sea-level rise, 2015–100
meters*

Scenario	2015	2030	2050	2075	2100
RCP 2.6: 5th percentile	0.02	0.06	0.11	0.17	0.23
RCP 4.5: 50th percentile	0.03	0.08	0.16	0.29	0.43
RCP 8.5: 95th percentile	0.04	0.13	0.28	0.59	1.03

Sources: Nicholls and others 2019, with representative concentration pathways (RCPs) derived from the Intergovernmental Panel on Climate Change.
Note: The base level from which sea-level rise is estimated is the 1985–2005 average level.

to be 1 percent of capital cost per year for sea dikes and surge barriers and 0.5 percent for river dikes.

The uncertainty regarding socioeconomic pathways and sea-level rise was factored in by modeling the cost of different strategies across multiple shared socioeconomic pathways (SSPs)—SSP 2, 3, and 5—and across multiple representative concentration pathways (RCPs) (table 5.3). All of these are drawn from the Intergovernmental Panel on Climate Change (IPCC) and Nicholls and others (2019).

Our analysis only considers relative sea-level rise due to the sum of climate-induced sea-level rise, glacial isostatic adjustment, and naturally occurring deltaic subsidence (caused by tectonics or the natural compaction of deltas' soft and easily compressed soils).[2] Human-induced subsidence in coastal cities (caused by excessive pumping of groundwater) can also be significant, with multiple meters of subsidence observed in cities such as Bangkok, Ho Chi Minh City, Jakarta, and Manila over the last few decades (for example, Kaneko and Toyota 2011; Nicholls 1995, 2018). In Asia, subsidence threatens coastal megacities as much as climate-induced sea-level rise (World Bank 2010).

Including city subsidence would not change the ranking of the different strategies or the global results. However, it would increase the costs of protection as well as the impacts if protection fails in some of these big cities (Hallegatte and others 2013). Thus, mitigation of human-induced subsidence should be considered wherever possible as an immediate preventive response available to cities. In Bangkok, extreme land subsidence was successfully reduced through regulations and restrictions on groundwater extraction.

River Floods

For river floods, Ward and others (2017) explored three protection strategies, similar to the ones explored for coastal protection: (a) achieving an optimal level of protection based on a simple cost-benefit analysis, (b) keeping the current *absolute* level of flood risk in each country constant, in U.S. dollars, and (c) keeping the current *relative* level of flood risk constant in each country, as a percent of GDP.

They explored how the global costs and benefits of river flood protection change in each of these strategies with socioeconomic change, climate change, and construction costs. They used the same socioeconomic scenarios as for the coastal protection analysis. For climate change, they explored more scenarios because there is more uncertainty regarding future precipitation patterns than future sea-level rise. Thus, they explored all RCPs using five different global climate models to capture this uncertainty.

FUTURE INVESTMENT COSTS DEPEND ON CONSTRUCTION COSTS AND RISK AVERSION

The main conclusion of our analysis of the possible costs of four coastal protection strategies and three river protection strategies over the 2015–100 period is that uncertainty regarding socioeconomic changes and climate change is small compared with the uncertainty around construction costs and tolerance to risk.

Coastal Protection: The Optimal Protection Strategy Requires More Investments Than One That Maintains Absolute Risks Constant

Capital costs range from US$2 billion to US$56 billion per year, on average, between 2015 and 2030, depending on construction costs and the protection strategy pursued. This represents between 0.006 percent and 0.05 percent of LMICs' GDP per year, on average, for the least expensive strategy (constant relative risk) and between 0.04 percent and 0.19 percent of LMICs' GDP per year, on average, for the most expensive one (optimal protection) (figure 5.1). For comparison with other sectors, these numbers include all LMICs in the denominator, including countries without a coast. But removing countries with no coast from the sample has little impact—costs would still range between 0.05 percent and 0.20 percent of LMICs' GDP per year, on average, by 2030—as landlocked countries tend to be small and relatively poor.

Capital investment costs are the lowest in scenarios with low construction costs and a risk-taking strategy in which coastal communities only maintain protection levels to keep current average losses constant relative to their GDP (figure 5.1). Conversely, investment costs are highest in the low-risk-tolerance strategy and in the optimal protection strategy, especially if construction costs are high.

Between 2015 and 2030, investment costs are of the same order of magnitude for the optimal protection strategy and the low-risk-tolerance strategy, indicating that the level of protection pursued in the low-risk-tolerance strategy (the one that limits losses to 0.01 percent of GDP) is close to the economic optimum as derived from a cost-benefit analysis. However, further analysis of the scenarios found that, when construction costs are low, the optimal protection strategy results in higher levels of protection (hence greater investments) than in the low-risk-tolerance strategy. Thus, if construction

FIGURE 5.1 Construction costs, combined with risk aversion, shape coastal protection capital costs

Average annual cost of investment in coastal protection, by construction costs and risk-taking strategy, 2015–30

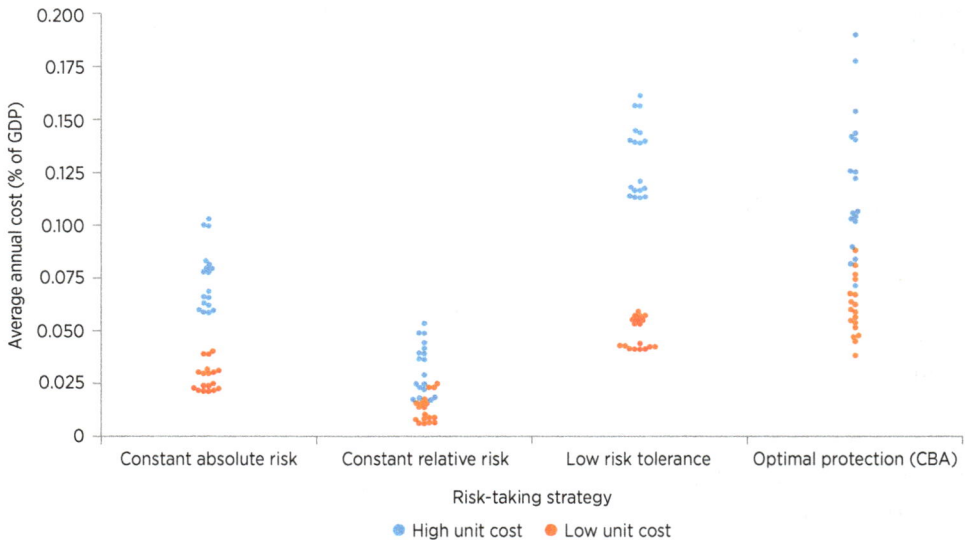

Source: Based on Nicholls and others 2019.
Note: Each dot represents one scenario, with the 18 scenarios in each subgroup derived by combining the three socioeconomic pathways, three representative concentration pathways, and two choices of technology (river dike or storm surge barrier). Numbers exclude high-income countries. If low- and middle-income countries with no coast were excluded, the points would be between 0.05 percent and 0.20 percent. The graph (like others in this chapter) is a "beeswarm" plot, which plots data points relative to a fixed reference axis (the x-axis) in a way that no two data points overlap, showing not only the range of values but also their distribution. CBA = cost-benefit analysis.

costs are low, the benefits of limiting average annual losses to less than 0.01 percent of GDP outweigh the costs, at least in some cities.

If capital and maintenance costs for both coastal protection and residual flood risk are accounted for by construction, the optimal protection strategy is much less costly than the other strategies by the end of the century (figure 5.2). The reason why the optimal protection strategy is costlier in the short run (2015–30) is because higher capital investments are needed initially to deal with suboptimal existing protection. After 2050, the higher cost of the other strategies springs from higher residual risks, rather than from higher investment costs. This outcome implies that the low-risk-tolerance strategy allows for greater risk than the economic optimum and "accepts" higher average annual losses.

A final note here is that these three strategies assume increased protection up to 2100. In the absence of adaptation, by 2100, 0.2 percent to 4.6 percent of the global population could be flooded annually, with expected annual losses equivalent to 0.3 percent to 9.3 percent of global GDP (Hinkel and others 2014). Coastal protection investments—or retreat—are thus critical to maintain future risk under acceptable levels.

FIGURE 5.2 **The optimal coastal protection strategy based on CBA reduces long-term costs**

Average annual cost of investment and maintenance in coastal protection, plus residual risk, by risk-taking strategy and time frame, 2015–100

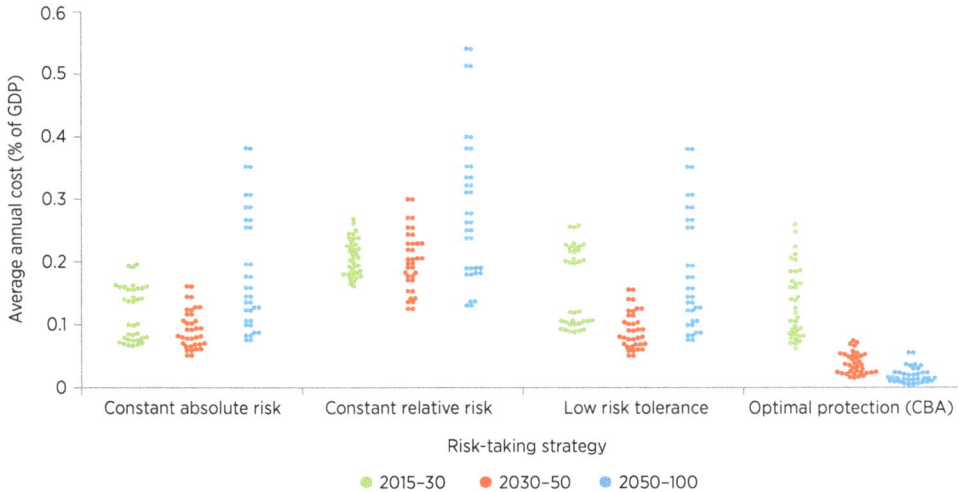

Source: Based on Nicholls and others 2019.
Note: Each dot represents one scenario, with the 36 scenarios in each subgroup derived by combining the three socioeconomic pathways, three representative concentration pathways, two choices of technology (dike or storm surge barrier), and high or low cost of the technology. Numbers exclude high-income countries. If low- and middle-income countries with no coast were excluded, the points would be between 0.006 percent and 0.57 percent. CBA = cost-benefit analysis.

River Floods: The Optimal Protection Strategy Requires *Less* Investment Than One That Maintains Absolute Risks Constant

Capital costs for river flood protection range from US$14 billion to US$847 billion per year, on average, between 2015 and 2030, depending on construction costs and the protection strategy pursued. This represents between 0.04 percent and 0.47 percent of LMICs' GDP per year, on average, for the least expensive strategy (optimal protection) and between 0.15 percent and 2.4 percent of LMICs' GDP per year, on average, for the most expensive one (constant absolute risk) (figure 5.3).

Construction costs for dikes are difficult to assess because they are highly heterogeneous (they vary with soil characteristics and availability of nature-based solutions) and depend on the selected technology and material costs (which are challenging to predict as they vary with availability and cost of sand and cement). Ward and others (2017) varied unit costs from one to nine between the low- and high-cost scenarios. However, in their detailed analysis of unit costs, Nicholls and others (2019) found that costs only varied from one to three within one country.

If we use the middle-cost estimate from Ward and others (2017), which falls within the range defined by Nicholls and others (2019), investment costs for river flood protection range between 0.05 percent and 0.26 percent of

FIGURE 5.3 **The choice of protection level, combined with construction costs, shapes river flood protection capital costs**

Average annual cost of investment in river flood protection, by construction costs and risk-taking strategy, 2015–30

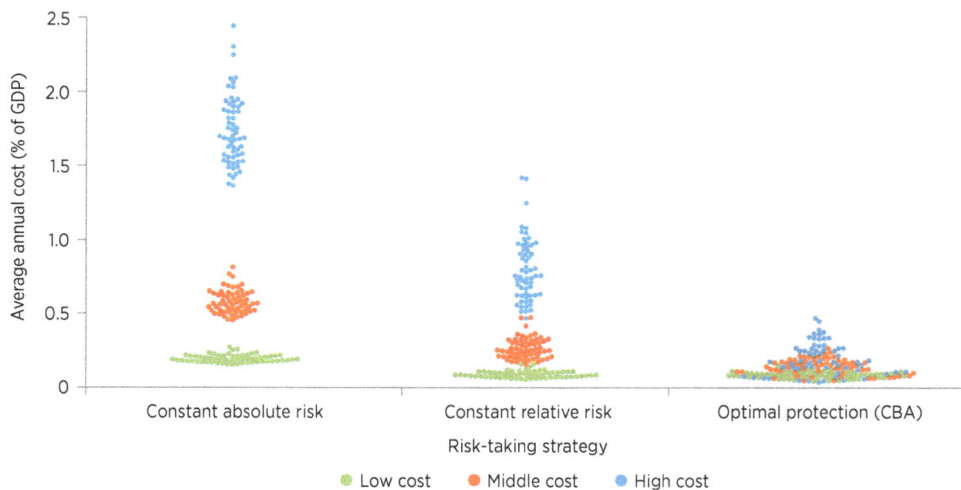

Source: Based on Ward and others 2017.
Note: Each dot represents one scenario, with the 60 scenarios in each subgroup derived by combining the three socioeconomic pathways, four representative concentration pathways, and five global climate models. Numbers exclude high-income countries. CBA = cost-benefit analysis.

LMICs' GDP for the optimal protection strategy and between 0.45 percent and 0.81 percent of GDP for the constant-absolute-risk strategy.

Contrary to coastal flood protection, where investments are the highest under the optimal strategy, for river floods, investment costs are more than twice as high in the low-risk strategy (to keep absolute risk levels constant) as what the cost-benefit analysis suggests is the optimal level of investment. This is because 1 kilometer of dike at the coast can protect, on average, many more square kilometers of land than 1 kilometer of dike along a river.

If hard infrastructure is too expensive, other options are available to reduce river flood risks. Flood management is better designed as a system and at the scale of the river basin (van Stokkom and others 2005), especially because nature-based solutions can reduce the need to invest in hard infrastructure. Wetlands, forests, and other natural areas located upstream of human settlements can absorb water and reduce peak river runoff, making it easier and less costly to manage floods (Browder and others, forthcoming; Hey and Philippi 1995; Ming and others 2007).

Land-use planning can also contribute to reducing investment needs, by ensuring that new construction does not take place in areas that are difficult and expensive to protect (Burby and Dalton 1994; Burby and others 2000; Burby and others 2006; Kousky and others 2006). Investment needs in flood protection are much higher if private construction is allowed in flood-prone areas than if strict zoning policies are implemented. And the willingness of government to fund flood protection in densely populated areas may even create an incentive for individuals to settle in at-risk areas, thereby increasing investment needs. This said, the cost of restrictive land-use planning should not be ignored, and flood-prone areas may be desirable locations (for the amenities, agglomeration effects, or network effects they offer)—even if they increase the need for investment in flood protection (Hallegatte 2017; Viguié and Hallegatte 2012).

HOW DIFFERENT REGIONS FARE DEPENDS ON THE PROTECTION STRATEGY

The protection strategy chosen also plays an important role at the regional level. For river flood protection, while the three protection strategies cost less than 0.5 percent of regional GDP in most regions, costs can go up to 1.5 percent of GDP annually in Latin America and up to 4 percent of GDP annually in Sub-Saharan Africa for the constant-absolute-risk strategy (figure 5.4). The optimal strategy would require investing 0.08 percent of GDP, on average, in Latin America and the Caribbean and 0.38 percent of GDP, on average, in Sub-Saharan Africa, but would "accept" risks that are higher than today (2015) as cities grow and the climate changes.

FIGURE 5.4 For river floods, maintaining 2015 risk levels might be unaffordable in Sub-Saharan Africa

Average annual cost of investment in river flood protection, by region and risk-taking strategy, 2015–30

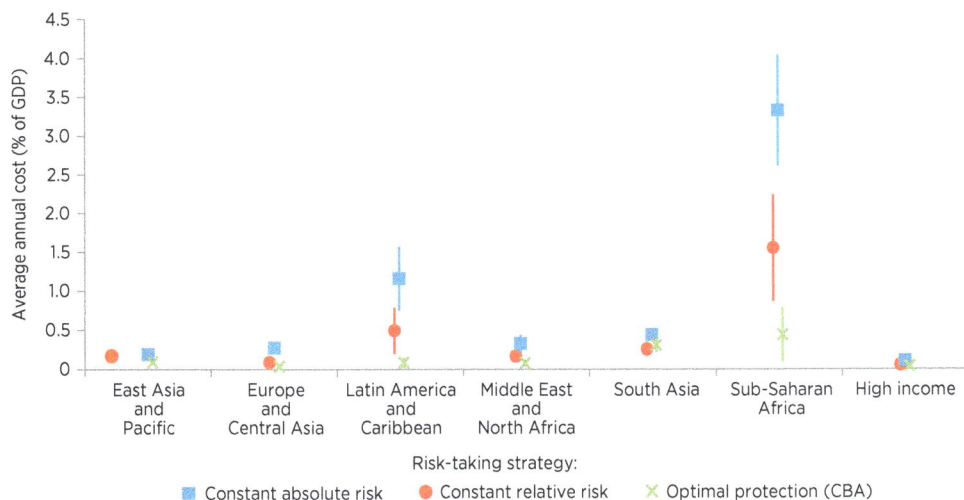

Source: Based on Ward and others 2017.
Note: The markers represent the average across all 60 scenarios for a given strategy (using the middle estimate for construction costs), and vertical bars represent the range.

The uncertainty around costs in figure 5.4 is driven mostly by the socio-economic scenarios as costs are much higher in a scenario with high GDP growth and urbanization (SSP 5) than in a scenario with slow GDP growth and slow urbanization (SSP 3). This is particularly true in Africa.

For coastal protection, while most regions invest less than 0.1 percent of regional GDP per year in the constant-absolute-risk strategy, there is much greater regional variation in the optimal protection strategy—from 0.005 percent for Europe and Central Asia to 0.05 percent for Sub-Saharan Africa, on average, over all scenarios (figure 5.5). In Latin America, high-income countries, and, to a lesser extent, East Asia, investment costs are lower in the optimal protection strategy than in the low-risk-tolerance strategy. This indicates that, for some coastal cities in these countries, it might not be economically optimal to build strong protection.

In fact, while an estimated 24 percent of the world's coast is protected today, by 2030 the low-risk-tolerance strategy would protect 26 percent of the world's coast, and the optimal protection strategy would protect only about 22 percent. The decrease in protection mostly comes from high-income countries (with a small decrease in Latin America), while protection "length" increases 150 percent in South Asia, 70 percent in Sub-Saharan Africa, and 30 percent in East Asia and Pacific (Nicholls and others 2019).[3]

FIGURE 5.5 **For coastal floods, the optimal protection strategy based on CBA invests more than the low-risk-tolerance strategy only in South Asia and Sub-Saharan Africa**

Average annual cost of investment in coastal protection, by region and risk-taking strategy, 2015–30

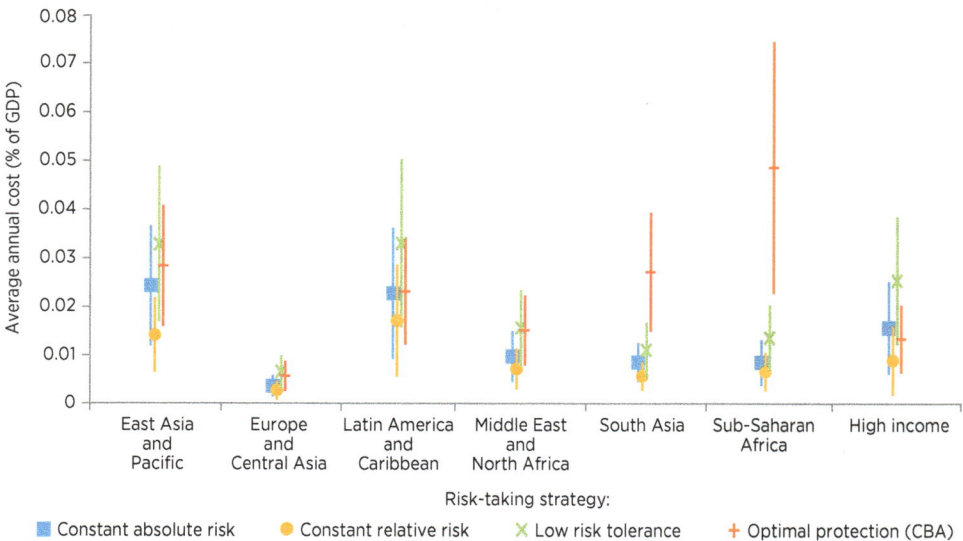

Source: Based on Nicholls and others 2019.
Note: The markers represent the average across all 36 scenarios for a given strategy, and vertical bars represent the range. High-income countries are included here for comparison but are not included in the total numbers given in the text. If countries with no coast were excluded, the points would be between 0.001 percent and 0.09 percent. CBA = cost-benefit analysis.

The remaining 74 percent to 78 percent of world coasts that are not protected evolve more naturally—using low-cost ecosystem-based or nature-based approaches, along with retreat (Temmerman and others 2013).

This redistribution of investments from high- to lower-income countries in the optimal protection strategy suggests that low-income countries are investing too little in coastal protection compared with what would be the lowest-cost strategy. This underinvestment in protection is often referred to as the "adaptation deficit," which we estimate here as the difference in investment costs between the optimal protection strategy and current protections in 2015, as estimated by Nicholls and others (2019).[4] This deficit ranges between US$0.7 billion in Latin America and US$75 billion in East Asia and Pacific (table 5.4).

However, this result should be taken with caution. At this stage, empirical observations of protection standards are extremely limited, so our analysis may rely on underestimates or overestimates of current protection levels. Further, traditional cost-benefit analysis cannot capture risk aversion, efficiency of institutions, and uncertainty around whether governments will undertake the needed maintenance.

Besides, the uncertainty pertaining to future sea-level rise and future exposure to coastal floods prevents decision makers from designing "optimal" protections. Instead, they need to focus on "robust" investments that will maintain future losses below a given acceptable level—no matter what happens to future climate and socioeconomic conditions—or on flexible investments that can be upgraded over time as conditions change (Hallegatte 2009).

Furthermore, risk assessments based on asset losses favor richer communities even though the poorest suffer the most from disaster losses (Hallegatte and others 2016; Hallegatte and others 2017). It is thus vital to complement measures of asset losses with a measure of socioeconomic resilience to account for inequalities in the impact of disasters on people's well-being.

TABLE 5.4 East and South Asia and Sub-Saharan Africa have the highest adaptation deficits in coastal protection

Adaptation deficit in coastal protection across scenarios, by region, 2015

Region	Adaptation deficit in coastal protection in 2015 (US$, billions)
East Asia and Pacific	75.0
Europe and Central Asia	1.8
Latin America and Caribbean	0.7
Middle East and North Africa	6.0
South Asia	49.0
Sub-Saharan Africa	28.0

Source: Based on Nicholls and others 2019.
Note: The adaptation deficit in coastal protection is calculated as the difference between the optimal protection strategy and estimated current protections in 2015, averaged across scenarios.

Depending on the scale of the assessment, doing so might prioritize different regions or neighborhoods (Hallegatte and others 2017).

Finally, in the absence of funds for financing dikes, countries can use cheaper options for protection—like nature-based solutions that have proven to be more cost-effective than infrastructure in certain areas (Reguero and others 2018). Another option is planned retreat, in particular, in areas that cannot afford to pay for protection or where population density does not justify the investment. Retreat can have important social consequences and should be managed carefully, which can also imply high relocation costs.

PROTECTION STRATEGIES SHOULD BUDGET FOR LONG-TERM MAINTENANCE EXPENSES

Flood protection infrastructure creates countervailing risks (Wiener 1998). This occurs because protection creates an incentive for people to settle in at-risk areas, especially if the infrastructure is paid for through nationwide taxes and people do not pay directly for the additional risk that their choice of location creates. These countervailing risks reinforce the importance of the commitment made by the initial capital investment. Indeed, neglecting maintenance could put the lives of many people at risk.

Over the 21st century, the cost of maintaining existing and future coastal protection infrastructure is between 0.008 percent and 0.04 percent of LMICs' GDP per year, on average—depending on the protection strategy chosen and construction costs (maintenance costs are estimated as a fixed fraction of construction costs). For river flood protection, the cost is between 0.006 percent and 0.10 percent of LMICs' GDP annually by 2100 for new protection.

Although these costs appear affordable, the development of appropriate institutions and governance mechanisms to deliver maintenance as well as the necessary funding streams are essential for an infrastructure-based protection strategy to be effective. The Netherlands and the Thames Estuary (London) are good examples of major flood defense systems that were built decades ago and have been actively maintained and upgraded as needed (Lavery and Donovan 2005; Ranger and others 2013; Stive and others 2011; Tarrant and Sayers 2012; Van Alphen 2015). These systems are linked to strong flood management institutions and long-term planning that looks many decades into the future. For protection to be successful elsewhere, similar arrangements would be required, notably to guarantee the funding streams for maintenance (Hinkel and others 2018).

The danger of focusing on defense without this institutional support is to lull society into a false sense of security, leading to bigger losses when defenses fail. Historic precedent shows that complacency in this regard can lead to disasters—Hurricane Katrina's devastation of New Orleans in 2005 being a recent example. Thus, any coastal society following a protective infrastructure approach needs to recognize protection as a long-term commitment.

If this commitment cannot be delivered, alternative coastal adaptation approaches are recommended—such as accommodation, retreat, or nature-based solutions (if these can also be protected over time). Further, even if defenses are well maintained, they will always be associated with residual risk, meaning that appropriate measures will need to be put in place for their management, especially in coastal cities (Hallegatte and others 2013). Appropriate flood warnings and disaster preparedness mechanisms remain essential, even if a good protection and maintenance regime is in place.

IN SUM

Total investment needs in coastal and river flood protection, as derived by a cost-benefit analysis and assuming perfect foresight, would cost LMICs between 0.1 percent and 0.5 percent of GDP annually including both new capital investments and maintenance, with the exact amount depending mostly on GDP growth, urbanization, and the impacts of climate change.

In practice, however, few countries other than the Netherlands apply a cost-benefit approach. Most countries do not have strict rules regarding the level of protection that is to be provided to the population. New York City is not even protected against events that happen every 100 years, while some towns in Germany and the Netherlands are protected against events that happen every 10,000 years. The difference in protection levels does not come principally from different risk tolerance levels, but rather from different institutional systems and funding mechanisms. In addition, implementing a strategy based on heavy protection is risky if institutions and financial resources are not in place to ensure constant maintenance over time and to upgrade the protection as sea levels rise and rainfall patterns change.

Given the often-limited budgets for flood protection and maintenance, cities will likely have to use a combination of structural approaches and nature-based solutions, as well as residual risk communication and early-warning systems, as illustrated by the case of New Orleans (box 5.1). In rapidly urbanizing countries, land-use management to prevent urban expansion in new flood-prone areas would also be more cost-effective than hard protection.

Next steps could involve seeking a better understanding of the cost of land-use management and its effect on rents, the feedback effects between protection investment and increased risk (when people settle behind the defenses), and the cost of retreat. More research is also needed on the potential of nature-based solutions for future flood protection.

PROTECTING NEW ORLEANS FROM FLOODING

Contributed by Dr. Denise Reed

New Orleans is a coastal city on the banks of the Mississippi River, separated from the Gulf of Mexico by 100 kilometers of coastal wetlands and shallow open-water bodies. Protection from river flooding is provided by a system of dikes and floodways built and maintained by the U.S. government. Given high rates of deltaic subsidence, New Orleans and the surrounding Mississippi Delta illustrate the challenges faced by many coastal cities.

The failure of the protection systems surrounding New Orleans during Hurricane Katrina in 2005 brought to light many issues surrounding how the protection "system" had been planned, implemented, and maintained, forcing Louisiana to rethink its approach to coastal protection.

Following Katrina, Louisiana joined its flood protection and land-loss functions under a single state authority, the Coastal Protection and Restoration Authority, and mandated the development of a Coastal Master Plan to be refined and updated every five years. The planning process looks 50 years into the future and considers how degradation (or restoration) of the surrounding wetland landscape influences the threat of flooding in New Orleans and how the process changes under different scenarios of sea-level rise and subsidence.

For previous coastal protection efforts, planning was undertaken for a specific level of protection, resulting in the prioritization of projects with very high costs for which funds were not readily available. This led to protracted construction and made it difficult to integrate new knowledge over time, even when circumstances changed. To address this, the Coastal Master Plan uses a cost-constrained approach to identify the most cost-effective projects to pursue—given an ambitious, but not out of the question, funding level for all protection projects (US$25 billion). Scientific analyses are used to predict future coastal conditions and project benefits based on different assumptions about sea-level rise, subsidence, and other key external drivers (Peyronnin and others 2013).

As the plan is updated every five years, new understanding can be incorporated and used to determine (a) which projects should be pursued in which areas, (b) what level of protection should be provided, and (c) whether the approach should be structural or nonstructural. The effect of coastal wetland dynamics can also be considered. Such an analysis can show the extent to which wetland restoration can lower flooding levels and how wetland self-adjustment to sea-level rise may offset some of the effects of climate change on flood risk.

Importantly, the 2017 Coastal Master Plan does not seek to eliminate flood risk; instead, it seeks to identify a cost-effective path forward, paying continued attention to persons in flood-prone areas and to the residual risk that exists and will remain even after implementation.

NOTES

1. Numbers in this chapter include all LMICs, for comparison with other chapters. If countries without a coast were excluded from the total GDP of LMICs, the numbers would barely change (see the technical appendix for a list of these countries).
2. Glacial isostatic adjustment is the rising (falling) adjustment that the land once under (around) the ice of the last ice age is still undergoing. Even though the ice melted long ago, the land once under and around the ice is still adjusting to the melting of its ice-age burden and will continue to do so for centuries. Deltaic subsidence is the soil compression that happens to delta plains as a result of natural tectonics, compaction, sedimentation, and anthropogenic causes (such as drainage and pumping of the underground oil, gas, or water that support the deltas' soft and easily compressed soils).
3. Even within high-income countries, some cities increase protection under the optimal protection strategy while others decrease it.
4. The adaptation deficit is usually defined as the difference between the optimal protection or resilience investments needed by a country in the absence of climate change relative to their current level of protection. Many LMICs are indeed not well protected against even historical floods (World Bank 2010).

REFERENCES

Browder, G., S. Ozment, I. Rehberger Bescos, T. Gartner, and G. M. Lange. Forthcoming. *Integrating Green and Grey: Creating Next Generation Infrastructure*. Washington, DC: World Bank and World Resources Institute.

Burby, R. J., E. L. Birch, and S. M. Wachter. 2006. "The Problems of Containment and the Promise of Planning." In *Rebuilding Urban Places after Disaster: Lessons from Hurricane Katrina*, edited by E. L. Birch and S. M. Wachter. Philadelphia: University of Pennsylvania Press.

Burby, R. J., and L. C. Dalton. 1994. "Plans Can Matter! The Role of Land Use Plans and State Planning Mandates in Limiting the Development of Hazardous Areas." *Public Administration Review* 54 (3): 229–38.

Burby, R. J., R. E. Deyle, D. R. Godschalk, and R. B. Olshansky. 2000. "Creating Hazard Resilient Communities through Land-Use Planning." *Natural Hazards Review* 1 (2): 99–106.

Hallegatte, S. 2009. "Strategies to Adapt to an Uncertain Climate Change." *Global Environmental Change* 19 (2): 240–47.

———. 2017. "A Normative Exploration of the Link between Development, Economic Growth, and Natural Risk." *Economics of Disasters and Climate Change* 1 (June): 5–31.

Hallegatte, S., M. Bangalore, L. Bonzanigo, M. Fay, T. Kane, U. Narloch, J. Rozenberg, D. Treguer, and A. Vogt-Schilb. 2016. *Shock Waves: Managing the Impacts of Climate Change on Poverty*. Washington, DC: World Bank.

Hallegatte, S., C. Green, R. J. Nicholls, and J. Corfee-Morlot. 2013. "Future Flood Losses in Major Coastal Cities." *Nature Climate Change* 3 (9): 802–06.

Hallegatte, S., A. Vogt-Schilb, M. Bangalore, and J. Rozenberg. 2017. *Unbreakable: Building the Resilience of the Poor in the Face of Natural Disasters*. Washington, DC: World Bank.

Hey, D. L., and N. S. Philippi. 1995. "Flood Reduction through Wetland Restoration: The Upper Mississippi River Basin as a Case History." *Restoration Ecology* 3 (4): 4–17.

Hinkel, J., J. C. J. H. Aerts, S. Brown, J. A. Jiménez, D. Lincke, R. J. Nicholls, P. Scussolini, A. Sanchez-Arcilla, A. Vafeidis, and K. Appeaning Addo. 2018. "The Ability of Societies to Adapt to Twenty-First-Century Sea-Level Rise." *Nature Climate Change* 8 (7): 570.

Hinkel, J., D. Lincke, A. T. Vafeidis, M. Perrette, R. J. Nicholls, R. S. J. Tol, B. Marzeion, X. Fettweis, C. Ionescu, and A. Levermann. 2014. "Coastal Flood Damage and Adaptation Costs under 21st Century Sea-Level Rise." *Proceedings of the National Academy of Sciences* 111 (9): 3292–97.

Kaneko, S., and T. Toyota. 2011. "Long-Term Urbanization and Land Subsidence in Asian Megacities: An Indicators System Approach." In *Groundwater and Subsurface Environments: Human Impacts in Asian Coastal Cities*, edited by M. Taniguchi. Tokyo: Springer.

Kousky, C., E. F. P. Luttmer, and R. J. Zeckhauser. 2006. "Private Investment and Government Protection." *Journal of Risk Uncertainty* 33 (1): 73–100.

Lavery, S., and B. Donovan. 2005. "Flood Risk Management in the Thames Estuary Looking Ahead 100 Years." *Philosophical Transactions of the Royal Society A: Mathematical, Physical and Engineering Sciences* 363 (1831): 1455–74.

Lincke, D., and J. Hinkel. 2018. "Economically Robust Protection against 21st Century Sea-Level Rise." *Global Environmental Change* 51 (July): 67–73.

Ming, J., L. Xian-guo, X. Lin-shu, C. Li-juan, and T. Shouzheng. 2007. "Flood Mitigation Benefit of Wetland Soil: A Case Study in Momoge National Nature Reserve in China." *Ecological Economics* 61 (2–3): 217–23.

Nicholls, R. J. 1995. "Coastal Megacities and Climate Change." *GeoJournal* 37 (3): 369–79.

———. 2018. "Adapting to Sea-Level Rise." In *Resilience: The Science of Adaptation to Climate Change*, edited by K. Alverson and Z. Zommers. Amsterdam: Elsevier. In press.

Nicholls, R. J., J. Hinkel, D. Lincke, and T. van der Pol. 2019. "Global Investment Costs for Coastal Defence through the 21st Century." Background paper prepared for this report, World Bank, Washington, DC.

Peyronnin, N., M. Green, C. P. Richards, A. Owens, D. Reed, J. Chamberlain, D. G. Groves, W. K. Rhinehart, and K. Belhadjali. 2013. "Louisiana's 2012 Coastal Master Plan: Overview of a Science-Based and Publicly Informed Decision-Making Process." *Journal of Coastal Research* 67 (Special Issue): 1–15.

Ranger, N., T. Reeder, and J. Lowe. 2013. "Addressing 'Deep' Uncertainty over Long-Term Climate in Major Infrastructure Projects: Four Innovations of the Thames Estuary 2100 Project." *EURO Journal on Decision Processes* 1 (3–4): 233–62.

Reguero, B. G., M. W. Beck, D. N. Bresch, J. Calil, and I. Meliane. 2018. "Comparing the Cost Effectiveness of Nature-Based and Coastal Adaptation: A Case Study from the Gulf Coast of the United States." *PLOS ONE* 13 (4): e0192132.

Sadoff, C. W., J. W. Hall, D. Grey, J. C. J. H. Aerts, M. Ait-Kadi, C. Brown, A. Cox, and others. 2015. *Securing Water, Sustaining Growth: Report of the GWP/OECD Task Force on Water Security and Sustainable Growth*. Oxford, U.K.: University of Oxford.

Stive, M. J. F., L. O. Fresco, P. Kabat, B. W. A. H. Parmet, and C. P. Veerman. 2011. "How the Dutch Plan to Stay Dry over the Next Century." *Proceedings of the Institution of Civil Engineers–Civil Engineering* 164 (3): 114–21.

Tarrant, O., and P. Sayers. 2012. "Managing Flood Risk in the Thames Estuary—The Development of a Long-Term Robust and Flexible Strategy." In *Flood Risk: Planning, Design and Management of Flood Defence Infrastructure*, edited by P. Sayers, 202–326. London: ICE Publishing.

Temmerman, S., P. Meire, T. J. Bouma, P. M. J. Herman, T. Ysebaert, and H. J. De Vriend. 2013. "Ecosystem-Based Coastal Defence in the Face of Global Change." *Nature* 504 (7578): 79–83.

Van Alphen, J. 2015. "The Delta Programme and Updated Food Risk Management Policies in the Netherlands." *Journal of Flood Risk Management* 9 (4): 310–19. doi:10.1111/jfr3.12183.

van Stokkom, H. T. C., A. J. M. Smits, and R. S. E. W. Leuven. 2005. "Flood Defense in the Netherlands." *Water International* 30 (1): 76–87.

Viguié, V., and S. Hallegatte. 2012. "Trade-Offs and Synergies in Urban Climate Policies." *Nature Climate Change* 2 (5): 334–37.

Ward, P. J., B. Jongman, J. C. J. H. Aerts, P. D. Bates, W. J. W. Botzen, A. Diaz Loaiza, S. Hallegatte, and others. 2017. "A Global Framework for Future Costs and Benefits of River-Flood Protection in Urban Areas." *Nature Climate Change* 7 (9): 642–46.

Wiener, J. B. 1998. "Managing the Iatrogenic Risks of Risk Management." *Risk* 9 (1): 39–82.

World Bank. 2010. *Economics of Adaptation to Climate Change: Synthesis Report.* Washington, DC: World Bank.

———. 2017. *Climate Vulnerability Assessment: Making Fiji Climate Resilient.* Washington, DC: World Bank.

6

Infrastructure and Disruptive Technologies

MICHAEL M. LEIFMAN, MARIANNE FAY, CLAIRE NICOLAS, AND JULIE ROZENBERG

KEY MESSAGES

- New technologies will likely be available to disrupt infrastructure systems by 2030 in low- and middle-income countries (LMICs), potentially allowing for better service at lower costs.

- The impact and spread of these disruptive technologies depend on the ability and success of governments, planning authorities, and regulatory authorities to fulfill their enabling and distributive functions.

- By enabling function, we mean their ability to put in place enabling measures (like backbone infrastructure and regulatory framework) and to remove or minimize barriers. By distributive function, we mean their role in enacting measures that ensure that the spread of new technologies is not limited to the wealthy and does not result in a decrease in opportunities and access for the rest of the population.

INTRODUCTION

This report so far has relied on scenarios to explore uncertainty regarding key cost drivers of infrastructure investments: socioeconomic trends, climate change, and, to a modest extent, technology. We modeled technology mostly as a choice between the "high" (expensive) and "low" (inexpensive) options or between the "low-carbon" and "business-as-usual" ones. The scenarios made some assumptions about the pace of innovation, its diffusion, and the evolution of cost curves, but the diffusion and adoption of innovation were barely discussed.

In this chapter, we dig deeper into the pathways through which new technologies can disrupt infrastructure sectors. These technologies can come from cross-cutting innovations (such as the Internet of Things [IoT], artificial intelligence, machine learning, 3-D printing, and batteries) or from sector-specific ones (such as autonomous vehicles, electric vehicles, or new biological water filtration techniques). The disruption lies in how they are adopted and spread, not simply in their availability, and it can have positive or negative impacts.

One aspect of the disruption is that these new technologies allow for more decentralization of infrastructure services. This decentralization makes it possible for people who can afford it to buy the service directly from the private sector and thereby get around large-scale infrastructure networks and the cross-subsidies that historically have funded service for poorer individuals. For example, in cities the availability of ride sharing and autonomous vehicles can encourage the better-off to shift from mass transit to private rides, thus threatening to bankrupt mass transit agencies. And "grid defect" is a serious concern of power utilities, which often subsidize low-income consumers through cross-subsidies borne by more profitable ones.

Another aspect is the fact that technology disruptions create losers and winners. Failing to smooth the transition sufficiently for the incumbents and, alternatively, offering excessive protection for the incumbent are twin risks that need to be navigated carefully.

As in other chapters, we explore scenarios depicting the ways in which infrastructure sectors can evolve as a result of innovations and how negative impacts can be avoided. But instead of using models as in the other chapters, the exploration was done through expert elicitation, both through structured interviews and in the context of a workshop (annex 6A). The resulting scenarios describe how various policy choices and external forces could lead to sharply different futures for infrastructure.

The key message that emerges from this expert elicitation is that the main force that distinguishes the scenarios—that is, that distinguishes the way in which technology will affect infrastructure and the services it provides—is the ability and success of governments, planning authorities, and regulatory authorities to fulfill their enabling and distributive functions. By enabling function, we mean their ability to put in place backbone infrastructure, financial incentives, and regulatory frameworks. By distributive function, we mean their role in enacting measures to ensure that the spread of new technologies is not limited to the wealthy and does not decrease opportunities and access for the rest of the population.

Thus, according to our experts, the technological uncertainty relevant to infrastructure futures (at least in the next 15–20 years) is not about the success of technology research and development, but rather its deployment in LMICs. That deployment, in turn, depends on how effective governments are in their enabling and distributive functions. For that reason, throughout this report, we consider it appropriate to treat technology as a policy choice, rather than as an uncertainty outside the control of decision makers.

The chapter begins with a review of innovations that are critical to infrastructure, how these innovations are expected to mature, and the potential transformations they could bring to infrastructure. It then explores the uncertainty surrounding how these technologies may or may not spread across three different futures—(a) a leapfrog scenario, (b) a lopsided development scenario, and (c) a lock-in one—and what the spread of technology would mean for infrastructure. The chapter wraps up with a discussion of what governments need to do to avoid lopsided development or lock-in, and how well-designed public policies can increase the likelihood of a leapfrog scenario.

NEW TECHNOLOGIES ARE ENABLING DISRUPTIONS AND TRANSFORMATIONS

A fairly well-identified set of technology innovations—ranging from artificial intelligence and robotic function to sensors and low Earth orbit satellites—is opening up new options for infrastructure service delivery (box 6.1). For example, our experts anticipate that services can be delivered much more efficiently via digitally connected systems or a robust Industrial Internet of Things (IIoT). The IIoT would depend on sensors, which are increasingly inexpensive to manufacture and increasingly easy to embed into a product's original design (such as using 3-D printing to convert circuitry into a part). The sensors would rely on an advanced communications infrastructure combining 5G technology and low Earth orbit satellites for extremely low-latency communications between devices or extremely large amounts of data transfer.

These innovations are additional to some sector-specific technologies or business models, like mini-grids for the power sector or mobility as a service for the transport sector. We can group them by how they might affect infrastructure and service delivery.

Power Grids: IIoT and Machine Learning

Optimizing power systems to balance supply and demand is a complicated task because of the numerous components of the system (power plants, grid, substations), fluctuating sources of demand, scarcity of storage, and difficulty of knowing the state of various components. IIoT could provide continuous real-time information about those states and relay the information to

BOX 6.1

HOW OUR EXPERTS SEE A LIKELY TECHNOLOGY FUTURE (BY 2040-ISH)

Against a backdrop of fast-maturing enabling technologies, our experts point to a world in 2040 that features the following:

- Artificial intelligence and machine learning technologies continue to scale up rapidly, permitting optimization of operations in virtually all industries and walks of life.
- Robotic function has risen dramatically in perception and cognition (ability to understand and react to the surrounding environment), ambulation, motion and fine-motor movements (ability to interact physically with the environment), and interagent coordination (ability to coordinate complex tasks across multiple robots).
- Sensors are available to be used in all devices.
- 5G or better communications are widely commercially available.
- Low Earth orbit satellites are widely deployed, with 5G, enabling a true Internet of Things economy.
- Advanced manufacturing techniques like additive manufacturing (also known as 3-D printing) have altered how things are built, how efficiently they use energy, and how equipment and structures communicate.
- Tools like augmented reality, natural language processing, and delivery drones have begun to change the geography of production.
- Batteries for electric vehicles are significantly less expensive and longer-lasting than today.
- Batteries for grid storage are much less expensive and longer-lasting than current technology.
- Advances in chemistry, filtration, ultraviolet purification, and detection and sensing of contaminants enable new service offerings in water delivery and sanitation.

machine learning algorithms that could, in turn, indicate the next optimal action to undertake. This system can be used at various scales:

- By grid operators to ensure stability of the grid via better communication with producers and consumers (by modifying the price signal to incite them to modulate generation or demand)

- By power plant operators, for example, to maximize a wind park's production by optimizing the way the various turbines work together

- By mini-grid operators to coordinate with the central grid (when a connection exists) via improving decisions regarding whether the mini-grid should supply power to the grid, receive power from the grid, or be islanded if an issue arises on the main grid.

IIoT and machine learning may also help to optimize the pricing and charging of electric vehicles, whether a building or a household stores the power it generates from a solar array in an on-site battery or sends the power to the grid, or whether a power plant may be about to experience a fault and should instead cycle down into a preventive maintenance mode.

The total effect could be fewer outages, greater reliability, less wear and tear on equipment, lower pricing, fewer pollutants, and any number of outcomes that result from better and more efficient operation.

Transport: Batteries, Artificial Intelligence, and Additive Manufacturing

Our experts anticipate that battery technology will continue to evolve at a very rapid pace and that costs will continue to drop. At some point, commodity prices will create a "floor" for how low prices can go, but a combination of new chemistries (beyond lithium ion), continued economies of scale (more giga-factories), "learning by doing," and competitive forces could keep prices on a downward trajectory for quite some time. Moreover, new chemistries and new manufacturing methods could optimize some batteries for very long discharge periods over long lifetimes (such as 8 hours of storage with thousands of cycles over a 25-year lifetime) and optimize other batteries for vehicle operation (that is, many stops and starts and quick recharging).

Our experts further anticipate that artificial intelligence and machine learning will continue to progress, such that fully autonomous vehicles (level 5) will be commercially available in a few years. Artificial intelligence will enable fully pilotless drones and efficient ground and urban air-traffic control systems to manage the flow of vehicles; 5G will facilitate vehicle-to-vehicle communication and vehicle-to-traffic-controller communication.

Finally, our experts anticipate that additive manufacturing (3-D printing) will continue to progress and commercialize. The current research and development paths for finding faster production and larger components will be successful. 3-D printing will enable lighter vehicles (extending the effective miles per charge from car and drone batteries) and enable novel vehicle designs that otherwise would not be possible to manufacture. These technologies could reshape transportation systems and their infrastructure in many ways.

Autonomous Vehicles and Electric Vehicles

A system of autonomous vehicles, coordinating with each other and with a traffic controller algorithm, could dramatically reduce traffic time, traffic accidents, and vehicular pollution. Alternatively, autonomous vehicles might increase sprawl by minimizing the opportunity cost of driving, thus encouraging people to live farther from their work. Lower-cost batteries and higher demand for electric vehicles have already prompted several carmakers to produce more hybrid, plug-in hybrid, and fully electric vehicles.

Drones

The most promising area with respect to transport infrastructure is for package delivery. Infrastructure for receiving packages from drones will be needed in buildings—or potentially "drone depots"—and roadway traffic may abate as fewer delivery trucks and motor scooters will be employed.

Ride Sharing

As ride sharing grows in popularity, cities may see fewer vehicles on the road, which would reduce car ownership and the need for parking spaces (see chapter 4 for a discussion). There is no consensus on whether ride sharing would increase total vehicle-kilometers traveled, but there is a consensus that planning and regulations can mitigate this potential effect. Mobility as a service is an extreme form of ride sharing, whereby all forms of transportation (car, bicycle, scooter, ride share, bus, and rail) are interlinked by an app.

Taken together, these developments could lead to a more agile, efficient, and environmentally friendly way of moving people and goods, but the outcomes depend on planning and regional coordination.

Water and Sanitation: IIoT, Artificial Intelligence, and Advances in Chemistry and Biology

Our experts anticipate that several of the same advances in technology that will enable disruptions in the power and transportation sectors will also affect the water sector. Data analytics spanning the entirety of water system operations are becoming more common, increasing efficiency and leading to operational improvements. A wholly different, but complementary, set of scientific breakthroughs will affect water purification and sanitation. The techniques will make centralized systems better and more effective, but also will enable decentralized innovations. Many of these technologies and techniques have already started deploying (Leifman 2019).

Water Resource Management

In water resource management, new "softer" physical techniques such as dry dams and movable, inflatable dams are being considered for flood control, rather than traditional dams or berms and levees. The sum effect of these and other technologies could be a lower risk of floods and droughts, reduced use of water in agriculture via precision water delivery, less loss of water via improved irrigation, and, in areas with depleted groundwater, reduced subsidence and, in estuarine areas, reduced salinity.

Water Distribution Systems

In water distribution systems, miniaturized robots are being tested for deployment within pipes to identify leaks. Combined with incentives to reduce leaks, the sum effect could be a reduction in leaks, breaks, and "nonrevenue" water, thereby improving the financial position of water utilities and their ability to deliver services.

Drinking Water Purification Systems

Drinking water purification systems using ultraviolet rays and photocatalysts or using traditional methods but powered by solar photovoltaic cells and batteries are being tested. The combined effect could be to reduce the costs of purification not only for utilities but also in decentralized systems. Desalination and water purification could become a viable option—even in remote areas and on a small scale—thanks to lower energy costs, lack of need for heavy chemical treatments, and modularity.

Sewage and Treatment Systems

In sewage and treatment systems, new trencher systems are replacing traditional excavators to make pipe laying much quicker and less costly, with far less disruption to street traffic. These developments could help not only centralized water utilities, but also decentralized systems—which could be introduced to remote areas, where laying miles of pipe would be very costly, or in dense urban areas, where land resources are scarce.

NEW TECHNOLOGIES COULD GIVE RISE TO VERY DIFFERENT FUTURES

How might these new technologies shape the future in LMICs? We explore this question by evaluating three scenarios—leapfrog, lopsided, and lock-in—that shed light on the key uncertainties identified by our experts (box 6.2). Contrary to our initial expectations, these uncertainties are not about the success of technology research and development, but rather technology's deployment. The scenarios are somewhat extreme versions of how various futures might play out and are not designed to be fully descriptive. Rather, their aim is to focus attention on choices that can be made (intentionally or not) and what the impacts and ramifications of those choices might be (see annex 6A for details on our workshop examining these scenarios).

As mentioned earlier, the premise that distinguishes the scenarios is the ability and success of governments, planning authorities, and regulatory authorities to put in place the means to adopt innovation (such as backbone infrastructure, financial incentives, and regulatory frameworks) and measures to ensure that the spread of new technologies is not limited to the wealthy and does not result in a decrease in opportunities and access for the rest of the population. Thus, the key difference across the scenarios is how well governments, incumbent institutions, and regulatory agencies manage the challenge of balancing the need to protect and improve social welfare with the need to reduce inequities. How might the power, transport, and water sectors develop under our three scenarios? Table 6.1 summarizes some of the possible ways, although in the real world, the results will be more complicated, likely blending elements of our different futures.[1]

BOX 6.2

OUR THREE TECHNOLOGY-DEPLOYMENT SCENARIOS

Leapfrog

- Technologies have advanced quickly—some exponentially—and cost and business models make them widely attractive.
- Policies, social habits, and institutions have adapted well and in a timely manner, enabling the technologies to diffuse quickly and equitably across all segments of society.
- Data collection and use are a core part of infrastructure planning.
- Building data infrastructure (such as laying fiber, building towers, and establishing satellite connections) and using data to facilitate new business models has been—and is—a core element of planning.

Lopsided

- Technologies have advanced quickly—some exponentially—and cost and business models make them attractive.
- Policy design does not allow for equitable use of the technologies.
- Social habits of the wealthy in low- and middle-income countries (LMICs) have mimicked those in high-income countries, public institutions have fought change, and some policies with competing aims remain in place.
- Technologies have diffused quickly, but only in selected areas and, even then, only for a portion of the population—resulting in social exclusion and a two-tier world of "haves and have nots," with respect to modern systems.
- Proactive use of data is largely in the domain of the private sector, with sporadic use by public agencies and little public-private coordination.
- Adequate data infrastructure exists only in pockets and is dictated more often by narrow private concerns than by public policy.

Lock-In

- Technologies have advanced, but barriers to adopting new business models sharply limit their attractiveness in LMICs.
- Policies and social habits have not changed or adapted as new technologies were introduced, some institutions have fought change, and policies with competing aims remain in place.
- Technologies have diffused in high-income countries, but LMICs have seen widespread use of older technologies.
- Data collection and data use continue to be an afterthought in planning.
- Building data infrastructure is not part of normal planning.

TABLE 6.1 **General levels of technology deployment, by scenario and sector**

Sector	Scenario		
	Leapfrog	Lopsided	Lock-in
Power			
Description	Internet of Things–based digital grid; acceleration of grid-scale renewable energy and battery storage; construction and incorporation of some electric vehicle charging stations; rapid diffusion of micro-grids	Investment in digital only in privately owned capacity; more renewables, but not well integrated; private micro-grids for fleet electric vehicle charging; micro-grids for gated communities	Lack of investment in digital smarts and communications infrastructure; more renewable capacity, but poor grid integration; grids too weak to support many electric vehicles; very few micro-grids
Indicative statistic	Electricity access improved ~95% vs. 2018 base	Electricity access improved ~65% vs. 2018 base	Electricity access improved ~75% vs. 2018 base
Transport			
Description	Shared, autonomous electric vehicles are the norm for millennials; single-passenger cars are a rare luxury; wide diffusion of mobility as a service; common package delivery drones; occasional, autonomous flying cars	Limited penetration of autonomous vehicles and electric vehicles; limited implementation of physical infrastructure; new technologies most common for the wealthy and new neighborhoods; resistance to transportation network companies and ride sharing	Requisite physical and communication infrastructure not fully arrived; resistance to transportation network companies and ride sharing; grids not capable of handling loads from electric vehicles; autonomous vehicles create new problems for "drivered" cars
Indicative statistic	50% of cars on the road are shared or autonomous electric vehicles	Passenger vehicle-kilometers traveled for the wealthiest is up by 20%–30%	No more than 5% of cars are shared or autonomous electric vehicles
Water			
Description	Water management agencies cooperate within and across boundaries; wide collection and use of data for resource and system management; substantial reduction of nonrevenue water; mix of new connections to the main system and distributed systems	Cooperation in closely politically aligned areas; advanced flood control in areas with industrial operations or wealth; private water utilities incorporate digital strategies to reduce nonrevenue water; wealthy neighborhoods are built with local water reclamation and purification	"Stove-piping" and little coordination of data; legacy data systems and untrained staff; little approval for spending on digital; few distributed systems; few "trenchers"; piping remains costly and disruptive
Indicative statistic	Safe water access improved ~70% vs. 2018 base	Safe water access improved ~40% vs. 2018 base	Safe water access improved ~50% vs. 2018 base

WHAT GOVERNMENTS CAN DO (AND AVOID DOING)

One of the central features differentiating the three scenarios is the extent to which governments perform their roles as enabling (that is, are policies designed to help or hinder innovations that improve service levels?) and distributive (that is, are policies designed to ensure that multiple segments of society reap the rewards of innovation?) entities. A key question here is how countries can avoid lock-in or how they might get derailed into a lopsided future. Some institutional "behavioral markers" stand out, although it is important to recognize that multiple combinations of these behaviors can lead to lock-in or lopsided development.

Getting to Lock-In or Lopsided

Lopsided is perhaps the most "natural" state and the one toward which all sectors and development paths tend. In real (policy) life, full consistency is unlikely, and "lopsidedness" can occur at various scales (continent, country, city, or neighborhood).

The Issue of Sprawl

In the transport sector, a lack of regulation disincentivizing sprawl could be a prelude to lock-in. Sprawl is both the outcome and the cause of unsustainable cities. With a sprawling city, service provision becomes more difficult because routes must be extended. On traditional bus commuting routes, without dynamic routing, large service areas may suffer from inefficient service and may experience long delays in traffic. On bus rapid transit routes, while traffic is eliminated, routes still cannot offer coverage as full as in more compact spaces. With rail or light rail, similar problems exist—namely, the more spread out the service territory, the greater the challenge of providing efficient service—but with the additional burden of maintaining the rails and potentially having stranded assets if populations move or preferences change. Sprawl is also detrimental to electricity service provision. For example, the greater the land area that distribution companies must cover, the more miles of transmission and distribution infrastructure that must be built in a traditional grid, and the more complicated it is to maintain reliable service at proper voltage.

What can be done to tackle this issue? One tool might be a coordinated use of data, given that sprawl may happen in the absence of countervailing interventions. For example, transit agencies are typically not involved in zoning decisions, but they do have data on people's movements. Transportation network companies and mobile telephony companies have even more detailed data at their disposal, but, being privately operated, they are at an even greater remove from government planning. If zoning agencies make use of the data available (while protecting the privacy of individual users' data), decisions about housing density, commercial and industrial land rights, and service provision (such as hospitals and first responders) could be informed by where and how people are moving around a metropolitan area. Following that, incentives can be put in place to encourage density in a way that optimizes the use of resources.

The conditions that create sprawl under lock-in can also be precursors for lopsidedness, as in the case where public transit agencies do not take advantage of new technologies, but private companies do. In a sprawling metropolitan area, the middle class and the wealthy will typically rely on the same service infrastructure as the poor and will likely subsidize the system. But if the wealthy have access to new technologies or business models that enable them to receive better or equivalent service while not subsidizing others, then a lopsided world may emerge. Lopsidedness could result from poor planning practices for energy, water, and transportation systems, including (a) lack of benchmarking, (b) lack of data transparency and availability, (c) overly rigid decision-making process, and (d) lack of coordination between market actors (including government, utilities, and corporations).

How Technologies Are Promoted

Promoting technology choices rather than their outcomes is another potential route to a lopsided future. If policy making is focused too heavily on technology, rather than on equitable service delivery, there may be unintended consequences. For example, tax credits for distributed renewable energy are likely to promote rooftop solar, which has positive externalities, but the direct beneficiaries would be property owners with roofs and a high enough appetite for tax credits. If, as a consequence of promoting rooftop solar, the distribution utility loses revenue to fund operations and maintenance (O&M) expenditure on the grid, the tax subsidy would lead to a lopsided result. A similar result is possible in transport. If the government were to subsidize private ownership, rather than use, of autonomous electric vehicles, then only wealthy citizens who can afford a car would benefit. If electric vehicles produce a burden on the grid, or if autonomous vehicles encourage worse sprawl and exacerbate traffic, then the result would be decidedly lopsided. Of course, lopsided worlds are especially difficult to escape, because of the power accumulated by special interests that can influence decision makers.

These types of lopsided regulatory outcomes can be the result of several other symptoms of lack of good governance, including (a) public institutions falling prey to corruption and "regulatory capture," (b) lack of commitment to reform, and (c) lack of visionary leadership and the transient nature of government officials or inadequately compensated and incentivized public sector officials.

Misguided Efforts to Bolster Local Economies

Policy efforts to boost local economic growth can sometimes lead to locked-in or lopsided futures. For example, protectionist trade policies imposed on imported goods (like local content rules or tariffs) can have unintended effects such as unacceptably costly production. If a law is written mandating that battery components have to be manufactured locally, battery manufacturers may choose to ignore the market, locking in the grid to a more restricted set of choices. Or if battery manufacturers choose to manufacture locally, the prices may be so high that only wealthy communities installing mini-grids or wealthy individuals buying high-end electric vehicles will use batteries—leading to a lopsided future with less adoption of clean technologies than otherwise may have been the case.

Other, similar actions, intended to improve local economies, could have the same type of effect. For example,

- A refusal to align with international standards (such as intellectual property and Web-hosting protocols) based on state protection of industries could lead to lock-in.

- Lack of truly competitive bidding and procurement policies could box out innovations, leading to lock-in.

"Sins of Omission"

Sometimes inaction can yield the same locked-in or lopsided result as a more active policy. For example, many new technologies require preferential financing at their start, possibly because they carry a higher risk premium or higher transaction costs. Thus, when governments do not actively provide financing assistance (for example, through loans or loan guarantees), new technologies may not get adopted, and incumbent technologies are locked in. Sometimes a government may offer a targeted finance mechanism, but its design inadvertently leads to lopsidedness. In addition, both governments and service providers may fail to communicate properly the benefits of new technology. The success or failure of a new technology may hinge on customer readiness—if customers are not "primed" by early and frequent communication about the technology in advance of its offering, the technology may never be adopted and deployed.

What, then, are some of the key questions that governments need to grapple with as they seek to play their role in ensuring that technology serves rather than hinders development? We look at four key topics.

Equity vs. Rapid Deployment

Policy makers are likely to encounter the inevitable tension between encouraging rapid deployment of innovation and ensuring that innovations are equitable. This issue is related to the core of how governments perform their enabling and distributive functions, except in this case the equity concerns are for the systems getting disrupted. For example, when transport network companies (such as Uber or Didi Chuxing in China) enter a city, governments must weigh the benefits of rapidly adding more transportation options with the costs of putting taxi drivers' investments and employment at risk.

Similarly, one of the broader conversations taking place across many domains is the tension between open-data standards and data protection. In the name of maximizing the power of "big data," the more that is shared, the better—although data sharing may infringe on data privacy protections that customers may expect or be guaranteed.

As Joseph Schumpeter noted, creative destruction is the essence of an innovation economy, and hence governments must always allow some degree of destruction for innovation to progress. But a failure to protect those who stand to lose might result in political backlash and the eventual blocking or slowing down of innovation.

Silos vs. Integration in Planning and Service Delivery

Cities are regions that are interconnected by both the flow of people and the flow of the resources they use. This means that each policy decision has ramifications well beyond the immediately obvious ones. Our workshop participants stress the paramount importance of coordinated, regional planning:

- If one of the broad aims of a metropolitan government is sustainability, then service-providing agencies can agree on metrics and reinforcing programs.

- If public transit is deemed a preferred means of mobility because of its lower energy use and emissions per person-kilometer, then transit agencies would budget for more buses or for rail lines. But if the buses are unable to provide service levels equal to private cars, then the transit system may become less productive, as it struggles with competition.

- If zoning permission is granted for a new "closed loop" industrial zone without a proper review of electricity distribution, the grid may weaken or require more carbon-intensive production elsewhere.

Yet government agencies typically are not nearly as interconnected as the resources they manage. There are many reasons why siloing and stove piping occur and why overcoming that tendency is so difficult. Among the "better" reasons are organizational expertise and O&M efficiency (units exist precisely so that their managers can oversee a reasonable number of people, topics, and budgets). Among the less appealing reasons are the tendency for rivalry and fiefdoms, the reinforcing effect of poor communication channels, and the absence of data sharing.

These organizational behaviors are widespread. Changing them requires a combination of top-down leadership as well as a new set of processes and incentives to change and shape managerial cultures.

Centralization vs. Decentralization

One of the commonalities in the disruptions in infrastructure is the trade-off between centralization and decentralization. Centralized systems are often thought to have the inherent advantage of economies of scale. With the ability to socialize fixed costs over a large number of users or customers and to amortize costs over longer lifetimes, centralized systems can be more efficient. Moreover, centralized systems serve many customers and segments of society, so, in theory, they are better able to engage in longer-term and broader-based planning; they should be more able to address inequities and execute socially desirable strategies.

However, as is evidenced by many public utilities in virtually all LMICs, large organizations with centralized service delivery struggle with multiple potential sources of inefficiency. These sources of inefficiency include stove-piped planning, underfunding, rent-seeking, cumbersome bureaucracy, uneven political power leading to inequities or simply poor choices, and often the need to cross-subsidize service delivery such that some customers are underserved and others overcharged.

Moreover, decentralized models of service delivery often have some advantages that large, centralized organizations do not. These advantages include nimbleness in decision making and implementation, fewer hurdles in adopting new technologies or business models, the ability to target products more specifically to individuals or customer groups, and minimal political patronage as a barrier toward service optimization. Even so, decentralized offerings have their own hurdles. Often, smaller-scale projects are not attractive to financiers, and the transaction costs of multiple, individual projects can break some companies (which are often private). Aggregation of multiple projects is sometimes an option, but then the sequencing of the projects itself becomes a "choke point" for deal flow. Lack of name recognition may hamper adoption, and lack of political power may slow acceptance.

The trade-offs are many, and each sector in the scenarios is confronted with the push-pull between centralization and decentralization. The trade-offs are most obvious in the power sector, where decentralized solutions (such as solar home systems and mini-grids or micro-grids) are increasingly appealing and are disrupting traditional models of service delivery. In water delivery, newer technologies are enabling dynamic models of service delivery, improving the economics of decentralized water purification and treatment. In transportation, the tension between the "Uberization" of transport and central systems is already evident in municipalities around the world. But if managed and planned properly, centralized and decentralized systems should be able not only to coexist but also to bolster each other and improve overall service levels.

Flexibility

Insightful scenarios notwithstanding, tremendous uncertainties face infrastructure, given how long-lived it is and the lock-in it invariably creates as households and firms make lifestyle and business decisions based on the infrastructure's nature and location. Thus, the emphasis needs to be on greater flexibility for institutions, regulations, and even the infrastructure itself.

Institutional Flexibility

Institutional flexibility is the quality that allows governments to enable innovations in an equitable way and incumbent firms to adapt. It can be born of a focus on the goals of service delivery rather than proxy metrics of success—for example, (a) focusing on people with electricity or new customers per year or kilowatt-hours per customer, rather than miles of transmission or number of electrified villages or (b) focusing on the number of people moved per day or the number of vehicle-kilometers traveled per day, rather than the number of roads built or bus routes. Focusing on service delivery enables a change in mind-set, because it aligns the institution's goals with the customer's goals; any new business model that achieves those goals would be welcome. Institutional flexibility can also be facilitated by smaller operating units, which maximize nimbleness in decision making and minimize the creation of bureaucratic fiefdoms and opportunities for politically motivated decisions.

Regulatory Flexibility

Regulatory flexibility is the quality of laws, incentives, policies, and regulations that enable multiple means of meeting a societal need. For example, (a) laws that mandate a level of water quality as opposed to specifying a treatment chemical, (b) incentives that encourage improved access to reliable electricity, as opposed to paying for transmission or a particular prime mover, and (c) regulations that allow competition in serving commuters, under a safety and privacy standard, rather than a blanket prohibition or a blanket permission of transportation network companies.

Infrastructure Flexibility

A key symptom of lock-in is having financed long-lived infrastructure that has become obsolete. If that occurs, infrastructure flexibility can take on different meanings. One meaning is favoring shorter-lived projects. This approach might lead to disregarding what might otherwise be valuable projects or, with innovative project managers, might incentivize new methods for building the same type of project. Could projects that typically require a 30-year financial life be redesigned to pay back in 15 years? A second meaning is encouraging a more modular or "Lego-like" approach. This approach could lead to a longer time to "ultimate" completion, or it could also result in faster delivery of service to some customers. A third is making the infrastructure itself flexible. Instead of designing infrastructure to last 60 years, it could be designed to last 20–30 years or be designed for repurpose and reuse. If a country determines that light rail is the optimal form of transportation for the next 10 years, how can the right-of-way be repurposed quickly for bus rapid transit or autonomous or electric vehicles?

IN SUM

No matter how clever the scenarios, they may still fail to account for the "black swan" or low-probability, high-impact type of event. Such events could be (a) cyberterrorism that threatens infrastructure systems and derails the "leapfrog" innovations that rely on networks or (b) the solving of nuclear fusion puzzles, creating virtually unlimited carbon-free energy. Massive infrastructure shifts would indeed follow. But the lessons to be drawn from the exercise would still hold: for technologies to live up to their potential, governments have to deliver on enabling and distributive policies. Innovation is simply not enough.

ANNEX 6A: METHODOLOGY TO DERIVE THE THREE SCENARIOS

In constructing our scenarios, we used three steps: interviews with both open dialogue and more formal, expert elicitation; scenario "strawman" construction; and an interactive workshop with multiple experts.

Interviews

In the interview phase, we spoke with sector experts from various organizations within the World Bank (including the International Finance Corporation) and sector and technology experts at external organizations. We spoke with experts in artificial intelligence, advanced manufacturing, including additive manufacturing (3-D printing), communications systems, water technology, battery technology, transportation and mobility, mini-grids, electric vehicles, water resource management, water utility systems, and more. In all, we interviewed nearly 50 experts (a complete list is available in Leifman 2019), some of whom also attended the workshop. For both technology and sector experts, we typically included various open-ended questions, as well as some narrower questions using techniques of formal expert elicitation.

Our technology experts were generally extremely confident that by 2040 all of the technologies we discussed would have developed substantially, that the current research problems would have been solved, and that the technologies would be widely commercially available. Our sector experts also were generally confident that the disruptive technologies under discussion would be widely available and generally confident that there would be some deployment. The main area of uncertainty was the *degree* of deployment, whether institutions in LMICs would adapt quickly, and whether customers would adopt widely.

Scenario Strawman Construction

In the second phase of scenario building, we took what we learned from the interviews and, using five principles of scenario construction (Leifman 2019), crafted three scenarios. Given that our experts were generally optimistic about the availability of technology, we chose to build the scenarios around the key uncertainty of *deployment*. The primary factor distinguishing the scenarios is whether the technologies are deployed extensively and equitably. The scenarios shine a light on (a) the enabling function of government: did it fulfill its responsibility to ensure that barriers to technology adoption are limited? and (b) the distributive function of government: did it fulfill its responsibility to all of its citizens or just some? So that the "efficient cause" is not the sole determinant of a future state, the scenarios also focus on the role that incumbent institutions play (such as transit authorities, power utilities, and water utilities).

We presented the scenarios to the workshop participants in advance, in written form, and in presentation at the workshop itself, as a strawman.

That is, we invited participants to rethink the premise, rewrite a scenario, or eliminate one altogether. Despite one suggestion to use only the "leapfrog" scenario, the broad consensus was to refine the scenarios, rather than to replace any wholesale.

Scenario Workshop

The workshop to flesh out the scenarios was held on April 24, 2018, in Washington, D.C. More than 50 people were in attendance, including several of our expert interviewees. The group included experts from the World Bank and the International Finance Corporation, the United Nations, the Organisation for Economic Co-operation and Development, universities, research laboratories, consultancies, and corporations.

During the full process, from interviews through the workshop, we also followed the scenario planning "dos and don'ts" of McKinsey Consulting (Erdmann and Yeung 2015). For instance, to counter the problem of "availability bias," we interviewed experts within and external to the World Bank, across multiple disciplines and geographies. To address "probability neglect"— the phenomenon of focusing too much and too early on numerical precision— our interviews combined open-ended questions with probabilistic ones, and our probabilities were described only qualitatively (for example, "likely," "very likely"). We avoided "stability bias"—that is, assuming that the future will look like the past—both by including great change in one of our scenarios and by focusing on the uncertainty identified by our experts (specifically deployment, not technology breakthrough). We dealt with the pitfall of overconfidence by using formal expert elicitation techniques in our interviews—asking experts to reconsider their answers—and by shuffling our experts in different groupings and in different scenarios during the workshop. These shuffled groups of experts were also designed to encourage free and open debate.

NOTE

1. A detailed description of what these technologies might imply for infrastructure and how market actors might evolve as a result is available in a background paper to this report (Leifman 2019).

REFERENCES

Erdmann, B. S., and L. Yeung. 2015. "Overcoming Obstacles to Effective Scenario Planning." McKinsey & Company, New York, June. https://www.mckinsey.com /business-functions/strategy-and-corporate-finance/our-insights/overcoming -obstacles-to-effective-scenario-planning.

Leifman, M. 2019. "Scenarios: Leapfrog, Lock-in, and Lopsided." Background paper to this report, World Bank, Washington, DC.

Technical Appendix

COUNTRIES OR ECONOMIES INCLUDED

Water and Sanitation, Irrigation, and River Flood Protection

East Asia and Pacific
American Samoa, Cambodia, China, Fiji, Indonesia, Kiribati, the Democratic People's Republic of Korea, the Lao People's Democratic Republic, Malaysia, the Marshall Islands, the Federated States of Micronesia, Mongolia, Myanmar, Palau, Papua New Guinea, the Philippines, Samoa, the Solomon Islands, Thailand, Timor-Leste, Tonga, Tuvalu, Vanuatu, and Vietnam.

Europe and Central Asia
Albania, Armenia, Azerbaijan, Belarus, Bosnia and Herzegovina, Bulgaria, Georgia, Hungary, Kazakhstan, Kosovo, the Kyrgyz Republic, the former Yugoslav Republic of Macedonia, Moldova, Montenegro, Romania, Serbia, Tajikistan, Turkey, Turkmenistan, Ukraine, and Uzbekistan.

Latin America and the Caribbean
Argentina, Belize, Bolivia, Brazil, Colombia, Costa Rica, Cuba, Dominica, the Dominican Republic, Ecuador, El Salvador, Grenada, Guatemala, Guyana, Haiti, Honduras, Jamaica, Mexico, Nicaragua, Panama, Paraguay, Peru, St. Kitts and Nevis, St. Lucia, St. Vincent and the Grenadines, Suriname, and República Bolivariana de Venezuela.

Middle East and North Africa

Djibouti, the Arab Republic of Egypt, the Islamic Republic of Iran, Iraq, Jordan, Lebanon, Libya, Morocco, the Syrian Arab Republic, Tunisia, West Bank and Gaza, and the Republic of Yemen.

South Asia

Afghanistan, Bangladesh, Bhutan, India, Maldives, Nepal, Pakistan, and Sri Lanka.

Sub-Saharan Africa

Angola, Benin, Botswana, Burkina Faso, Burundi, Cabo Verde, Cameroon, the Central African Republic, Chad, the Comoros, the Democratic Republic of Congo, the Republic of Congo, Côte d'Ivoire, Eritrea, Eswatini, Ethiopia, Gabon, The Gambia, Ghana, Guinea, Guinea-Bissau, Kenya, Lesotho, Liberia, Madagascar, Mali, Mauritania, Mauritius, Mozambique, Namibia, Niger, Nigeria, Rwanda, São Tomé and Príncipe, Senegal, the Seychelles, Sierra Leone, Somalia, South Africa, South Sudan, Sudan, Tanzania, Togo, Uganda, Zambia, and Zimbabwe.

Coastal Protection

The countries or economies are the same as above. The following countries do not invest in coastal protection but are included in the overall gross domestic product (GDP): Afghanistan, Armenia, Azerbaijan, Belarus, Bhutan, Bolivia, Botswana, Burkina Faso, Burundi, Cambodia, the Central African Republic, Chad, the Democratic Republic of Congo, Eritrea, Eswatini, Ethiopia, Gabon, Honduras, Hungary, Iraq, Jordan, Kazakhstan, Kenya, the Kyrgyz Republic, Lao PDR, Lesotho, FYR Macedonia, Malawi, Mali, Mauritania, Mauritius, Moldova, Mongolia, Namibia, Nepal, Niger, Palau, Paraguay, Rwanda, Serbia, Sierra Leone, South Sudan, Sudan, Tajikistan, Turkmenistan, Uganda, Uzbekistan, Zambia, and Zimbabwe.

Energy (Global) and Transport (Global)

The regions are the ones used by the Intergovernmental Panel on Climate Change (IPCC) for the shared socioeconomic pathways (SSPs).

Reforming Economies of Eastern Europe and the Former Soviet Union

Armenia, Azerbaijan, Belarus, Georgia, Kazakhstan, the Kyrgyz Republic, Moldova, the Russian Federation, Tajikistan, Turkmenistan, Ukraine, and Uzbekistan.

Asia, with the Exception of the Middle East, Japan, and the Former Soviet Union States

Afghanistan, Bangladesh, Bhutan, Brunei Darussalam, Cambodia, China (including Hong Kong SAR, China and Macao SAR, China, but excluding Taiwan, China), Fiji, French Polynesia, India, Indonesia, the Democratic

People's Republic of Korea, the Republic of Korea, Lao PDR, Malaysia, Maldives, the Federated States of Micronesia, Mongolia, Myanmar, Nepal, New Caledonia, Pakistan, Papua New Guinea, the Philippines, Samoa, Singapore, the Solomon Islands, Sri Lanka, Taiwan, China, Thailand, Timor-Leste, Vanuatu, and Vietnam.

Africa and Middle East

Algeria, Angola, Bahrain, Benin, Botswana, Burkina Faso, Burundi, Cabo Verde, Cameroon, the Central African Republic, Chad, the Comoros, the Democratic Republic of Congo, the Republic of Congo, Côte d'Ivoire, Djibouti, Egypt, Equatorial Guinea, Eritrea, Eswatini, Ethiopia, Gabon, The Gambia, Ghana, Guinea, Guinea-Bissau, the Islamic Republic of Iran, Iraq, Israel, Jordan, Kenya, Kuwait, Lebanon, Lesotho, Liberia, Libya, Madagascar, Malawi, Mali, Mauritania, Mauritius, Mayotte (France), Morocco, Mozambique, Namibia, Niger, Nigeria, Oman, Qatar, Réunion, Rwanda, Saudi Arabia, Senegal, Sierra Leone, Somalia, South Africa, South Sudan, Sudan, Syria, Tanzania, Togo, Tunisia, Uganda, the United Arab Emirates, West Bank and Gaza, the Republic of Yemen, Zambia, and Zimbabwe.

Latin America and the Caribbean

Argentina, Aruba, The Bahamas, Barbados, Belize, Bolivia, Brazil, Chile, Colombia, Costa Rica, Cuba, the Dominican Republic, Ecuador, El Salvador, French Guiana (France), Grenada, Guadeloupe, Guatemala, Guyana, Haiti, Honduras, Jamaica, Martinique, Mexico, Nicaragua, Panama, Paraguay, Peru, Suriname, Trinidad and Tobago, Uruguay, U.S. Virgin Islands, and República Bolivariana de Venezuela.

Cost Calculations

Throughout the report, costs are given either in U.S. dollars or as a percentage of GDP, and they include all low- and middle-income countries.

Costs in U.S. dollars are in 2015 dollars, are discounted with a 6 percent discount rate, and are annualized between 2015 and 2030 (unless otherwise indicated).

Costs as a percentage of GDP are an average between 2015 and 2030 of annual costs divided by annual GDP. GDPs vary across sectoral analyses depending on calibration year, but the GDP growth rates are all based on the Organisation for Economic Co-operation and Development quantifications of the various shared socioeconomic pathways (SSPs).

THE SSPs AND REPRESENTATIVE CONCENTRATION PATHWAYS (RCPs)

The analyses in this report rest on the SSPs, which are part of a framework that the climate change research community and particularly the IPCC has adopted to facilitate the integrated analysis of future climate impacts,

FIGURE A.1 Overview of the SSP space

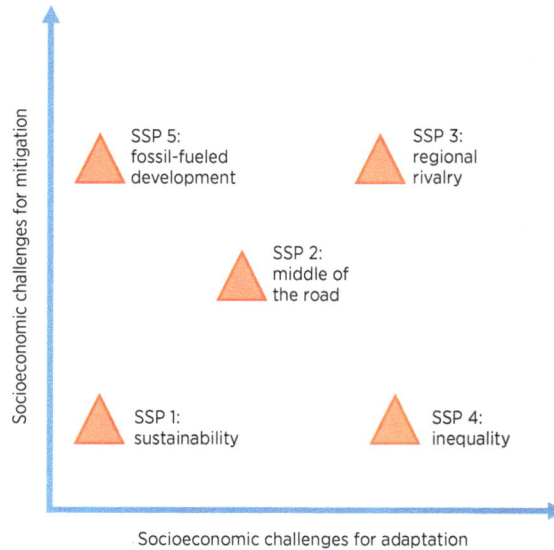

Source: Adapted from Riahi and others 2017.
Note: SSP 1 = low challenges for both mitigation (resource efficiency) and adaptation (rapid development); SSP 2 = medium challenges for both mitigation and adaptation (lopsided world); SSP 3 = high challenges for both mitigation (regionalized energy and land policies) and adaptation (slow development); SSP 4 = low challenges for mitigation (global high-tech economy) and high challenges for adaptation (regional low-tech economies); SSP 5 = high challenges for mitigation (resource or fossil fuel intensive) and low challenges for adaptation (rapid development); SSP = shared socioeconomic pathway.

vulnerabilities, adaptation, and mitigation. They describe five future potential socioeconomic pathways that the world could take in the absence of explicit additional policies and measures to limit climate change or to enhance adaptive capacity (figure A.1). They also provide quantitative projections for the main socioeconomic drivers of the SSPs: population, education, urbanization, and economic growth (figure A.2).

The five SSP narratives include (a) a world of sustainability-focused growth and equality (SSP 1), (b) a "middle of the road" world where trends broadly follow their historical patterns (SSP 2), (c) a fragmented world of "resurgent nationalism" (SSP 3), (d) a world of ever-increasing inequality (SSP 4), and (e) a world of rapid and unconstrained growth in economic output and energy use (SSP 5) (Riahi and others 2017).

Not all five SSPs are used in all sectoral studies. Most studies use SSPs 1, 2, and 3, but others use SSPs 4 and 5 to have more contrasted worlds in terms of GDP or urbanization. In general, when a "baseline" is used, it refers to SSP 2.

When climate change impacts are modeled (for irrigation and coastal protection), they are derived from the representative concentration pathways, developed in parallel to the SSPs by the IPCC community (van Vuuren and others 2011). The RCPs are largely independent from the SSPs, because previous scenario exercises demonstrated that many different socioeconomic pathways could lead to the same emissions concentration.

FIGURE A.2 Quantitative projections for demography, urbanization, and GDP in low- and middle-income countries, 2015–30

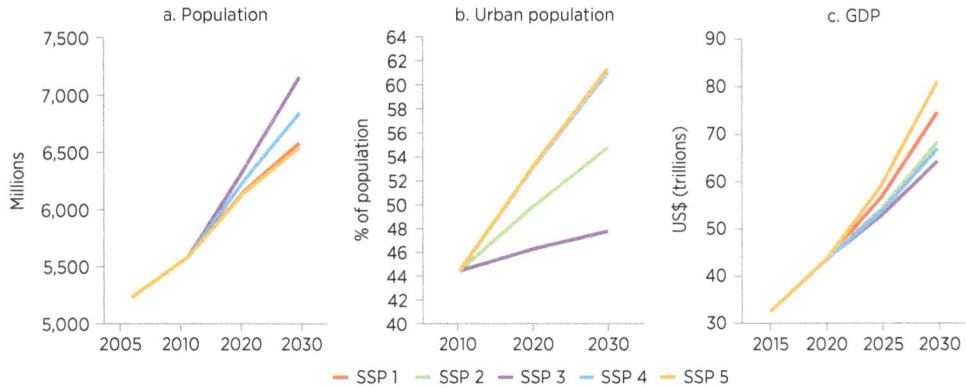

a. Population

b. Urban population

c. GDP

SSP 1   SSP 2   SSP 3   SSP 4   SSP 5

Source: Adapted from the International Institute for Applied Systems Analysis SSP database (https://tntcat.iiasa.ac.at /SspDb/dsd?Action=htmlpage&page=about).
Note: The five SSP narratives are explained in the text. GDP trajectories are calculated starting from current GDP and applying the Organisation for Economic Co-operation and Development SSP growth rates from the database. SSP = shared socioeconomic pathway.

REFERENCES

Riahi, K., D. P. van Vuuren, E. Kriegler, J. Edmonds, B. C. O'Neill, S. Fujimori, N. Bauer, and others. 2017. "The Shared Socioeconomic Pathways and Their Energy, Land Use, and Greenhouse Gas Emissions Implications: An Overview." *Global Environmental Change* 42 (January): 153–68. https://doi.org/10.1016/j .gloenvcha.2016.05.009.

van Vuuren, D. P., J. Edmonds, M. Kainuma, K. Riahi, A. Thomson, K. Hibbard, G. C. Hurtt, and others. 2011. "The Representative Concentration Pathways: An Overview." *Climatic Change* 109 (1–2): 5–31.

www.ingramcontent.com/pod-product-compliance
Lightning Source LLC
Chambersburg PA
CBHW080422270326
41929CB00018B/3130